THE RELIGION OF JESUS

The RELIGION of
JESUS

By WALTER E. BUNDY

Professor of English Bible in DePauw University

CASSELL & COMPANY, LTD
London.Toronto.Melbourne.&Sydney

FIRST PUBLISHED, 1929

Printed in the United States of America

To

CLAIRE, GEORGE,

VIRGINIA AND FRANK

Therefore let us also . . . lay
aside every weight, and the sin
which doth so easily beset us,
and let us run with patience
the race that is set before us,
looking unto

JESUS

THE AUTHOR AND PERFECTER

OF OUR FAITH

Heb. 12,1...2...

CONTENTS

CHAPTER   PAGE

     PREFACE   ix

  I THE RELIGIOUS GENIUS OF JESUS   1

 II THE RELIGIOUS FAITH OF JESUS   62

III THE RELIGIOUS CONSCIOUSNESS OF JESUS . .   141

 IV THE RELIGIOUS DEMANDS OF JESUS   210

  V THE RELIGIOUS AUTHORITY OF JESUS   271

BIBLIOGRAPHY   335

INDEX OF SUBJECTS   343

INDEX OF SCRIPTURE PASSAGES   355

PREFACE

JESUS was God's Galilean. No two words perhaps describe him in a more accurate and positive way. As a man of our human history, he was an early first-century Galilean. Judged in the light of the most distinctive thing in his personality, his utter religiousness, he was God's. It is to this distinctive thing that we devote our attention in the following study, the thing that made Jesus Jesus over against any other Galilean of his day— his own personal religious experience.

The present study, however, is not just another exposition of the religious teaching of Jesus, as important as such expositions are. It is much more than a study of what he said true religion is and ought to be. It is rather a study of Jesus' own personal experience of religion. Jesus as a religious personality was infinitely more than his religious teaching. All of his utterances are deeply personal; they are fresh extracts from his own experience. In the study of his religious teaching it is quite possible to miss Jesus entirely, especially if one has not sensed the intensely intimate character of all that he has to say about God in human experience.

The quest of the historical Jesus has been carried on for the most part in the seclusion of the study; and the findings, very often, have been phrased in a language that is foreign to the layman. But for once let the student leave off his critical crusade long enough to state very plainly, in the simple language of religious experience, the practical and personal results of his effort to recover Jesus as he actually was.

not too modest a claim

ix

Each one who approaches Jesus seriously will find something more, something new, something different. This is the prized privilege of his followers. The present study, then, is intensely personal. For this the author makes no apology. It is his own confession to Jesus, a purely personal confession, and this will explain for others the limitations of its worth as well as the extent of its weaknesses. But it could not be otherwise, for religion taken seriously is always intensely personal in the pressure it brings to bear on the individual.

The Jesus presented in this book is the Jesus whom the author knows through study and experience. It may not be the Jesus of some of our theologies, but for the author personally it is the Jesus of Matthew and Mark and Luke, the Jesus who was once a serious sharer of our common human experience, a real person of our human history, who knew God as intimately and genuinely as such knowledge is possible to our human equipment, who perfectly reproduced God in his own life and personality, and who devoted himself to the task of revealing God to men and of pointing them to and preparing them for God's great kingdom.

As an object of careful study Jesus raises more questions than he answers. This almost infinite suggestiveness seems to belong to the very nature of his genius. The author is clearly conscious of the fact that his task is not yet finished.

There is the psychological problem of the Christian will to recover Jesus, to see him as he was, with a view to his rehabilitation—a relatively new, but growing disposition.

There is the problem of recovering Jesus in the New Testament. To what extent do the New Testament writers turn to the human historical Jesus for permanent religious values? Do they know the religious Jesus? Do they understand Christianity as the adoption and faithful reproduction of his own personal piety?

There is the problem of the road to the recovery of Jesus. How shall we find our way back to him as he actually was? What of the spirit of those critical crusaders who have undertaken this pious pilgrimage, for it has been a discipline in piety? In the light of our best knowledge, what constitutes an adequate approach to Jesus?

There is the problem of the recovery of Jesus' social message. What are the social implications of Jesus' religious experience? What does he expect of men as groups? What does he demand in the way of group character and conduct? What has Jesus to offer in the way of social salvation?

There are the personal problems of Jesus—the dilemma of cause and cures, the Messianic issue, the ordeal of his fate. How did Jesus meet and find his way through these problems? What is his one aspiration in all of his inner struggles? Does he remain rigidly religious in all of these issues? Does he achieve personal religious triumph?

There is the problem of visions and voices in the religious experience of Jesus. Our best New Testament sources ascribe such to him. Were they sources of his religious convictions and certainties, or did he ever experience such?

More is to be said about the praying of Jesus. There

are the individual retreats for prayer. There are his seven personal prayers. How do they relate themselves to the total body of his religious experience?

These questions the author reserves for a companion volume in the near future, *Our Recovery of Jesus*. But even then he knows that he will not have said all that is to be said. Jesus grows and continues to grow for the careful student of his mind and life. And no student, even after he has done his best, will claim to have done Jesus more than relative justice.

Since the present study was completed, two important books on Jesus have appeared. The first is by Professor Shirley Jackson Case, *Jesus—A New Biography* (Chicago: University of Chicago Press, 1927). The author would direct the reader's attention to the last two chapters, on the religion lived and taught by Jesus. The second book is by Professor Rudolf Bultmann, of the University of Marburg, Germany, *Jesus* (Berlin: Deutsche Bibliothek, 1927). Those who read German will find it a very stimulating study.

To his friend and colleague, Professor William A. Huggard, of DePauw University, the author is deeply indebted for his great kindness in reading the original manuscript and offering many valuable suggestions and criticisms.

Greencastle, Indiana   W. E. B.
February, 1928.

THE RELIGION OF JESUS

THE RELIGION OF JESUS

CHAPTER I

THE RELIGIOUS GENIUS OF JESUS

THAT Jesus was a man with a religion, an exclusively religious personality, the whole of whose genius was launched in religion, is the most certain thing that we may say of him on the basis of the presentation made by Matthew, Mark and Luke—the most certain, because it is the clearest single feature in the Gospel picture. But when we come to seek out those formative factors and forces that contributed to the sum total of all that Jesus was and represented in the way of religion, the matter becomes almost hopelessly difficult, so far as an adequate analysis is concerned. The sources of his religious genius do not lie on the surface of the Synoptic story, nor can the most diligent research unearth all of the spiritual springs that had their issue in his religious experience. The most that we can do is our best, and, in the end, realize our serious limitations and the tentative character of our conclusions.

The difficulties that confront us in our quest of the sources of Jesus' religious genius are due, for the most part, to the limited character of our information. Our historical knowledge of him is deposited in literary records, none of which was written by Jesus himself. The fact that Jesus did not give literary expression to the great faith that possessed him, as did many of his prophetic predecessors and many of the champions of the Christian faith that succeeded him through nineteen

1

centuries, is a very serious handicap, and one that we are not in a position to overcome. In the quest of an adequate knowledge of any great man of the past, his own writings give us our most reliable information concerning his thought and teaching, his message and mission, his mind and experience, in short, concerning the man himself. It is thus that we come to know most of the great figures of the past, particularly those who have distinguished themselves in the field of religion. We have their literary productions, their journals and diaries, their autobiographies and confessions, their correspondence and notes, all of which are, at times at least, intensely personal and intimate, and they record those things which very often give us immediate access to the very pulse of their personalities, to the things that meant most, even everything, to them.

But Jesus, so far as we know, wrote nothing. Upon just one occasion do we read that he wrote, in the sand on the floor of the temple (John 7,53-8,11)—an act which, in the special situation, appears more as a mental preoccupation than as an expression of conscious thought. He has left us no autobiography, no confessions, no letters, no diary or journal, no literary record of his own religious mind and experience from his own hand. Our literary knowledge of Jesus is far from first hand, for it comes to us through the medium of the memory of the primitive Christian community—a medium that, by the very nature of its religious experience, communicated its faith in him rather than the facts from his life.

We have no materials from Jesus such as we possess from the hand of Paul, whose personal letters are a spontaneous expression of his own religious life and faith, non-literary products of an intensely religious personality, all the richer and more valuable because they were written with no thought of the remarkable literary future that was in store for them. In this respect, then, we are historically farther removed from Jesus than we are from Paul, for some of Paul's own letters have come down to us. Through these letters we can get back closer to the personal piety of Paul, closer to Paul himself than we can to Jesus. If we possessed documents from the hand of Jesus, written as spontaneously as Paul writes and coming with the same directness and freshness from his own personal piety as do many passages in Paul's letters, we would be infinitely closer to Jesus historically than we are. This lack of any personal documents from Jesus is a serious handicap in the way of the accomplishment of our present task, a serious impoverishment of our information concerning his experience of religion.

But when we approach this failure to give literary expression to his religious faith from the point of view of Jesus himself, it is no longer a serious problem. In the first place, there was nothing in his public career that demanded an extensive correspondence such as Paul was forced to carry on with his Christian communities scattered over the eastern half of the Roman Empire. Jesus' public work was restricted to a very limited area, the northwestern shore of the Sea of Galilee and its vicinity. He did not found communities of believers in the Galilean cities and villages where he worked; he attempted no organization. The followers who meant most to him were constantly in his company; separations between him and his chosen twelve were few and of brief duration. We can not imagine a circle of readers to whom he would have had occasion to address a personal or religious communication. In the second place, as we come to know

Jesus in the first three Gospels, we see that he was not the man to feel either the inclination or the impulse to write. Jesus was a teacher, the greatest of all teachers, but he was popular, never academic, in the matter and in the method of his teaching. He was not a man of the study; like Socrates, he was a man of the people, a man among the people. In the study of his words we never get the impression that they have been carefully planned and phrased, that he had carefully prepared beforehand just what he was going to say and just how he was going to say it. Just when and where he would meet his audiences, just who his audiences would be,—a gathering of country folk, a crowd of villagers, a synagogue assembly, a group of contentious authorities,—just what he would say to them, Jesus did not know. He met his audiences as occasion offered in a wandering itinerary. His audiences—sometimes great throngs, again small groups, even single individuals—he met by chance, not by schedule and appointment. They were not prepared for his coming, nor he for theirs. Jesus preached to the people as he met them, and they listened as they met him, on the mountainside, in the country, at the seashore, in the street and market-place, in private houses, in the synagogues and in the temple. On all occasions his message, both in form and in content, is free, frank and informal. Without exception, Jesus' words leave with us the impression of the spontaneous, extemporaneous and inspired speech of the intense prophetic personality.

In view of the above facts, it is not at all surprising that Jesus did not leave behind him written documents of a personal and intimate character that would help us back to the source-springs of his personal piety, documents that might give us invaluable aid in our effort to understand him better. Jesus never lets fall a single authentic hint to the effect that future generations may be interested in the preservation of personal memories of what he said and did, or who he was. Jesus knew but one future, that glorious future of the kingdom of God. Thus our literary records concerning him are the work of men who were removed from him by a Christian generation, men who were held to his memory by a strong bond of religious faith, but whose records were based, for the most part, upon the memoirs of those who, for longer or shorter periods of time, had been in his personal company, held to him by a deep personal devotion.

These records written by others are not biographies, accounts of the whole of Jesus' life. They are at best collections of reminiscences from his public career, the period in which he distinguished himself. Our best sources of information, the first three Gospels, neglect his prepublic life almost entirely. Mark does not devote so much as a line to Jesus' childhood, boyhood or youth. He brings Jesus on the scene of action by giving a compact survey of the work of the Baptist, which Mark regards as preparatory to that of Jesus. But of Jesus' life prior to his coming to John at the Jordan, Mark is silent. Mark has no Narratives of the Nativity, no Christmas stories with which Matthew and Luke open their accounts. Thus the earliest and most reliable account that has come down to us, the second Gospel, begins with his appearance in public. This would serve to show that the Narratives of the Nativity are a later addition, an aftergrowth, to the story, and that the earliest Christian interest in Jesus' life confined itself to his work in public and that it was only later that any interest was manifested in the circumstances of his birth.

But the birth traditions that have deposited themselves in the first two chapters of Matthew and Luke supply us with no additional biographical information about Jesus other than the name of his father, Joseph, and locate his birthplace as Bethlehem; and this second detail complicates rather than simplifies our problem. Mark knows nothing of Bethlehem as the birthplace of Jesus; this little village of David is not even mentioned in Mark's account. From Mark alone we would suppose that Jesus was not only a resident but a native of Nazareth. In Mark Nazareth is certainly the home of Jesus, and he is known as a Nazarene. His family is well known in Nazareth; the townspeople know his mother, four brothers by name, and they also refer to unnamed sisters. (Mark 6,1-6a.) Joseph does not figure personally in Mark; he is not even referred to by name or trade. Mary seems to be known as a widow in Nazareth, and the common supposition is that Joseph died long before his son began his public work. From Mark, then, all that we can gather of Jesus' prepublic life is that he was the son of Mary, that he had four named brothers and some unnamed sisters, that his home and that of his family was Nazareth, and that he was known there as a carpenter by trade.

Luke tells us (3,23) that Jesus was about thirty years of age when he began his public work of preaching and teaching. For us, then, the first thirty years are shrouded in darkness. We have very little, practically no reliable data from this important period, full data which would help us very materially in our quest of the sources of Jesus' religious life and experience. We have only the meager biographical details of the Narratives of the Nativity, and they are so meager that they render us no real aid. Luke gives us a single story from Jesus' boyhood. (2,41-52.) If this account is historical, the most that it tells us is that Jesus, at an early age, manifested the interests and inclinations, the predispositions and preoccupations which later, in mature years, consumed him entirely. But this great meagerness of materials on the prepublic period seems to fit the state of the facts—namely: No one seems to have known Jesus outside of Nazareth prior to his entrance upon his public work.

This obscure period of thirty years is commonly designated as *the unknown life of Jesus*. The loss in our knowledge of Jesus which this great gap involves has always been keenly felt by the Christian consciousness. Numerous attempts, both early and late, have been made to fill it up. Matthew and Luke made their contributions in their first two chapters, but they did not close up the gap. Somewhat later a whole body of Gospel literature sprang up, the apocryphal Gospels, dealing almost entirely with this obscure period, but this extensive literary activity made no real contribution toward our understanding, except to increase our appreciation of the less elaborate and less pretentious accounts of Matthew, Mark and Luke. Modern lives of Jesus have undertaken to supplement the meager Gospel accounts on the basis of generalities concerning the family and home life, the educational and religious training, the economic and social status of the Galilean Jews of Jesus' day—all or none of which might be true for Jesus in particular. But all of these attempts to write the unknown life of Jesus from Matthew and Luke down to our own day are, for the most part, the products of a reverent Christian imagination that expresses its faith rather than records fact.

We can not say a great deal about Jesus during this period. His religious training and education may have been the best that a plain laboring family of Nazareth could provide, but his personal religious life as we see it in mature form is much more than the religious education provided by the most pious Galilean family. Jesus nowhere refers to a strict religious training from youth up, of which Paul is proud to boast.[1] His home life may have been ideal, for, as modern biographers are fond of telling us, he thought and taught of God as the heavenly Father. Matthew's picture of Joseph in chapters one and two is friendly enough; Joseph appears as a pious patriarchal soul of Israel to whom God reveals himself in dreams. Luke's picture of Mary in 1,26-56 has always appealed to the Christian imagination, but in 2,22-52 Mary seems unacquainted with the future greatness of her son; with Joseph, she is astonished at the things Jesus says and that others say about him, and she seems to be gathering the first fond premonitions that something really great is in store for her son (Luke 2, 19 51b). But over against this traditional picture in the Christmas stories there stands in the same Gospels, and in Mark, the cold fact that none of Jesus' immediate family was in his intimate personal following and that he began and accomplished his public work without the support, perhaps without the sympathy, of his immediate kin.[2]

Thus we see that those imaginative attempts to get back at the factors in Jesus' prepublic life that contributed

---

[1]Cf. Acts 22,3; 26,5; Rom. 11,1; II Cor. 11,22; Phil. 3,5.
[2]Cf. Mark 3, 19b-21; 3, 31-35; Matt. 12, 46-50; Luke 8, 19-21.

to his making give rise to as many perplexities as they seek to remove. Consequently, others have turned away from the conventional sources of religious training and education to those natural forces that help men to make themselves. But when they have demonstrated, as is easily done, Jesus' keen sense for reality, his deep appreciation of the natural world, his penetrating insight into human nature—all natural rather than acquired gifts, we are still on the periphery of our problem and quite far from the real source-springs of his religious genius.

In our conclusions on the prepublic life of Jesus we may not demand too much detail, and we must learn to be satisfied with more general, yet safer materials. Historical research has opened our eyes to see that Jesus was really a genuine child of his land and people. The historical background against which he appears is the purely local and distinctly Jewish background of first-century Palestine, more particularly of Galilee. Nowhere does he betray an influence from the general atmosphere of the Greek culture and Roman civilization of his day. There is no evidence that he was acquainted with the Greek language. His mother tongue was a provincial dialect, Aramaic, the peculiar speech that betrayed the Galilean origin of one of his disciples. (Matt. 26,73; Mark 14,70; Luke 22,59.) It was in this dialect that Jesus thought and taught, preached and prayed, and cried to God in his direst need—*Abba,* in Gethsemane (Mark 14,36); *Eloi, Eloi,* on the cross when the Psalmist's classic cry of distress burst over his lips (Mark 15,34).

Not only does Jesus seem to have remained untouched by the currents of the world civilization and culture of his day, but he appears uninfluenced by the prevalent conceptions and practises of religion among the leaders of his own people, although he was intimately acquainted with their vagaries and extravagances. The personal piety of Jesus appears as the naive spontaneous piety of the Galilean peasant, a piety that was so deep-seated that it remained unspoiled by contacts with, at least by any influences from, the recognized religion of convention. He did not come from the professional religious classes. Jesus was a layman, a lay prophet and preacher of the kingdom of God. The whole of his religious constitution is that of the layman, a constitution as simple as it is susceptible to all that religion may mean in human life and experience. Jesus came from that social stratum of Israel that preserved its religion, unofficially to be sure, yet really, and where the great champions found the readiest response and the most genuine reception in revival and reformation. He belonged to Israel's *meek of the earth* (*die Stillen im Lande*) who furnished to this people the great body of its prophetic and religious genius. Thus Jesus' religious genius sprang from a very limited social and psychological environment, but it had its roots struck deep in the richest and most fertile deposit of religious life and experience known to the ancient world.

We could understand Jesus better if we knew and could relate more of his prepublic life. The early years, training and development of any great man are very important in our knowledge of him. In the case of Jesus, we know very little of those formative factors that contributed to his making, that prepared him for and brought him into public life with the greatest religious message and mission that human history knows. We should like very much to know all of the usual biographical details that belong to the complete story of any great man. We should like to know more of his maturing mind, how the things that later consumed the whole of his thought found their way into his attention and devotion, how and why he came to the great religious faith, not that he possessed but that possessed him, when and where his great religious convictions dawned upon him and claimed him for their own, how it was that he came to feel himself called and commissioned, completely consecrated to the championship of the life of God in the affairs of men.

Jesus the child, the boy, the youth, is lost to us for ever. We know him only in his maturity, the early maturity of the East. He is a man of mature mind when he makes his first appearance in the Gospel story, when he comes to John at the Jordan. The Gospels furnish us with no materials that would indicate any fundamental change, transition or development in Jesus. From the beginning to the end of his public life, he is the same. His religious thought is so compact and crystallized, his faith so firm and unflinching, that any changes or developments lie in the past prior to his decision upon a public career. Jesus is a man of full and finished faith when he appears before us, and, as we shall see, it is the fulness and firmness of this faith that brings him out of private life into public life. This faith never left him. He is often disappointed, troubled, uncertain, distressed, but his faith remains unbroken. There is no waning or weakening, no faltering or failing.

The great religious values to which Jesus committed and consecrated himself are clear enough, as clear as crystal, but how, when and where they came to dominate the whole of his life we do not know. Jesus possessed a religious faith without parallel, a faith that was as free and frank as it was fervent, but we are not in a position to locate all the fires of his faith, fires that flash high in exalted moments to subside again in a steady unfailing glow. Of the origins of his religious certainty we know little in detail. But it is enough to know that all of these things were his very own; it is enough that we may see them clearly, that we may sense them and share them, as he himself intended.

Even if we did possess a complete set of source materials, the real secret of Jesus' personality, as is usually the case with the genuinely religious, would elude an adequate and exhaustive analysis. As Professor Deissmann writes, "We are no longer in a position to reconstruct psychologically from the confessions of the mature man (Jesus) the various stages in his development."[3] But in the Synoptic picture we see what some of the contributing forces were. From the very prominence of certain factors, the important rôle played by some of them in his fully developed religious life, we may conclude that they were principal sources that made a substantial contribution to his personal piety. From the predominant elements in Jesus' mature mind we may, without making too heavy drafts upon the historical imagination, find our way back to at least some of the major matters that went into his religious making.

In the analysis that follows, sketchy rather than exhaustive, the author singles out four fundamental elements that contributed to the production of the religious personality of Jesus. The first is a matter of religious literature, the Old Testament; the second concerns itself with the heritage of a people's characteristic and

---

[3]*Evangelium und Urchristentum*, p. 83.

distinctive genius, the prophets of Israel; the third is the factor of contemporary influence, John the Baptist; the fourth is the fact of native and natural personal endowment, Jesus' own peculiar genius for religion. These four elements we shall treat in the order given under the titles: Jesus and the Old Testament; Jesus and his Prophetic Predecessors; Jesus and his Prophetic Contemporary; and finally, Jesus Himself.

JESUS AND THE OLD TESTAMENT

For students of the life of Jesus this is an old and almost threadbare subject. Our aim here is simply to emphasize a phase of this problem that has been neglected by not a few and that is of greatest importance in our study of Jesus as a religious subject—the distinctly individual contribution which the Old Testament made to his personal religious life.

There is not the slightest trace of evidence that Jesus read any other literature than the religious literature of his people. But that his acquaintance with the religious literature of his people was confined to the books which we know as the Old Testament is not at all a certain or necessary conclusion. From the prominence of the apocalyptic element in Jesus' thought we may conclude that it is not at all improbable that he was familiar with the religious literature of later Judaism that failed to win a place in the canonical collection of Old Testament writings. As we shall see when we come to his conception of the kingdom of God in the next chapter, there was a whole body of later Judaism's literature, represented only by Daniel in the Old Testament canon, which presents a form of religious thought and outlook very closely related to that of Jesus, but quite different from anything in the Old Testament, of course, with the exception of the book of Daniel. For our present purpose, however, we may look upon the Old Testament as we know it as the Bible of Jesus.

We have only one account of Jesus reading from an Old Testament writing, the scene in the Nazareth synagogue when he read a pertinent passage from Isaiah. (Luke 4,16-20.) But no one who reads the Gospels can doubt that Jesus was at home in the Old Testament and that he was thoroughly familiar with it from beginning to end, and it was a familiarity and command possible only for one who had lived in it and loved it. He often alludes to the outstanding Old Testament traditions—the creation, the garden of Eden, the fate of Sodom and of Lot's wife, to the popular stories connected with prominent Old Testament characters like Abel, Noah, Moses, David, Solomon, the Queen of Sheba, Elijah, Elisha and Jonah. His allusions to the Old Testament narratives are so numerous that, as Professor Wernle says, "one could compile a brief Biblical history from the words of Jesus alone."[4] Very often these allusions to the Old Testament Jesus uses to illustrate his teaching. On numerous occasions he makes direct quotations from the Old Testament, especially from the law and the prophets, to prove his points and to defend his positions both in his teaching and in his conduct. In many words that are not direct and conscious quotations there is an Old Testament ring, a tone and point of view that suggest at once some Old Testament passage. Jesus' Old Testament allusions and quotations, his words that have an

---

[4]*Jesus*, p. 1.

Old Testament atmosphere about them, have a surprisingly wide range; they strike three-fourths of the Old Testament writings. Outside of the Old Testament canon, certain words of his suggest passages in II Esdras, Tobit, Judith, the Wisdom of Solomon, Ecclesiasticus and I Maccabees.

In his use of the Old Testament an interesting and instructive light falls on the mind of Jesus. His method of approach to the religious literature of his people is as simple as it is sincere. There is no elaborate exegesis, no forced interpretations, no wearisome warpings, no painful pressing of passages until they yield the desired meaning, no subtle straining of the sense of the text. Jesus did not read his own thoughts into the Old Testament and then read them out again. In this respect Jesus bears none of the marks of the schools and schoolmen of his day and people, as does Paul in his typically Rabbinical exegesis with its strained senses, made meanings, and painful processes of proof and reasoning. In his use of the Old Testament we see no far-fetched allegories such as we find in I Corinthians 9,9-10, in Galatians 4, 22-31, or in I Corinthians 10,4 where Paul indentifies Christ with the rock in the wilderness. In Jesus' expositions of Old Testament passages we see no pressing of a singular such as we find in Galatians 3,16. Both Jesus (Mark 10,2-12) and Paul (I Cor. 11,6-10) cite the creation story, but in a very different way and from a very different point of view. In only one passage in each of the first three Gospels is Jesus credited with the use of the Rabbinical method, in the question of David's Son and David's Lord in Mark 12,35-37. (Matt. 22, 41-46; Luke 20,41-44.) Apart from the fact that he is here represented as provoking public discussion of a

theme which he regularly avoided and which he suppressed even in the privacy of his most trusted group,
the reasoning here is too delicately membered, the definition of terms is too careful and minute; in short, the whole
discussion is too academic and theoretical to be ascribed
to Jesus.

We also have no indication that Jesus read the Old
Testament with a view to procuring official credentials
for himself and his work as did his disciples after him,
who, like Paul, the author of the first Gospel and the
early Christian writers in general, sought and brought
from the Old Testament concrete Scriptural confirmations, not only for the major phases, but even for
the minor details of Jesus' life and work.   This process
of proof from prophecy is especially characteristic of the
author of the first Gospel, who sees in the flight of the
holy family into Egypt a fulfillment of Hosea 11,1 (Matt.
2,14-15), in the removal from Nazareth to Capernaum
a fulfillment of Isaiah 9,1-2 (Matt. 4,12-16), and in
the fact that Jesus taught in parables a fulfillment of
Psalms 78,2 (Matt. 13,35).   Now and again, the Christian point of view of the Gospel writers ascribes this
proof-passage use of the Old Testament to Jesus himself,
but, as we shall see presently, Jesus' use of the Old Testament has something so distinctive and characteristic about
it, his selections of Scripture are so pointed, personal and
pertinent, so different from and so superior to the Christian proofs from prophecy made by the Gospel writers
that we have no great difficulty in determining the passages actually used by him and the passages ascribed to
him by the later Christian point of view.   At times this
Christian use of the Old Testament does violence to the
picture of the historical Jesus, as is the case in Mark 4,

10-12 where he is represented as using parable to conceal rather than to reveal the truth, lest his contemporaries outside of the circle of the twelve might understand, repent and their sins be forgiven them—a passage and point of view (Isa. 6,9-10) that contradicts every authentic feature of the historical Jesus and that presents one of the most vicious doctrines in the history of Christian thought.

Is this a correct exposition of Mark 4:10-12?

The early Christian use of the Old Testament was Christocentric, a searching of the Scriptures for Messianic momenta to which the life and work of Jesus would measure up. Jesus' own use of the Old Testament is never egocentric. In only one passage (Luke 4,16-21) does he bring the Old Testament (Isa. 61,1-2) to bear directly upon himself, but even here he does not cite the Isaiah passage as an official confirmation of his identity. His use of Isaiah on this occasion is purely devotional. In other words, he finds in this Isaiah passage an anticipation of his own prophetic consciousness of personal call and commission to the work of God. Jesus' conscious relationship to the Old Testament was not Christocentric. It was purely personal, and if we were to leave off our study of Jesus and the Old Testament at this point, we should miss entirely the great contribution which it made to his own personal piety and religion.

Jesus read the Old Testament for the religious message that it contained, and in his use of it we see him pressing his way to the very heart of its religious meaning. In his reading of the Old Testament Jesus stands apart in the sureness with which he grasped the finest elements of its writers' faith, in his ability to single out the essential and vital, to make this live again in its primitive purity and power, and to carry it on to its natural and complete culmination. For Jesus the Old Testament was much more than a familiar field of religious literature from which he could draw at will instructive illustrations; it was much more than a source-book of proof-passages with which he could establish, defend and reinforce his points and positions. For Jesus the Old Testament was something more living, something more intimately and intensely personal.

Jesus did not read the Old Testament as the scribe of his day, nor as the professional Biblical scholar since, as the modern Old Testament exegete. He read the Old Testament as a layman, in the spirit and with the understanding and hope with which the devout soul resorts to its religious literature. He turned to the Old Testament with the same purpose that Jews and Christians have had when they turn to the twenty-third Psalm or to the ninety-first, both of which breathe that pure atmosphere of lay piety in which Jesus grew up. For Jesus the Old Testament writings were devotional documents. They were sources of personal religious light and strength, which is all that the religious consciousness may, with right, expect and demand of its Scriptures.

The Old Testament played a prominent rôle in the religious experience of Jesus; it is always an authoritative element in his religious consciousness. The Old Testament, as we see it contributing to the religious life of Jesus, supplies solid substance for his religious certainties and gives support to his religious convictions. It was a guide for religious character, a code and control for religious conduct. At decisive moments we see him resorting instinctively to his people's Scriptures. At important junctures in his religious experience the Old Testament determines his decisions and choices. It becomes the promoting factor in some of his religious acts. In an hour of deepest distress, in the throes of severest personal struggle, its classic passages burst from his lips as the only adequate expression of the hurt of his soul, or as expressions of comfort and consolation when calm confidence and composure have been restored.

It is important that we see when, where and under what conditions Jesus resorts to the Old Testament as a source of personal religious light and strength. Such personal and intimate scenes as this requires are not numerous in the Gospels, for there is a reserve and reticence in the religious constitution of Jesus that keeps most of these things from our eyes, and they were seldom witnessed by his contemporaries and disciples. It was in the sacred precincts of his own soul that he faced and fought through his personal problems. But now and again, Jesus does disclose the struggles through which he has passed or is passing. Sometimes the pressure is so great that he acts or speaks forgetful of the presence of others, or the stress of the moment is so severe that he is alone with his God even though a multitude looks on. Such intimate occasions are rare, but they are so clear that we sense at once the sacred significance which the Old Testament had for Jesus' personal religious life. Here we single out two principal passages in which the personal contribution of the Old Testament is unquestionable—the threefold temptation of Matthew 4,1-11 and Luke 4,1-13, and two of his prayers on the cross (Matt. 27,46; Mark 15,34; Luke 23,46).

Jesus, as is universally true of the genuinely religious consciousness, passed through the experience of severe test and trial. In a symbolical and figurative form that doubtless goes back to a rehearsal of Jesus himself, Mat-

thew and Luke report three specific temptations that he
faced immediately prior to his appearance in public.
Each of the three presents a particular personal problem
which he was forced to face, and each ends with a
definite decision at which he arrived. Further, each of
the three decisions makes it clear to us how important
was the place which the Hebrew Scriptures occupied in
the personal piety and religion of Jesus. In each case he
repulses the tempter with a pertinent passage from the
Old Testament, and each word quoted affords us an
intimate insight into the Old Testament sources of his
religious life.

"Man shall not live by bread alone, but by every
word that proceedeth out of the mouth of God."
(Deut. 8,3.)
"Thou shalt not make trial of the Lord thy God."
(Deut. 6,16.)
"Thou shalt worship the Lord thy God, and him
only shalt thou serve." (Deut. 6,13.)

These replies to the tempter are the only replies possible for the pious Israelite who is loyal to the best of
his faith. In them Jesus reveals to us very clearly that
the Old Testament belongs to the very nerve and fiber
of his religious life, that he presses his way to its very
heart, and that it is in the light and terms of the purest
piety of the Old Testament that he makes critical choices
and lasting decisions and that he solves his most pressing
personal problems. For Jesus the Old Testament was
a source of religious triumph in the severest struggles of
soul.

Mark does not have these temptations in the figurative

form which they assume in Matthew and Luke, but he has them none the less. In Mark they are actual historical situations in which Jesus finds himself. In Mark's Galilean account we see Jesus in the same situations, confronted with the same problems, and making decisions identical with those in the threefold temptation of Matthew and Luke. In Mark all three tests have their historical parallels and psychological points of contact in the public life of Jesus; all three fit vitally and organically into his subsequent experience, where historically, logically and psychologically they belong, and not in his immediate prepublic life as Matthew and Luke represent.

The first temptation (Matt. 4,3-4; Luke 4,3-4) has its historical parallel in Mark 1,35-38—the fourth and closing incident of Mark's first day of Jesus in public, the famous day in Capernaum (Mark 1,21-38). It has been an eventful day, a day full of new experiences both for the Capernaum crowds and for Jesus. It begins on a Sabbath with Jesus teaching in the synagogue and curing the demoniac, his first cure, in Mark 1,21-28. Then follows the scene in Simon's house where he cures his wife's mother (1,29-31), and at sunset on this Sabbath the Capernaum people throng the street at Simon's door that he may heal their sick (1,32-34). The day has been consumed by cures, resulting in great popularity. But the events of the day have confronted him with a new experience, his strange personal power to cure and to heal, and the appearance of this surprising power which, rather than his message, attracts all Capernaum brings his mind into a state of serious solicitude. He finds that the people respond to his cures rather than to the cause of God which he preaches. Early the following morning, according to Mark, "a great while before day," he withdraws from Simon's house to a desert place for prayer. (1,35-38.)   And in this retreat to solitude we find Jesus in exactly the same dilemma that Matthew and Luke present in figurative form in the first temptation.   In both he is confronted with the presence and proper place of his phenomenal personal powers.   Both situations are alike seductive in that they appeal to the use of these personal powers in behalf of natural and legitimate human needs.   In both his choice is the same; he decides in favor of message rather than miracle, in favor of cause rather than cures, as the essence of his mission.   For Jesus to return to Capernaum and cure would be to turn stones into bread.   It is in connection with this early morning struggle that Deuteronomy 8,3 must have come to him as a source of religious light and strength. Jesus' decision here in Mark 1,35-38—

"Let us go elsewhere into the next towns, that I may preach there also; for to this end came I forth"—

must have been reached under the influence, if not at the direct dictation, of such a passage as Deuteronomy 8,3:

"Man shall not live by bread alone but by every word that proceedeth out of the mouth of God." (Matt. 4,4.)

The second temptation of Matthew 4,5-7, the third of Luke 4,9-12, has its historical and psychological parallel in the demand for a sign in Mark 8,11-12.[5]   The Gospel writers give us no details concerning the scene, but the

[5]*See* parallels in Matt. 16,1-4; 12,38-42; Luke 11,16 29-32.

opponents in Mark 8,11 seem to demand personal credentials as does Satan when he suggests that Jesus leap from the pinnacle of the temple. In Mark 8,11-12 Jesus is in the same situation, confronted with the same dilemma, and his decision is identical with that in the second temptation of Matthew and the third of Luke. In an hour and scene such as we have in Mark 8,11-12, a precept of Old Testament piety must have come to his mind:

"Thou shalt not make trial of the Lord thy God."

Jesus, who trusted in God as none before or after him, refused, in the light of Deuteronomy 6,16, to make trial of the Lord his God. And this attitude dominates the whole of his life, so far as it is accessible to us. It is not for him to challenge God to public performance; his task is to meet the tests which God sets before him. He puts his God to tests and trials, but of a very different order. Like every pious Israelite, he refuses to make trial of Israel's God, but upon his God Jesus places those severer tests of personal religion. In his own personal piety he demands and draws upon those divine resources that are indispensable to the life of the genuinely religious consciousness.

In the third temptation of Matthew 4,8-10, the second of Luke 4,5-8, we find a figurative presentation of a Markan scene. This temptation has its historical and psychological parallel in Mark 8,32b-33 (Cf. Matt. 16,22-23), "where Jesus hears the tempter speaking through the mouth of an intimate disciple. Peter's rebuke would as completely turn him from the divinely appointed path as if he were to fall down and worship Satan."[6] The parallelism here is the clearest of all; it

---

[6] *The Psychic Health of Jesus*, by W. E. Bundy, p. 157. Courtesy of The Macmillan Company.

is apparent even in the details. Jesus' word to Simon Peter, "Get thee behind me, Satan," (Mark 8,33) is identical in point with his parting parry to Satan in Matthew 4,10: "Get thee hence, Satan." And in some manuscripts his word to Satan in Matthew 4,10 is verbatim his word to Simon Peter in Mark 8,33. In such a situation as we have in Mark 8,32b-33 where he for the first time speaks to his disciples of his fate, and when one of them, well meaning but misunderstanding, would turn him from the passion path which he regards as the divine will for himself, Deuteronomy 6,13 must have come to Jesus as a source of religious strength,

"Thou shalt worship the Lord thy God, and him only shalt thou serve."

All three scenes in Mark (1,35-38; 8,11-12; 8,32b-33) belong to the religious life of Jesus, and the three temptations of Matthew and Luke are simply these three scenes reset in the language of religious experience.

Not all of Jesus' temptations are reported to us, perhaps for the reason that he did not choose to reveal all of his inner struggles with conflicting forces. Luke tells us that Satan departed from him "for a season" only (4,13), and we see him in the throes of personal religious struggle from his first day in public (Mark 1,35-38) to the last (Mark 14, 32-42; 15,34). On the last night of his life Jesus reviews his public career as an unbroken series of temptations. (Luke 22,28.) How prominent the Old Testament was in his triumphs over other temptations we can not say, but we may conclude that it was an important factor simply on the basis of the threefold test in the wilderness.

Temptation was not the only religious experience in which Jesus resorted to the Old Testament, or more accurately, in which the Old Testament offered itself to him. Two of his words on the cross, both prayers, are verbatim from the Psalms. And it is only as classic expressions of Old Testament piety make such involuntary invasions into his prayer-life that we realize fully the important rôle which the Old Testament played in the religious life of Jesus. According to Matthew 27,46 and Mark 15,34, Jesus' only intelligible word on the cross was a cry of distress, a verbatim quotation of Psalms 22,1:

"My God, my God, why hast thou forsaken me?"

Luke's last utterance of Jesus is, with the exception of the first word, a sentence verbatim from Psalms 31,5:

"Father, into thy hands I commend my spirit."

These two paradoxical prayers—one, a distressed protest; the other, a calm commitment—present a strange contrast that is characteristic of the picture of the dying Jesus as presented by Matthew and Mark over against Luke. According to Matthew and Mark, Jesus dies in the throes of struggle, uttering a poignant protest to his God. According to Luke, he dies in a state of calm composure, dispensing forgiveness to his executioners (23,34), promising Paradise to a fellow victim (23,43), and at the last committing himself to the Father in complete confidence (23,46).

Most students of the life of Jesus reject one of these paradoxical pictures in favor of the other. Usually

Luke's picture is rejected because Luke himself, it is thought, seems to take offense at Mark's realistic picture in which Jesus dies in dire distress and therefore provides a more idealistic picture more in conformity with his own conception of Jesus. Those of this opinion point to the Gethsemane scene where Luke has eliminated the perturbed state of Jesus' emotions, and they conclude that he has done the same in the crucifixion scene. But the psychology of religious experience leaves it for ever possible, even probable, that both pictures are true to fact. The history of religious experience has produced just such paradoxes in which a stunning sense of divine desertion is reversed into a state of complete confidence and trust, and the subject calmly commits himself to the One who, it seemed, a moment ago was gone for ever out of his life.

For us here it is not important that we decide against one picture or the other, or that we accept both. But it is important in our study of the contribution of the Old Testament to Jesus' religious life that we see here how, in two diametrically opposed states of religious emotion, prayer passages from the Psalms escape his lips. Jesus, like Luther, Pascal and Bunyan, prayed in the words of his Scriptures.

"Often in time of need, quite unconsciously and without realization of it, a man will seize upon a fixed formula of prayer, or better, the formula presents itself to him, and into it he will pour the whole of his feeling. Thus the fixed, impersonal formula is filled with personal life."[7]

---

[7]Heiler, *Das Gebet*, p. 50.

The two Psalm passages on the cross are not conscious, deliberate quotations; they are involuntary invasions from the prayer-life and literature of his people. Soederblom says of the first, "He did not choose, nor did he reflect; he poured forth his distress."[8] As Professor Deissmann says of the first, we may say that both are "his very own, secured by his heart's blood."[8]

Thus far we have pointed out Jesus' familiarity with the Old Testament, how he used it to illustrate his teaching and to reinforce his points and positions, how it was for him a source of personal religious light and strength; in short, we have pointed out his natural religious dependence upon his people's Scriptures. But there is yet another element in Jesus' attitude toward the Old Testament that is as important as it is characteristic of all that we know of him in this respect. Over against his devout dependence there stands his sovereign personal freedom, a freedom that has the courage to reject as well as the loyalty to reproduce certain elements of its piety.

As every loyal Jew, Jesus revered the Old Testament as the one great religious heritage of his people. The Old Testament was Holy Scripture, sacred and inspired, revealing God's will to His people; it was God's word, a religious authority. But for Jesus the Old Testament was not an object of religious worship. There is nothing of the Bibliolatry in his personal attitude toward his sacred Scriptures such as has been so prominent both among Jews and among Christians since. He did not worship a book, or a collection of books; he worshiped the God revealed in Scripture. He read the Old Testa-

---

[8]Quoted by Heiler, *Das Gebet*, p. 355,

ment with characteristic Jewish vividness of imagination and tenseness of feeling, but such never led to the impairment of his critical judgment. His reverent attitude did not exempt the religious teaching and message of the Old Testament from his incisive criticism. The literary and historical questions of the modern Old Testament critic never crossed his mind. It never occurred to him to question the traditional positions with regard to the authorship, date and composition of the Old Testament writings, the historicity of any of their narratives. For Jesus Moses was the author of the Pentateuch, David the author of all the Psalms; Noah built the ark; the flood came; fire and brimstone rained down on Sodom; Lot's wife turned into a pillar of salt. In all such questions his attitude toward the Old Testament was just as uncritical as that of the most naive of his contemporaries.

Nevertheless, Jesus was a critical reader of the Old Testament. His criticism was not literary and historical, but religious, personally religious—a criticism born of a deep experience of God in his own life. This criticism resulted in an attitude that was freely selective, never slavish, over against the Old Testament religious teachings. Jesus was always reverent in his reactions to the Old Testament religion, but he could be radical in his rejections because he knew a source of religious authority that is always high above and more living than a body of religious literature. In the history of modern Biblical criticism it would be difficult to find a more severe critic of the Old Testament than Jesus was. He called in question certain long-accepted elements of Old Testament piety, and for himself and his followers he replaced them with a fuller and deeper understanding of religion.

In the slow struggle through which modern Biblical criticism has passed, on more than one occasion, to more than one honest critic, Jesus' famous series of statements in the Sermon on the Mount,

"Ye have heard it said of old . . . but I say unto you,"

has come as a source of consolation and comfort.[9]

Certain of the Old Testament writings seem to have made very little impression on Jesus, particularly those writings that were the products of official and organized religion. A book like Leviticus he neglects almost entirely; from its heart he extracts its one great passage,

"Thou shalt love thy neighbor as thyself." (19,18.)

Jesus seems to have reacted most strongly to those writings which sprang from prophetic and personal religion. His reactions to this personal prophetic type are usually favorable, but now and again most unfavorable when the religious motive becomes unworthy. We have seen that the Psalms were one of the richest sources of his personal piety, but the imprecatory Psalms he rejected outright. Without specific reference to this element in his people's religious literature, he nevertheless exercised most cutting criticism upon it. Jesus' word, "Hate thine enemy," ascribed to tradition by him, is not found in the Old Testament as a specific statement, but it exists as an actual attitude in the imprecatory Psalms. To these outbursts of feeling in the name of religious faith that would bring the divine wrath and judgment down upon the heads of Israel's enemies, national and personal, he replied,

---

[9]Matt. 5,21-24; 27-30; 31-32; 33-37; 38-42; 43-48.

"Love your enemies, do good to them that hate you, bless them that curse you, pray for them that despitefully use you." (Luke 6,27-28.)

And for Jesus this is more than a pious precept; on the cross it becomes his own personal prayer. (Luke 23,34.)

Further, Jesus could answer Scripture with Scripture. From Psalms 91,11-12 there radiates the cheerful warmth of a trustful piety,

"He shall give his angels charge concerning thee: and on their hands they shall bear thee up, lest haply thou dash thy foot against a stone." (Matt. 4,6; Luke 4,10-11.)

But this peaceful passage has hardly occurred to Jesus when there sweeps across his soul that stern statement of a more critical piety,

"Thou shalt not make trial of the Lord thy God." (Deut. 6,16; Matt. 4,7; Luke 4,12.)

Jesus manifests here, not a naive but a critical type of piety. Over against the unquestioning assurance of the Psalmist that trusts itself to divine deliverance he sets, and accepts for himself, a more critical piety that refuses to make trial of God. The antithesis here set between Psalms 91,11-12 and Deuteronomy 6,16 reveals to us the intelligent and critical reflection to which Jesus subjected the most familiar teachings of his Bible and how, within the sacred Scriptures themselves, he rejected one type of piety in favor of another.

We may conclude our sketch of Jesus and his religious relation to the Old Testament as follows. In him we see a genuine, but intelligent devotion to his people's Scriptures. The Old Testament and its religion are nerve and fiber of his own personal piety. His criticisms are never of a learned and academic type such as prevailed in his own day and since. His criticisms were born in the depths of his own personal religious experience. He reproduced and rejected on the sole basis of the Scripture's contribution to a personal knowledge of God and His will. But, all in all, Jesus felt himself a constructive critic; he "came not to destroy, but to fulfil." (Matt. 5,17.)

JESUS AND HIS PROPHETIC PREDECESSORS

Jesus was a prophetic personality. This is the impression that he left with his contemporaries both in the matter of his message and in the manner of his mission. In connection with Herod's superstitious opinion that Jesus was the resurrected Baptist, Mark reports other rumors generally current:

"But others said, It is Elijah. And others said, *It is* a prophet, *even* as one of the prophets." (Mark 6,15.)

And when Jesus, for the only time, questions the twelve with regard to public opinion concerning himself, they reply,

"Some *say* John the Baptist; some, Elijah; and others, Jeremiah, or one of the prophets." (Matt. 16,14.)

In his person and work, Jesus' contemporaries felt that

they were experiencing a real rebirth of Israel's long lost religious gift—and they were not mistaken.

Jesus is the last of that long line of Israel's prophets, a strange and sensitive strain of religious genius peculiar to Israel, who brought the religious life and thought of this people to its most exalted elevations and gave to both their pure and classic expressions. The prophets of Israel from Amos down to John the Baptist furnished the religious background out of which it was historically possible for Jesus to appear. Without the prophets from Amos down to John, from the strictly historical point of view, there could have been no Jesus. Apart from them there would have been no historical antecedents, no sources of religious genius, that could furnish the conditions necessary for the production of a prophet like Jesus—the prince of them all.

The prophetic religion of the Old Testament constituted the solid substratum for all of Jesus' thinking and teaching, feeling and faith. In him the best of the prophets lived again—Amos, Hosea, Micah, the Isaiahs, Jeremiah. Jesus was the spirit of their spirit. It was in the religion of the prophets that he schooled and steeled himself. He drew deeply and much from all that they represented in the way of religion. With a peculiar fineness of feeling he entered into the highest sentiments, into the deepest convictions, into the most exalted faith of the prophets. With an immediate intuition he sensed the spirit of their thought, teaching and faith. This spirit Jesus brought to new life, always enriched and enhanced in his own personal experience. He seems to have desired nothing more than to fulfill the prophetic religion of his people, to carry it on to its full and fruitful culmination. Jesus thought of himself as a prophet.

This he was, through and through a prophetic mind and personality.

The prophetic elements in Jesus' person and work are so clear that they need hardly to be pointed out. He belongs to the ranks of Israel's prophets by virtue of his religious thinking and teaching. In his conception of the essence of religion as reverence and righteousness he is prophetic. On his lips we hear Israel's great confession of its prophetic faith:

"Hear, O Israel; the Lord our God, the Lord is one; and thou shalt love the Lord thy God with all thy heart, and with all thy soul, and with all thy mind, and with all thy strength." (Mark 12, 29-30.)

To this classic expression of religious reverence and devotion he adds its prophetic correlate on religion as righteousness,

"Thou shalt love thy neighbor as thyself." (Mark 12,31.)

With the characteristic proneness of the prophets to focus faith on principal points, to simplify its statements, and to intensify its feeling and fervor, Jesus declares these to be the two great commandments, the sum and substance of all that religion requires of men. Both of these Old Testament commandments are the crystallization of the religion of the prophets. In his conception of religion as moral and ethical, as inward, as purity of heart, Jesus is prophetic.

Jesus often quotes the prophets.[10] Not a few of his words, that are not explicit quotations, are clear echoes

[10]As examples of direct quotations, see: Hosea 6,6 in Matt. 9,13 and 12,7; Isa. 29,13 in Mark 7,6-7; Isa. 61,1-2 in Luke 4,17-19.

and recasts of prophetic utterances.[11] Apart from these direct reflections of prophetic utterances, his point of view, the whole of his religious approach is prophetic. In his attitude toward official and organized religion he is a true son of his prophetic predecessors. He confronted the conventional religion of his day with a skepticism that comes straight from the spirit of the prophets, and his criticisms and indictments are prophetic in position, uttered in the prophetic fearlessness that does not hesitate to reject long-accepted traditions in favor of the religious truth revealed in personal experience. Jesus' future for Jerusalem, the temple, and his people is the prophetic picture. Jerusalem is the Holy City, "the city of the great King"; he weeps over it, and forecasts its fall. His indictments against a religion of cult are not as prominent as in some of his forerunners. He seems more indifferent toward it than incited to speech by it, but he is still the prophet when cult and ceremony are the sole fruits of piety. He never attacks the cult worship of the temple. For Jesus, the temple is holy because of Him who dwells therein; it is God's house, a place to worship, to which he goes immediately upon entering the Holy City. His act of cleansing the temple is a prophetic act, prompted by prophetic piety, and accomplished in prophetic zeal. In cleansing the temple of its trade and traffic Jesus does not have in mind the purity of a center of cult, but of a house of prayer. (Mark 11,15-17; Isa. 56,7; Jer. 7,11.) Yet over against his love for the temple stands his announcement of its destruction, an echo of Isaiah, Micah, Jeremiah and Ezekiel. (Mark 13,1-2.)

---

[11]Cf. Mic. 7,6 and Matt. 10,35; Mic. 6,8 and Matt. 23,23.

The national and political element is not as prominent in Jesus' thought as it is in the Old Testament prophets. Although Jesus loved his people with typical prophetic passion and restricted his work to them, he is not the intense patriot that some of his predecessors were, nor does he undertake the rôle of the statesman as some of them did. However, his picture of the future is painted in Jewish colors. He sees his disciples sitting on twelve thrones judging the twelve tribes of Israel (Matt. 19,28; Luke 22,30b), and he pictures Abraham, Isaac and Jacob reclining at the Messianic feast. These features belong to the Jewishness of Jesus, but they are not genuine Jewish particularism. He promises that the peoples shall come

"from the east and west, and from the north and south, and shall sit down with Abraham, Isaac, and Jacob, and all the prophets, in the kingdom of God." (Luke 13,28-29; Matt. 8,12.)

Like the prophets before him he preached a future theocratic society, but it was a universally human, not a distinctly Jewish value. Jesus began where his last great predecessor, Second Isaiah (40-66), left off.

The great themes of Israel's prophetic message reappear in the message of Jesus—repentance, warning, judgment to come, a day of God in the future. His style of presentation is, in general, prophetic—directly to the point, clear, compact, vividly projected in graphic pictures. In Jesus we see the tense, terse treatments of a great theme very like the prophets. In a single picture he casts his thought into a rough relief that strikes the hearer and that sends the message home to his heart.

However, he is much more matter-of-fact, much less fantastic in his style than some of the prophets who present
their thought in an unreal and extravagant imagery that
is often hard to fathom.   Jesus possessed a sense for the
real world that the more temperamental of his prophetic
predecessors lacked.

Like the prophets, at least the majority, Jesus' manner
of presentation is impromptu, offhand, extemporaneous.
His speech is the spontaneous inspired speech of the
prophet—a style of speech that nature gives, that men do
not learn.   Like the prophets, he is convinced of the divine inspiration and origin of his message.   But in his
words the stereotyped formula of the prophets is not to
be found, "Thus saith Jehovah," and God does not appear as the real spokesman in the first person with the
prophet only His mouthpiece.   Often in the prophetic
utterances it is the divine ego, not the prophet, who is
speaking.[12]   In these formulas, "Thus saith Jehovah,"
and in their I-style (*Ichstyl*) which presents God as the
real speaker, the old prophets practically disclaim all
personal responsibility for the origin and content of their
message, and in some cases the prophetic personality is
wholly submerged by the divine ego.   But this element
has no counterpart in the experience of Jesus.   He never,
in the first three Gospels, disclaims his message as his
own.   His own ego is never submerged by the divine
presence and pressure that possessed the more primitive
prophetic personality.   He feels himself to be God's
spokesman; his message is from God.   But this conviction of the divine origin and content of his message never
results in a complete or partial suppression of his normal

---

[12]Cf. Amos 3,7-8; 5,2 16-20; 8,11-13; Isa. 1,10-17; Mic. 1,6; 2,3;
Nahum 1,14; 3,5-6.

and natural self-consciousness. He did not present his message as dictated by the divine. Consciously, his message was derived from his own personal experience of God.

Jesus has the passionate, tense type of utterance characteristic of the prophet. He preaches, as he prays, under a genuine personal pressure, with a prophetic passion. His words are always intense, but always intelligible. His utterances do not pour forth in the violent volume of some of the prophets, which often resulted in a turbulent turmoil of thought and which left the hearer in a state of confusion. Jesus' words carried their own conviction with them; he spoke as one having authority, but he does not seem to have spoken under the intense, often uncontrolled, personal pressure of some of the prophets before him.[13]

Jesus is prophetic also in his general experience of religion. His sources of religious knowledge are prophetic, immediate personal experience. His religious certainties are prophetic, born of deep inner conviction. He feels himself called of God, commissioned to a very definite task in behalf of the divine cause, and it is in the light of an Isaiah passage (61,1-2) that he interprets for himself this call and commission (Luke 4,16-21). In the whole of his religious consciousness Jesus was prophetic. But this topic is reserved for a later chapter, and we may anticipate here by saying that, in his religious convictions and certainties, in his attitudes and aspirations, in his enthusiasm and in his earnestness, in the fineness of his feeling and in the firmness of his faith, in

---

[13]For examples of this prophetic pressure, *see*: II Kings 5,26; 19,14; Jer. 6,11; 20,7-9; 23,18; Amos 3,8; 7,14; Isa. 6; Ezek. 1; 3,14-15; Zech. 1,7*ff*.; 3,1*ff*.

his manner and mood, in his tense temperament, in the substance of his thought, in the tone of his message, in his passion and zeal for his work, Jesus was true to the type, a genuine prophetic genius.

But there is one respect in which Jesus, in his experience of religion, stands quite apart, not only from his prophetic predecessors but from the great representatives of religious genius generally, both before and after him. Here we have in mind the rôle which unusual psychic phenomena—visions and voices, ecstasies and exaltations of spirit—have played in the experience of great religious genius.[14]

JESUS AND HIS PROPHETIC CONTEMPORARY

Any inquiry into the formative factors and forces that contributed to the sum total of all that Jesus was and represented in the way of religion must include the person and work of that rugged Jordan prophet, John the Baptist, Jesus' great prophetic contemporary. We do not know a great deal about the Baptist.[15] As Professor Deissmann writes, "Only the shadow of the Baptist falls across the scene of the Gospel story, but it is a truly great shadow."[16]

[14]This topic is reserved for special study: *Visions and Voices in the Religious Experience of Jesus.* Cf. p. xi.

[15]The following references present a complete list of the New Testament material on the Baptist and his following: Luke 1,5-25 57-80; Matt. 3,1-17 and Mark 1,1-11 and Luke 3,1-22; Matt. 4,12 and Mark 1,14; Matt. 9,14 and Mark 2,18 and Luke 5,33; Matt. 11,2-19 and Luke 7,18-35; Matt. 14, 1-12 and Mark 6,14-29; Luke 9,7-9; Matt. 16,14 and Mark 8,28 and Luke 9,29; Matt. 17,13; Luke 11,1; 16,16; Matt. 21,25-26 and Mark 11,30-32 and Luke 20,4-6; Matt. 21,32; Acts 1,5 22a; 10,37b; 11,16; 13,24-25; 18,24-19,7.

[16]*Evangelium und Urchristentum,* p. 81.

What we know of the Baptist shows us that he was true to the type, a genuine prophetic genius. So far as we know he did not belong to the literary prophets in that he or his disciples committed his message to writing, as is the case with the majority of the prophets of Israel known to us. Nevertheless, he belongs in the ranks of the great prophets of Israel by virtue of the theme, character and tone of his message. Such remnants of the Baptist's message as we possess remind us at once of the stirring preaching of Amos and Micah. "John the Baptist stands alongside Isaiah and Jeremiah, the gigantic figures of the Semitic East."[17] Not only the message, but the person of the Baptist is genuinely prophetic. In his personality he resembles most two of the outstanding preliterary prophets, Nathan and Elijah. His championship of the sanctity of the family and his rebuke to Herod (Matt. 14,3-4; Mark 6,17-18; Luke 3,19-20) recall at once the religious thought and the fearless directness of expression of Nathan (II Sam. 12,1-15). If Herod had been better versed in the history of Jewish prophecy, he would probably have seen in the Baptist the ghost of Nathan, as his superstitious mind saw in Jesus the resurrected Baptist. (Matt. 14,1-2; Mark 6,14-16; Luke 9,7-9.) Upon the general public that saw and heard him, the Baptist seems to have left the impression that he was, either in reality or in interpretation, Elijah returned.[18] The Baptist's own followers seem to have found in him the Elijah (Luke 1,13-17) who, according to popular thought, had not died but would come again in fulfillment of Malachi 4,5-6. For the general public of

---

[17]Deissmann, *Evangelium und Urchristentum*, p. 82.

[18]Cf. Matt. 11,14; 14,1-2; Mark 6,14-16; Luke 9,7-9; Matt. 17,10-13; Mark 9,11-13; Luke 1,5 25.

his day, the Baptist was a prophet of God, preaching a heaven-sent message, and practising a God-given religious rite.   He was a prophet of tremendous popularity. Herod hesitated to carry out his plan against the Baptist's life, because he feared John (Mark 6,20), and the multitude counted him as a prophet (Matt. 14,5). Even some months after his death public sentiment in Jerusalem was so strong for the Baptist that the religious authorities there did not dare to disclaim the divine origin of his baptism.[19]

John the Baptist was not a Christian but a Jew. And it is difficult for us as Christians, even with the historical point of view and interest, to project a Jewish picture of the Baptist, one that does him real historical justice as a prominent figure in the religious history of his people. This task is difficult, for we involuntarily think of him in his relation to Jesus, who towers so high in Christian conception and conviction that the Baptist appears at a distinct disadvantage, a disadvantage that is unfair to the true historical significance of the Baptist and the place he really occupied in the religious life of his own day and people.

This Christian point of view and interest goes back to the New Testament itself. The New Testament picture of the Baptist is Christianized, but in it we can still detect something of his independent greatness apart from his relation to Jesus. And from our present point of view of gaining an adequate picture of the Baptist and of estimating his contribution to Jesus, we must realize that he receives from us historical justice only when we see in him a great independent prophet and preacher of Judaism

[19]Cf. Matt. 21,25-26; Mark 11,30-32; Luke 20,4-6.

with a message and mission of his own. The Baptist really bursts the bands of Judaism because he is too great to be cramped within the narrow confines of Judaism's ceremonial practise and conventional conception of religion. The Baptist, like Jesus, marks a rebirth of prophetism which always meant for Israel a shattering of the ceremonial and conventional casings that confined the free spirit of Hebrew religious genius and which required a return to those fresh clear springs from which religion, in its purity, flowed forth in a vast and vigorous volume.

Our New Testament materials on the Baptist's message and mission are almost discouragingly meager. Hardly more than a dozen sentences ascribed to him have come down to us. But the meagerness of these materials is so offset by their distinctive character that we can hope to secure a very fair idea of what he said and hoped to accomplish. Among the first three Gospel writers, Mark's account of the Baptist is briefest and most inadequate. (1,2-8.) The independent aspects of the Baptist's message and mission receive only incidental notice. Mark gives us no extracts from the Baptist's preaching of repentance; he presents only his announcement of the Coming One. Mark is interested only in the Messianic, the distinctly Christian aspects of the Baptist's ministry. For Mark, the Baptist's work exhausted itself in announcing and preparing the way for the Coming One; he is the herald, the advance-agent, the forerunner of the Messiah who, for Mark, is Jesus. In Mark's picture we see the natural Christian neglect of the independent features of the Baptist and his work and the natural Christian inclination and interest in his dependent relationship as a subordinate contributor to Jesus and his work.

We are indebted chiefly to Matthew (3,1-12) and Luke (3,1-18) for our knowledge of the independent phases of the Baptist's ministry. Both preserve extracts from his message of repentance. (Matt. 3,7-10; Luke 3,7-9.) These extracts are very brief, but they are distinctive in character, and they serve to show very clearly that in the Baptist we have before us a genuine prophet and a real revival of the long lost prophetic fire and fearlessness. His sermon on repentance in Matthew and Luke is a sterling prophetic message. With the traditional sternness and vigor of Israel's prophets he preaches a reconstruction of mind and life in view of threatening judgment. Like Amos, his view of the future is primarily pessimistic; for Israel there is coming, and that soon, the judgment of God, in which there is to be no preference for the sons of Abraham. Thus, for Matthew and Luke, the Baptist's significance does not exhaust itself in his dependent relationship to Jesus. He is not merely the herald, the advance-agent, the forerunner of the Messiah. The announcement of the Coming One is only one element, perhaps not the principal element, in his public work. The Baptist appears as a great prophet and preacher with a message and mission of his own, a man of powerful personality who hurls prophetic warnings into the face of his complacent contemporaries demanding repentance in view of God's imminent judgment.

To Luke (3,10-14) we are indebted for a further phase of the Baptist's independent work. In the demands which he makes of the various classes of his contemporaries he strikes upon the same simple, yet fundamental themes that run through the messages of some of the greatest of his prophetic predecessors, and he, as they, insists upon the moralization of religion. Here the Baptist's religious thinking calls to mind at once that of Amos and Micah.

In his announcement of the Coming One, the Baptist recognizes and confesses the limitations of his own person and work, and he welcomes the advent of one greater than himself, before whom he passes into insignificance. Here the Baptist reveals a modesty that belongs to true greatness, and this genuine consciousness of self-limitation is one of the clearest features of his personality in the Gospel picture. Naturally, such fitted into the Christian estimate of the Baptist, but there is a genuineness about it even in the Christian picture that assures us that we meet here the native nobility of his prophetic personality, consecrated completely to the divine cause. The Baptist of history did feel himself the called and commissioned prophet of God whose contributions were insignificant when compared with the consummation to be accomplished by the Coming One.

Matthew (3,4) and Mark (1,6) furnish a brief notice, neglected by Luke, concerning the Baptist's personal habits of dress and diet. He is clad in primitive garments, which according to Zechariah 3,4 are the mark of the prophet, camel's hair and a leathern girdle about his loins; his food consists of locusts and wild honey. These eccentric habits of life brought upon him the ridicule of the religious leaders whom Jesus quotes as saying, "He hath a demon." (Matt. 11,18; Luke 7,33.) In his strange apparel the Baptist appears as a striking figure, leading the secluded, yet vigorous life of the wilderness prophet. His ascetic habits throw an interesting and instructive light on his character; he appears as strict in his demands upon himself, in his own self-discipline, as in his demands upon others. Jesus refers to him as a prophet who came "eating no bread nor drinking wine." (Matt. 11,18; Luke 7,33; 1,15.) But his own eccentric habits and ascetic self-discipline he does not seem to have required of others. His followers fasted (Mark 2,18), but they do not appear to have been an ascetic sect withdrawn from the regular social order. This fact is also instructive, for it shows that the Baptist, with all of his aggressiveness, was in mind and disposition free from religious fanaticism.

In one of his great addresses Jesus characterizes the Baptist, first in a negative way, as not "a man clothed in soft raiment," "gorgeously apparelled," "living delicately," then in a brief positive statement, as "a prophet," even "more than a prophet." (Matt.11,7-9; Luke 7,24-26.) Just such a staunch and stalwart prophetic character the Baptist's contemporaries seem to have found in him. The thronging of the crowds to the withdrawn scene of his work testifies to the power of the personality of this Jordan preacher. He does not go to the people; they seek him out. At the center of such a situation the Baptist must have stood as a man of great personal powers, as a decidedly capable and forceful character, delivering an unusually striking and powerful message.

All of the Gospel writers open their accounts of Jesus' public life with a brief treatment of the Baptist and his work. The New Testament accounts of Jesus and John are linked firmly together for the reason that such was the state of the facts. Apart from the fact that the Baptist fitted quite naturally into the account of Jesus as his forerunner according to the Christian point of view, the Gospel writers were forced to devote some attention to the Baptist under the very pressure of historical fact. They could not ignore the Baptist entirely, for Jesus and John were too close together in every way. Apart from such general considerations as the fact that Jesus and John were of the same race, that they were contemporaries, that they worked among the same people, and that they appeared in immediate succession in point of time, there are other facts that would make these two great prophets historically inseparable. John was Jesus' predecessor in public; he was on the scene of action first, delivering a striking message that brought great crowds to hear and to heed, and carrying on an important work that was in an advanced stage when Jesus joined his audience. Jesus was so deeply impressed by the Baptist that he too was baptized by him. He held John in highest esteem, and he spoke of him on more than one occasion. The very importance, as well as the number, of Jesus' references to the Baptist would demand that the Gospel writers, sooner or later, give some account of him and his work. And it would be impossible for any Christian writer, whether early or late, with any sense of personal or historical justice to give an account of Jesus, who had so much in common both in message and in mission with his great contemporary, without giving at least some appreciative notice to John the Baptist such as the author has tried to do in the above sketch. Now we may turn to our main question: Did John the Baptist make a real contribution to Jesus? If so, what was it?

According to the New Testament account, Jesus and John met but once, at the Jordan—a meeting that seems to have meant more for Jesus than it did for the Baptist. In spite of Matthew's recognition scene (3,14-15), there is no reason for supposing that the Baptist recognized

Jesus, either personally or officially. In Mark the personal contacts between Jesus and John begin and end at the Jordan. In Matthew and Luke, however, they are brought together indirectly by the Baptist's deputation of some of his disciples to Jesus with the question, "Art thou he that cometh, or look we for another?" (Matt. 11,2-7; Luke 7,18-24)—not necessarily the question of one who has believed and later falls into doubt, as is the common Christian conception, but very probably the question of one who, for the first time, begins to reflect on the possibilities of Jesus' person. What Jesus came to mean for the Baptist we do not know, but what the Baptist meant for Jesus is quite clear; at least, there comes to Jesus from the Baptist an imposing impression and, what is still more, a deep personal influence.

The frequent allusions of Jesus to the Baptist, both in public and in private, are evidence enough of the fact that he was acquainted in detail with his message, mission and person. In the message of Jesus we hear clear echoes of the message of the Baptist, not only in the general theme of repentance, but in expressions and figures used by the Baptist which later come from the lips of Jesus,[20] and in one case, at least, a verbatim extract.[21] The full effect of the Baptist's message on Jesus, however, is not revealed in such reproductions of it as Jesus makes, but in his act of presenting himself to John for baptism. This act is a tremendous tribute to the Baptist, his message and ministry; and his response to the religious values represented by the Baptist makes it clear be-

[20]Cf. Matt. 3,7 and Luke 3,7b with Matt. 12,34; 23,33; Matt. 3,12 with 13,30b; Matt. 3,9 and Luke 3,8a with Matt. 7,16-18; 12,33 and Luke 6,43-44.
[21]Cf. Matt. 3,10 and Luke 3,9 with Matt. 7,19.

yond all possibility of doubt that the Baptist made upon Jesus a profound and deep impression.

But the Baptist's contribution did not exhaust itself in this deep impression. Matthew and Luke preserve to us one of the greater addresses of Jesus which has for its theme the Baptist and his work and which is commonly known as his address on the Baptist. (Matt. 11,2-19; Luke 7,18-35.) This is the only occasion upon which Jesus ever digresses from his main theme of the kingdom of God—but even here he does not desert it entirely— and devotes a series of statements to a person. This passage is very important for our present problem of determining the Baptist's contribution, for it preserves to us Jesus' estimate of John. His statement here shows very clearly that he did not look upon the Baptist merely as his own personal advance-agent and announcer, but as a popular and powerful preacher of repentance. Jesus' personal view of the Baptist is more Jewish and less Christian than that of the Gospel writers and the traditional Christian view since. Within the New Testament, Jesus does the Baptist the greatest historical, religious and personal justice. He does not take a Messianic view of the Baptist in the sense that the Baptist is his own personal forerunner. In his address on the Baptist, he brings this Jordan prophet into a direct relationship with his own cause, the kingdom of God. He felt that the Baptist's work had an important bearing on his own, and it is in the light of the Baptist's bearing on his own work, rather than on his own person, that he gives his estimate. John is "much more than a prophet." For the thought of Jesus, it is John and the kingdom of God, not John and the Messiah.

One of the most enigmatic of all of Jesus' words has to do with the Baptist and the kingdom of God:

"From the days of John the Baptist until now the kingdom of heaven suffereth violence, and men of violence take it by force."   (Matt. 11,12; Luke 16,16.)

At least one thing is quite clear in this puzzling utterance: Jesus brings John the Baptist and the kingdom of God into a vital relationship.   Between the Baptist and himself he established a purely personal rather than official bond.

"Among them that are born of women there hath not arisen a greater than John the Baptist."   (Matt. 11,11; Luke 7,28.)

Such is his own personal estimate of the Baptist.   In other words, John is, in the opinion of Jesus, the greatest man that ever lived.   This is a striking statement for any person to make about another, and John must have been a most extraordinary figure to call forth such an exalted tribute.   This almost extravagant statement makes it clear that the Baptist must have exercised on Jesus a strong and lasting influence, for it is inconceivable that one man could entertain of another such an exalted estimate without having been greatly influenced by him.

Just what this personal influence was we are not in a position to say; our sources of information are too inadequate.   Some are of the opinion that Jesus was the Baptist's voluntary successor; he took up the divine cause where the Baptist was forced to lay it down.   Matthew seems to have something of this view in 4,12 when he

relates that the news of the Baptist's imprisonment brings
Jesus into Galilee for his public work. Others agree
with the Gospel writers that the Baptist was one of the
principal promoting factors and forces that brought Jesus
out of private into public life: "the holy spark had lept
from the Baptist to Him."[22] But Professor Deissmann,
I think, is nearer the facts when he makes the Baptist's
contribution even more personal, "The significance of the
Baptist for Jesus, and thereby for the religious history
of mankind, is that he, by his powerful message, released
in the life of Jesus what had been deposited there as prophetic tension, and which, once released, was to work
itself out in the gospel."[23]

For the historical student, there must have been some
vital personal contribution of the Baptist to Jesus, of
which Jesus himself was clearly conscious. And in our
task of seeking out the forces and factors that contributed
to the making of a religious genius like Jesus, the only
great one of a personal sort upon which we can determine
definitely is John the Baptist. From the strictly historical point of view, the Baptist seems to have played a
more important rôle—a rôle that amounted to a strong
and lasting influence—in the life of Jesus than any other
individual known to us. But from the very evident fact
that Jesus was strongly influenced by the Baptist we must
not, however, draw the false conclusion, to which not a
few have been led, that he was an imitator of the Baptist. Jesus was more than a disciple of the Baptist, and
none knew this better than Jesus himself.

In conclusion on the subject of Jesus and his pro-

[22]*The Religion of Jesus and the Faith of Paul*, by A. Deissmann,
p. 129. Published by Doubleday, Doran and Company.
[23]*Evangelium und Urchristentum*, p. 83.

phetic contemporary, we may bring the two into brief comparison in order that we may appreciate the elements which they have in common and the differences which preserve the individuality of each.

Both Jesus and John were unconventional and uncompromising preachers of religion. Both were unprofessional preachers, laymen from the rank and file of the Jewish people as were the great majority of their prophetic ancestors, lay prophets who championed the divine cause to which they felt themselves called and commissioned.

Jesus and John had much in common in the theme and character of their message. Both preached repentance in view of the impending future, which for the Baptist was the divine judgment to be accomplished by the Coming One; for Jesus this future was the kingdom of God in which the elements of judgment, to be accomplished by the Son of man, were not lacking. The message of Jesus has a greater variety in presentation than that of John, whose message would present more variety perhaps if we had a fuller record of it. (Luke 3,10-14.) However, the character of the Baptist's thought does not suggest the rich and attractive variety of that of the mind of Jesus. But in the Gospel picture of Jesus and John, each has a style of his own, a manner and method that is natural, and we are grateful to the writers of the first three Gospels for preserving to us the individuality of each.

In the temper of their thinking Jesus and John have much in common. Both look upon the present order of things as on the verge of being supplanted, and that soon. The Baptist, however, seems more persistently pessimistic in his view of the impending events. There is a prominent strain of optimism in the thought of Jesus for this world, its human life and history, not to be found in that of John. Jesus takes a world-affirming attitude not apparent in the thought and temper of the Baptist.

Both Jesus and John broke with family ties for the sake of complete consecration to the divine cause which they championed. One lived the life of a wilderness recluse, and his work had its scene far apart from the regular social order. The other lived among men as they lived and took pleasure in the regular affairs and conventions of society; he worked in the midst of the thoroughfares of the people, calling and challenging men where he found them.

Jesus did not practise baptism[24] as John did. Even a command for baptism in the first three Gospels is found only on the lips of the Risen Lord. (Matt. 28,19; Mark 16,16.) In this religious rite we are followers of the Baptist rather than of Jesus.

In their personal habits of life and conduct Jesus and John differ greatly. Jesus did not share the Baptist's eccentric peculiarities of dress and diet, nor his ascetic self-discipline. John was condemned for his asceticism, and Jesus for his indulgence. Here they stand at opposite extremes. This contrast Jesus brings out clearly at the close of his address on the Baptist:

"For John the Baptist is come eating no bread nor drinking wine; and ye say, He hath a demon. The Son of man is come eating and drinking; and ye say, Behold, a gluttonous man, and a winebibber, a friend of publicans and sinners." (Luke 7,33-34; Matt. 11, 18-19.)

---

[24]*See* on the contrary John 3,22-26, where Jesus is represented by the Fourth Gospel as practising baptism; *see also* the correction, or contradiction, of this in 4,2.

Both Jesus and John had a group of intimate personal followers or disciples that survived after their death. The following of the Baptist presents certain elements of religious organization in the observation of certain rites and practises. In the following of Jesus all such elements are missing. Jesus' disciples were held to one another and to him by a purely personal bond which must have been present to some extent in the relationship between John and his disciples.

On the general public Jesus and John seem to have left something of the same impression; both revive the memory of Elijah, and some, with Herod, regard Jesus as the Baptist come to life.[25] The fates and fortunes of the two men are much alike. Both were successful with the general public and unsuccessful with the recognized religious leaders. Both suffered martyrdom for the divine cause which they championed.

Between these two great prophets of religion there seems to have been no rivalry, but there was between their followers. (Mark 2,18; John 3,22-26.) The immeasurably greater of the two held the other in highest respect and in deepest appreciation.

JESUS HIMSELF

Thus far we have sought to point out those factors and forces in Israel's religious past that contributed to the production of a religious genius like Jesus, elements that reappear in his own religious personality as solid and substantial contributions—the Old Testament, the prophetic genius in general, and John the Baptist in particular.

---

[25]Cf. Matt. 14,1-2; Mark 6,14-16; Luke 9,7-9; Matt. 16,13-14; Mark 8,27-28; Luke 9,18-19.

Jesus was not an isolated figure in human history, a super-natural intervention unconnected with the past and present of his people. To isolate him from the religious life of his people is not only an injustice to both Jesus and his people, but to the plainest facts of the Gospel records and to the simplest sense of the historian. It is equally unjust to explain Jesus exhaustively by pointing out his dependence upon the religious heritage behind and around him. Very often we meet these two extremes. Some emphasize the remoteness of Jesus from his people and their religion and will see him only as entirely new and different. But, as we have seen, there are important elements common to Jesus and his people, and equally essential to both. Others have stressed his closeness to the past and present to such a degree that Jesus as an independent personality is entirely submerged in the religious history of his people. But, as we shall see, Jesus is more than a mere mosaic of moral precepts from the Jewish law and prophets; his personal religion is more than a frail framework of religious maxims from his people's past.

In every feature of the Gospel picture one is impressed with the genuine Jewishness of Jesus. In religious thought and teaching, in feeling and faith, he was a true son of Israel. He lived and moved and had his being in the rich devotional life of his people. His personal piety roots deep in all that is best in the religious traditions and genius of his race. Of this organic bond that held him to his people and their faith Jesus was fully conscious. The fulfillment of the law and the prophets he regards as his life's work. (Matt. 5,17.) His own disciples saw him in this light. On the mount of transfiguration they beheld him transfigured between the two great representatives of Old Testament religion, Moses and Elijah. Here Jesus belongs, for in his message and mission, in his person, the best of both reappears, renewed, refreshed and reinforced. The three disciples on the mount of transfiguration saw more than they knew when they beheld Jesus in communion with Moses and Elijah. In him the spirit of both men lived again—the conscientious code of character and conduct of the Mosaic law, and the prophetic passion and personal piety of Elijah and his eighth and sixth century successors. Thus Jesus stands in the purest waters of that strong steady stream of Israel's religious genius and faith. But in him that stream is widened and deepened, and its current becomes a rushing torrent that sustains and supports, and that pours forth its power into every accessible channel, into every available course of human life.

Jesus was much more than a faithful reproduction of Israel's religion, much more than the compact summarization of all that went before him. In him we see the perfection of Israel's purest piety, the natural and organic culmination of his people's peculiar genius for religion. Jesus is Israel's reason for existence; in him her historical task is accomplished. Jesus should be the chief pride of the Jewish people; he is the finest flower of its religious life. May the day come, and that speedily, when liberal Jews and liberal Christians will forget those unpleasant historical developments, and both in a spirit of profound reverence approach, appraise and appropriate Jesus for the intrinsic religious values which he alone perfectly represents!

Much of Jesus' personal piety is simply a loyal reproduction of the traditional religion of his people. Great fundamentals of the religion of Israel reappear in him

THE RELIGIOUS GENIUS OF JESUS 57

perisheth, and the skins: but *they put* new wine into
fresh wine-skins."

But in another word, Jesus brings the new and the old
into an organic bond. They merge; each loses its identity; there is no new, no old; both have disappeared to
reappear in the freshness of a living personality, as is
clear in the parable in Matthew 13,52:

> "Therefore every scribe who hath been made a dis-
> ciple of the kingdom of heaven is like unto a man that
> is a householder, who bringeth forth out of his treasure
> things new and old."

It would be difficult to find a more accurate statement
of the relation of the new and the old in the religious
experience of Jesus than we find in this parable. From
his treasure house, his own personal religious experience,
he brought forth things old and new. And as Loisy
writes, "The importance of these elements depends neither on their antiquity nor on their novelty, but on the
place they fill in the religious teaching of Jesus, and on
the value that Jesus himself attached to them."[28] It is
important to know just what Jesus accepted and rejected
in the religious past of his people, to know how he
recast and appropriated that which he inherited, for his
revisions and rejections reveal the very essence of his
experience of religion. He retained more than he rejected, and his sense in selection, his care in criticism,
testify to the purity and power of his own personal piety.
He subjected certain precepts of the past to the most
cutting criticism; his revisions often amount to rejections;

---

[28] *The Gospel and the Church*, by A. Loisy, p. 11. Published by Charles
Scribner's Sons.

he revolted openly against the inherited practises, interpretations and neglects of his contemporaries. But that
great body of Israel's religion, with the fine fiber of its
prophetic faith and the sound tissue of its moral law,
Jesus not only accepted but assimilated as his own.

In Jesus' personal position with regard to the religious
past of his people, we see a series of strange contrasts
and contradictions: a reverent conservatism over against
a radical criticism, a faithful reproduction followed by a
total rejection, a fidelity accompanied by a sovereign
freedom. But just such contrasts and contradictions
form the stuff that new life is made of, and in Jesus we
see that pressure of paradox that only truly great personalities can bear. Jesus is conservative in his attitude toward tradition, but he appears thus only because he is
actually above it. It is the exalted elevation of his experience of religion that causes him to appear conservative.
In reality, Jesus is never uncritical. For both the old and
the new he sets the test of validation in his own religious
experience; both must verify themselves for him personally. This type of criticism is born only of a deep personal experience of God in an individual life. Such a
criticism can conserve, yet it can cut to the very core. But
in the Gospel picture, whether we come upon new or old,
we are always confronted with Jesus himself.

There can be no doubt but that a great many, even important, elements in Jesus' personal piety came to him by
social inheritance. No man of that early date had behind
him a richer religious heritage than Jesus, who sprang
from a pious race whose religion had already reached a
remarkably high level and was the central element and
interest of its culture. But the personal piety of Jesus has
something much greater than the authority of tradition

behind it. It is exactly at those points where the best of his religious heritage reaches the deeper sources of his personal life and finds validity and warrant in his own religious experience that Jesus makes his great contribution. In spite of all the elements that held him reverently to the past, it is clear that Jesus belongs on the side of the religions of the spirit over against the religions of authority. For Jesus, the sources and standards of religious authority are not located in the past; they are in the present, a matter of personal experience. As Professor Coe writes, "Religious experience itself is a revaluation of values."[29]

Jesus is not to be measured over against his past or present by an absolute originality but by the contribution that comes in his experience of religion. The distinctive elements are not what he shares in common with his religious past or present, nor in those things which appear to be new, but in those things, whether inherited or original, which command his own religious loyalty and upon which his religious faith and devotion center. The very weight of Jesus' religious convictions, the certainty with which he expresses them, is something new in the religion of his day and people. It was this unique religious experience that brought him out beyond the confines of his people's past and present; it came by an irresistible inner necessity that operated at the very core of his being.

There are lines, divergent and convergent, that lead down to Jesus. We can trace our way back to some of the major sources that lay in the religious past from which he sprang. We can locate certain stimulations in the surroundings in which he lived that account for some

[92] *The Psychology of Religion,* by G. A. Coe, p. 222. Published by the University of Chicago Press.

of the particular attitudes which he took in religious matters. These things may not be overlooked as contributing factors, but when all has been said and done, we have not explained Jesus himself. Even if we had far more materials concerning his religious development and his mature experience of religion than we possess, the final analysis and reconstruction would be a mere patchwork. The religion of Israel is only the historical background before and out of which Jesus arose as something different, great and grand. Jesus is positively unique, creatively genial, both in the purity and in the power of his personal piety. In the last analysis he stands before us as the prince of humanity's prophets, the perfection of religious genius. Even the most searching psychology can not press its way into the sacrosanct, into the soul habitat of Jesus. We can not analyze it, but we are permitted to know that it is there. In Jesus we see an inexplicable mystery and depth of personality, a genuine genius whose holy element is religion. We call Jesus a religious genius, but in this we have only given him a name that leaves him as much of an enigma as ever. As an historical fact he stands as incontestable as he is inexplicable, and as such he commands the investigator's recognition and reverence.

The plainest human personality remains for us a problem and a mystery. But when personality reaches the peaks and pinnacles that are clearly in view in all their grandeur and glory and yet tower high above us, then we begin to feel, to use the language of Professor Otto, that we are in the presence of *the holy*; we feel that it is *wholly other* than ourselves, and yet we are irresistibly drawn to it. Such is the case in Jesus. There is in him that *unexplained residuum*, that *personal X*, that defies definition yet very clearly demonstrates itself. For want of a better term, we call it *religious genius*. It is that *something besides, above* and *beyond,* that *elusive extra* which we can not explain. It bewilders and baffles the understanding; yet we sense it clearly and we feel unmistakably that it seeks to impart itself to us.

We are not in a position to unveil the deepest secrets of Jesus' religious personality. As in the case of other great geniuses, we may approach, admire, appreciate, appropriate, but we can not explain Jesus. In our study of him, sooner or later, we must halt in reverence because we have gone as far as we may go. And for all practical purposes we may stop here, not only because we must, but because we can see all that we are in need of seeing in order to know him and to become his intelligent followers. Our task is not to explain Jesus, but to learn to know him. We are in a position to do this; we do have the materials for the construction of a very clear picture of him, of his pure personal piety, his deep experience of God and religion. And this is all that really matters in our practical problem of deriving from him the highest religious helpfulness. To assist ever so modestly in the winning of an adequate knowledge of the religious experience of Jesus is the hope behind the chapters that follow.

CHAPTER II

The Religious Faith of Jesus

In the study of any great religious genius it is of paramount importance that we learn what he believed, that we come to some adequate understanding of his religious faith; otherwise, we stand little chance of knowing the man himself. The religious faith of the great genius is the key to his whole life. It accounts for all that he is and hopes to be, all that he says and works to accomplish. It is his personal faith that the great figure of religion seeks to share with others. He does not seek to give himself to others except as this is the natural issue of his faith, and usually it is. He gives himself first of all to his faith. This faith is always intensely personal; it commands completely the whole of his life; it reaches down to the last details of his existence. It accounts for his utter and unreserved devotion to a few things and for his indifference to many things. This personal faith is firm and unfailing because it springs from the depths of great inner conviction and certainty. It gives him his life-task; it brings him into it; it carries him through to its accomplishment. His religious faith gives him his message; it is his faith that he preaches.

This faith centers upon certain religious values which he regards as infinite and permanent, the supreme concerns of human life. To these values he commits himself so completely that all else falls into the background of his attention. Every other issue he sees only in its relation to them. He is a man of few thoughts and interests, but about these few the whole of his conscious existence

62

centers. It is this intense concentration upon a very limited scope that enables him to make his great contribution. The religious faith of the genius who makes a permanent contribution focuses upon God and His cause among men. He is wholly convinced that God has a cause in human life and history, that He will accomplish it, and that soon. This is the very pulse of his religious life; it is the most certain, the clearest single element in his experience.

In the case of Jesus a study of his religious faith is absolutely indispensable, for apart from it he is wholly unintelligible. It was his religious faith that made him what he was, that accounts for all that he said and did. We must ask ourselves the question: *What* did Jesus believe? And equally important is its natural correlate: *How* did Jesus believe? These questions historical Christianity has never taken seriously, but for us to-day in our religious approach to Jesus they furnish the one key to all that he represents in the way of religion, to the whole of his personality. The answers to these questions are not to be found in the official beliefs of historical Christianity; they are not guaranteed in the formal and recognized statements of faith. We must turn directly to the Gospel picture and let Jesus speak for himself so far as this is possible. He will not say all that we should like to hear, but he alone can give us an adequate answer. The ability to answer these questions does not require a complete critical equipment, for the religious faith and beliefs of Jesus are as clear as any feature in the Gospel picture; they are unmistakable even for the devotional reader.

By the religious beliefs of Jesus we mean those elements in his thinking and feeling that are essential and distinctive, those elements that mark and make him as other and different from any Galilean Jew of his day. Many of Jesus' beliefs were simply the common property of his contemporaries. His beliefs in heaven and hell, in Satan and his demons, in the resurrection and the judgment, in angels and the future life, all are simply the reflections of the religious views, ideas and conceptions of his people and day. All of these things came to him by way of social inheritance from his religious past and contemporary religious environment. On them he exercised no criticism; he made no important revisions or rejections; in their main body he simply accepted them. In all of these matters Jesus was as orthodox as any of his contemporaries. We might single out all of his words on these subjects, systematize all of his statements in which these themes are involved, and in the end have only a cross-section of the religious thought-world of first-century Judaism. All of these matters are purely secondary and incidental. They are characteristic of him, but equally characteristic of his contemporaries. Some of these questions were involved in the sectarianism of Jesus' day, but over against the factions that fought their forensic fights on these issues he stood with a sovereign freedom and independence. The distinctive elements of his faith fall entirely outside of these things. It was not his religious opinions that separated Jesus from his contemporaries, but his religious experience that expressed itself in a great personal faith that was entirely his very own.

The personal religious faith of Jesus is much more than a group of beliefs. When we come to those distinctive elements in his faith, to those things that are essential to the understanding of him, we shall find that they are much more than mere matters of intellectual acceptance and entertainment. A compendium of his religious beliefs, ideas and conceptions might be exhaustive and yet miss entirely the really distinctive features. Religious beliefs and theological views may be ever so widely and loyally accepted, and yet mean little in the life of the individual or group that entertains them. They are often the source of bitter prejudice and feeling, but they do not alter perceptibly the actual living of the individuals and groups concerned. They are not commanding values according to which men shape their actions, speech and spirit. Real religious faith, on the other hand, is something that men live by; it offers to them the supreme values which they in turn seek to attain. They mold the whole of their existence according to the intrinsic substance of the objects believed in. The objects of real religious faith are utterly commanding, and men feel the compulsion of living according to all that they require. This faith builds itself into the very fiber and tissue of their lives. Real religious faith is not just held and entertained; it becomes the creative element in individual character and the controlling force in social conduct.

Jesus was not a man of many beliefs. He was not an advocate of religious opinions, theological views or special ideas. He was the spokesman of God, the preacher of what God can and may mean in human life, and this meaning of God was what he himself had found God to be in his own personal experience. To speak of the religious beliefs of Jesus is not entirely to the point. It is better to speak of his personal religious faith because there is too much intense conviction and certainty in his experience, and in his expressions of this experience there is too little of the formal character, too little of the careful systematic statement and logical definition that belong to belief.

Jesus was a man of great religious faith. But what was this faith? What were the religious objects to which he accorded reverence and personal devotion? Where did his religious loyalties center? What were the great religious truths that Jesus lived by? Upon what great central issues did his personal faith focus? What were the high goals of his religious aspiration for himself and for men generally? What were those supreme values which he preached, for which he prayed and set everything else at naught?

When we come to answer these questions we shall find that any attempt to systematize the religious faith of Jesus is doomed to complete failure. If we succeed in securing the system, we also succeed in losing Jesus in the system. The religious faith of Jesus is not intricate and involved, but intimate and intense. It is not to be systematically stated, but very simply sensed. It is his very own, and because it is so much his own, it is full of paradox and impossible of systematization. At its original sources religious faith is always a simple thing, at least in its statement, although it may involve the whole of human life in its outlook. It must be simple because it springs from the heart of some great religious personality. It is only when faith has departed quite far from the personal sources from which it sprang that it becomes intricate and involved, and in proportion as it becomes intricate and involved, it loses its primitive power and persuasiveness.

The personal religious faith of Jesus can be summed up in a single simple statement, and this simplification comes from Jesus himself. The very heart of all that he believed and hoped he put in a single sentence,

"The kingdom of God is at hand, repent ye." (Mark 1,15.)

God and His kingdom are the focal points. They do not represent two different and independent religious values. They are one and inseparable. Jesus knows of no God apart from His kingdom, of no kingdom apart from God. Jesus brought them together—in his experience they were never apart—in that one invariable and constant expression, the kingdom of God. We begin with Jesus' faith in God for the reason that the kingdom as his message and cause is the natural and organic issue of the meaning of God in his own personal experience.

JESUS' FAITH IN GOD

The belief in God in some form or other and the belief that He means something in human life and experience are characteristic of every known religion. Even atheism has its belief about God, and the very denial of God means something for the atheist himself. Most religions distinguish themselves by their belief in God, the kind of God believed in, the difference He makes and what He matters in human life, and the meaning He has in the experience of the believer.

This is still more true of the great religious genius. We can not come to an adequate understanding of him apart from his experience of his relation to his God, apart from the meaning that God has for him personally, for in the experience of the great religious genius it is

God who means most, even everything. The whole
of his life is theocentric; he lives a God-centered existence;
God and his experience of Him are the very core of his
being.

A study of the personal piety of Jesus must begin with
his faith or belief in God, not only because it is the polar
point of all personal piety, but because "Jesus' faith in
God is the basis of the whole of his message and the
foundation of the whole of his life and work."[1] Here
we have in mind not so much his teaching about God as
his experience of God. As we shall see, Jesus' teaching
about God is only a reflex of something deeper and more
vital, his personal experience of God. Too often these
two things have been separated, or even worse, the second
has been neglected entirely. We are beginning to realize
that Jesus' teaching about God was not an academic
subject-matter that he thought out and presented in an
attractive way to his contemporaries. His teaching on
this point is purely personal, autobiographical, an announcement of what he has found God to be in his own
personal experience. Therefore we shall avoid the
beaten paths of New Testament theology in search of
those more personal elements that belong to Jesus'
experience of God.

Jesus' faith in God came to him by way of social inheritance and, in its main outlines, it is fundamentally that of
his people. Nowhere in the Gospels do we read that
Jesus leaves the impression with his contemporaries that
he is preaching a new God such as the early Christians
left with certain circles of their hearers. Biblical theology
would describe Jesus' belief in God as the ethical
monotheism of Israel—the belief that there is only one

[1]Wernle, *Jesus*, p. 41.

true God and that He is good. Jesus never questions the traditional conception of God that had been held by his people for at least eight centuries. He never undertakes a refutation of polytheism either for himself or for his contemporaries. He never seeks to validate ethical monotheism either for himself or for his hearers. On this point neither Jesus nor his audiences stood in need of conviction.

A doubt concerning the existence of God seems never to have crossed Jesus' mind. He never seeks to prove God's reality to his hearers. It was as unnatural for them as it was for him to entertain any skepticism on this point. The stock arguments for the existence of God that have appeared in Christian theology and philosophy did not occur to Jesus; in fact, they were historically impossible as elements in his thought. He knows nothing of the cosmological, ontological and teleological arguments for God's existence. He seems to have felt no need for such proof. He was too much prophet, too little philosopher and theologian, to feel any such need. The reality of God presented no problem to his religious thinking. On this point Jesus' thought springs from the primitive piety of his people, and to any one that would have suggested doubt concerning God's existence he would have turned in amazement and have answered as any pious Israelite: Has not God chosen and led His people? Has He not given to them His law? Has He not spoken to them through His prophets? Do we not know Him *now* as our Father?

The stock phraseology of Christian theism does not appear in the simple religious language of Jesus. That God is infinite, unchangeable, eternal, essential, indivisible, self-existent, that He is mind, wisdom, thought, intelligence, will, purpose, power, that He is the Supreme Person, Activity, Value, Pure Being, the Absolute, the First Cause, he never said and felt no need for saying. At the foundation of his faith in God we find no rationalistic grounds. The arguments for the character of God that are common in Christian theism have no counterpart in his religious thinking. He felt no theistic problems such as Christian theologians and philosophers have felt. The God of theology and philosophy is not the God of Jesus. The God of Jesus is the God of primitive personal piety; His existence and ethical character are assumed without question and assured without formal proof. There is nothing of abstract intellectualism in his thought of God. The God of Jesus was not born in a moment of intellectual illumination. His thought of God is not burdened and beset with intellectual problems and puzzles. In his thought there are no theological speculations, no philosophical abstractions, no sharp definitions, no carefully framed concepts; in fact, Jesus would not be Jesus if we found such. He needed no theoretical supports and confirmations, no rationalistic arguments to give content, conviction and certainty to his faith in God. As we learn to know Jesus in the first three Gospels, we see that such would never have satisfied him.

For Jesus, God is not a problem to be solved in the terms of speculative thought, but an intensely personal problem to be solved in the terms of the sum total of individual and social experience. That such is true to the Gospel picture is clear from the fact that Jesus speaks of God only in the concrete and universally intelligible terms of individual and social experience, in those intimate phrases that belong to personal piety in its purity. The prophets before Jesus wrestled with two great problems concerning the God of Israel: What God is to be worshiped, and how is He to be worshiped? The prophetic answers to these questions are the background of all that he thinks and teaches of God, but they are not problems for Jesus himself. Christian thought has sought to define God in every conceivable term of philosophy and theology, but for Jesus God was more than a problem of theoretical thought. For Jesus, as we shall see in the next chapter, God was a problem involving the sum total *God* of human experience: How may men, individually and collectively, come to know God and to do His holy will? In his experience God was primarily Holy Will that orders the last detail of human existence. Human religiousness is the problem of the discovery of this Holy Will and its accomplishment in our human life. Jesus' own problems concerning God were not those of impersonal speculation, but intensely personal problems involving the quest and performance of this Holy Will.

For Jesus, then, God is not just a belief or a group of beliefs; He is not just an abstract concept or system of concepts. For Jesus, God is an intensely personal matter of concrete human experience. Henceforth we shall not speak of Jesus' belief in God, but of his experience of God*, his very own in the strictest sense of the term. Thus God in the experience of Jesus becomes purely personal, and it is just for this reason that he made his great religious contribution.

God in the experience of Jesus is paradoxical, and the paradox goes deep. But this is not at all surprising, for

---

*For a compact but fine study of Jesus' experience of God, *see* Johannes Leipoldt, *Das Gotteserlebnis Jesu im Lichte der vergleichenden Religionsgeschichte.*

personal piety in its purity always contains a certain amount of paradox; in fact, personal piety at its best seems unable to exist without paradox. We note this paradox in his experience of God because it actually exists and it warns us against the attempt to introduce a psychological system. In Jesus' experience of God we meet two paradoxical elements: on the one hand, his experience of God as *Holy;* on the other hand, his experience of God as *Father.*

Jesus' Experience of God as Holy

The experience of God as holy was not new with Jesus, and it is just here that he proves the genuineness of his religious consciousness. It is this experience of God as holy that calls forth the most elemental of the religious emotions—fear, awe, dread, reverence. These emotions are fundamental to the religious consciousness, whether primitive or cultured. They are so characteristic of the religious consciousness in all its forms that not a few regard these emotions as the original source of that peculiar type of human experience which we call religious. In primitive man's experience there is always that unintelligible and incomprehensible element in the Divine which he senses clearly, in his thought of which there is a strong strain of superstition, and which causes him to fear and to dread. The presence of the Divine is terrible and awful, and primitive man felt himself confronted with that which was *Wholly Other* than himself. Religious experience in its more intelligent forms strips its thought of primitive superstitions; it ceases to fear certain elements and objects that caused primitive man to shudder and to dread because he felt that he was in the presence of the *Holy*. But religious experience even on its most cultured levels and most exalted ethical elevations never loses these primitive emotions apart from which there is no genuinely religious consciousness.

Even in a highly purified religion like that of prophetic Israel this primitive religious recoil is not only present, but predominant. For the pious Israelite God was *terrible, awful, fearful, dreadful, sublime, sacred, majestic, mysterious*; His name must not be spoken; no man can see His face and live; God is *holy*, the *mysterium tremendum*, the *Wholly Other*, the *Numinous*. This primitive experience of God has its classic Old Testament expression in Isaiah's *Trisagion*,

"Holy, holy, holy, is Jehovah of hosts." (6,3.)

And again in 55,8-9:

"For my thoughts are not your thoughts, neither are your ways my ways, saith Jehovah, for as the heavens are higher than the earth, so are my ways higher than your ways, and my thoughts than your thoughts."

As Professor Rudolf Otto has shown in such a brilliant way, these non-rational elements in the experience of God are absolutely basal in all genuine religious experience.[2]

"A God, wholly comprehensible and comprehended, is no God."[3]

---

[2]*Das Heilige: Ueber das Irrationale in der Idee des Goettlichen und sein Verhaeltnis zum Rationalen*, now translated into English by John W. Harvey, *The Idea of the Holy. An Inquiry into the Non-rational Factor in the Idea of the Divine*. Quotations in this book are from the ninth German edition, and the words printed in italics in the present section are for the most part the terminology of Professor Otto.

[3]Terstegen, quoted by Otto, *Das Heilige*, p. 28.

In all its forms the genuine experience of God includes those elements that can not be rationalized, and that will fit into none of the usual categories of thought. A God that could be completely conceived and wholly understood, about whom there was left nothing of the inscrutable, the unintelligible, the incomprehensible, whose presence did not give rise to those elemental emotions of holy horror, fear, dread, awe and reverence, could never remain the object of either enlightened or unenlightened religious faith. All religions hold that God reveals Himself, but in all religions it is equally true that God remains *holy, different, other* in His real essence and being, which for man is impenetrable, unfathomable and inaccessible.

These non-rational elements in the experience of God reappear at the very depths of the religious life of Jesus. Christian thought has never been really sensitive to these non-rational elements in his religious experience. In its advanced stages Christian thought has neglected them entirely, sometimes deliberately, for the queer feeling of a contradiction with its own faith pressed upon it. The Christian consciousness with its exalted estimate of Jesus has overlooked entirely the clear Gospel fact that his own consciousness was genuinely religious in this respect. The Christian boast has always been that Jesus made the unapproachable God of Israel approachable, and the unnamable God of Israel he addressed as Father. Christianity may with right be proud of this religious triumph of Jesus, but it must not do violence to historical fact or to the religion of the New Testament. As Professor Otto writes, "The God of the New Testament is not less holy than the God of the Old Testament, but more so; the chasm between Creator and creature is not less, but absolute; the worthlessness of the profane over against Him is not eliminated, but sublimated."[4]   The Christian consciousness may never lose those elemental feelings in its experience of God, that sense of the *Holy*, that belongs to all truly religious experience.   If it does, it will become untrue to its best sources, the religious experience of Jesus and of the early Christians, and will cease to be really religious.

Jesus was a true son of Israel in his experience of God. For Jesus God is the Holy One; He is the *Numinous*, the *mysterium tremendum*, the *Wholly Other*.   His God is *fearful, sublime, sacred, majestic, mysterious*; He is *inscrutable, incomprehensible, impenetrable, unfathomable*; He is all that is *high* and *holy*.   In fact, these non-rational elements in his experience of God are fully as distinctive as the rational elements.   No religious genius of history entertained and expounded a clearer conception of God as moral will and ethical goodness, a more simple idea of God and His relation to humankind, yet in Jesus' experience there still remain those non-rational elements that make the Heavenly Father of his experience a God before whom he stands in awe and reverence, to whom he prays in fear and dread.   As Professor Otto points out,[5] Jesus did rationalize, moralize and humanize the idea of God, but for Jesus personally God still continues to come into his experience as the *Dreadfully Divine*, arousing in him the most elemental emotions of the primitive religious consciousness.   The Heavenly Father could not have been God for Jesus apart from those non-rational elements which in his religious experience appear in their highest and richest forms.

[4]*Das Heilige*, p. 73.
[5]*Ibid.*, p. 102.

Jesus' experience of God as *Holy* and *Other* is clear and strong in his words, acts and attitudes. His word,

> "Judge not that ye be not judged. For with what judgment ye judge, ye shall be judged, and with what measure ye mete, it shall be measured unto you," (Matt. 7,1-2)

springs from that primitive feeling of the religious consciousness that judgment belongs to the Divine alone.

His word on oaths springs from an elemental emotion of awe and reverence before the *mysterium tremendum* (Matt. 5,34-37):

> "Swear not at all; neither by the heaven, for it is the throne of God; nor by the earth, for it is the footstool of his feet; nor by Jerusalem, for it is the city of the great King. Neither shalt thou swear by thy head, for thou canst not make one hair white or black. Let your speech be, Yea, yea; Nay, nay: and whatsoever is more than these is of the evil *one*."

The whole of Jesus' quest of the divine will is a reflection of his experience of God as *Holy*. Before the mysterious majesty of God and His holy will he trembles, and at the heart of his personal struggle in Gethsemane are those primitive emotions aroused by the experience of God as *Holy Will*. As Professor Otto writes of the Gethsemane scene, "Whoever believes that he is not able to discover the Holy One of Israel in the God of the Gospels, must find him here, if he is able to see at all."[6]

---

[6]*Das Heilige*, p. 106. Cf. Mark 14, 33-44.

We also possess a prayer of Jesus that comes straight and strong from his experience of God as *Holy*. On the cross he does not cry, *Father, Father,* but,

"My God, my God, why hast thou forsaken me?" (Mark 15,34)

—an outburst of deep dread and fear in the presence of God as *Wholly Other* and *Numen,* of the primitive sense of dreadful distance that separates man from his Maker. As Bousset writes, "He experienced the fact that God is fearful, that He is enveloped in a darkness of uncertainty and awe even for those who are nearest him."[7]

Jesus' experience of God as *Holy* is specially prominent in his prayer-life. He praises God, petitions God, and protests to Him, but the primitive sense of being in the presence of the *Holy* never leaves him. The great majority of Jesus' prayer-words reflecting this religious fear and awe also reflects their paradoxical counterpart, an attitude of trust and confidence. This mingled state of religious feeling—awe and fear with complete trust and confidence—appears in not a few of his words. This contrast, this paradox of piety, is clear in the opening words of the *Lord's Prayer*:

"Our Father who art in heaven. Hallowed be thy name." (Matt. 6,9.)

It is clear in the address of his prayer of praise,

"Father, Lord of heaven and earth." (Matt. 11, 25.)

---
[7] *Jesus,* p. 51.

In its most compact form this paradox appears in his experience of God as *Heavenly Father*.

In Matthew 10,28 Jesus expresses that primitive fear and awe of God that is essential to all true piety,

> "Be not afraid of them that kill the body, but are not able to kill the soul: but rather fear him who is able to destroy both soul and body in hell."

But this word is followed at once by an expression of unreserved trust and confidence:

> "Are not two sparrows sold for a penny? and not one of them shall fall on the ground without your Father: but the very hairs on your head are all numbered. Fear not therefore: ye are of more value than many sparrows." (Matt. 10,29-31.)

In the Gospel picture we find that Jesus' experience of God includes the awe and reverence that separate man from his Maker, but we discover also that he feels himself irresistibly drawn to the Holy One who inspires trust and confidence. This brings us to the second element in Jesus' experience of God, as *Father,* a sense and attitude so prominent in his experience that it has occupied the whole foreground of Christian interest.

Jesus' Experience of God as Father

The idea of God as Father was common in the religions of the ancient world. Practically all of the peoples of the Roman Empire addressed God as Father—Romans, Greeks and Jews. That God is a Father, that

men are His children, and that God loves men as a father
loves his children, are religious experiences that found
expression in the devotional literature of Israel.[8] In
Psalm 103 we meet a God of love, a truly evangelical
piety,

"Like as a father pitieth his children, so Jehovah
pitieth them that fear him."

But the use of the term *Father* in addressing the deity on
the part of the Jewish and other peoples of antiquity does
not in the least compromise Jesus' tremendous contribution to the human experience of God in this respect. As
Professor Deissmann says, "God as Father is an ancient
gold coin. But where does it bear the stamp that Jesus
gave it?"[9] And Professor Wernle writes, "What a difference it makes whether a man simply calls God his
Father or whether he trusts Him as completely as a child
trusts his father."[10]

God the Father was not wholly original with Jesus,
but any casual reader of the Old Testament and the
Gospels can see that God the Father in the experience
of Jesus is something quite different from anything that
we find in the Old Testament. What in the religious
experience of Israel is only occasional and sporadic becomes in the experience of Jesus essential and distinctive.
The high peaks of Old Testament piety that now and
again reached up into the experience of God as Father
are the constant unbroken level on which Jesus lives and

---

[8]Cf. Psalms 27,10; 29,1; 82,6; 89,27; Isa. 1,2; 63,16-18; 64,7;
Hos. 2,1; 3,1; Jer. 3,19; Mal. 1,6; 3,17; Sir. 23,14; 51,10; Wisd.
Sol. 2,13 16; 14,1*ff.*; 18,5; III Macc. 5,7.

[9]*Evangelium und Urchristentum*, p. 103.

[10]*Jesus*, p. 23.

moves and has his religious being. Here again we meet Jesus' relation to the religious past of his people, and again it is not a question of his absolute originality but of his distinctive contribution to the religious experience of Israel. The experience of God as Father is the very heart and pulse of Jesus' personal piety, and in spite of all its antecedents in the ancient world, God as Father stands as his distinctive achievement in the field of religious experience.

This element is so prominent in Jesus' experience of God that other elements, such as the experience of God as holy, are easily overlooked. It invades every avenue of his religious life. In prayer he addresses the Holy One of Israel as Father, a tremendous triumph in the human quest of God. Father, in the religious feeling and faith of Jesus, expresses the deepest secret in the human experience of the Divine. It is at this point that he exercised his most direct and lasting influence on historical Christianity. God as Father is one of the few vital elements in Jesus' religious experience that have survived in historical Christianity and have found their way into Christian confession and creed.

Jesus tells us practically nothing in a direct way of his experience of God as Father, but we see it reflected in his attitude toward the world and the sum total of the concerns of human life. As a true son of the religious genius of his people he saw God in nature, in human history, in the fates and fortunes of the individual and the group. For Jesus God bore a direct relationship to every detail of human existence. He saw God present and at work in the most prosaic and matter-of-fact items of human life and experience. And the God whom he saw everywhere is always the Father revealing His love and care for His children. As Professor Wernle writes, "This is one of the most significant things that Jesus has to say to all ages."[11]

Before the wonders of the natural world Jesus stands in awe as before the Holy One, yet he is not a worshiper of nature. His words on nature possess a beauty that is close to the poetic (Matt. 6,25-34), yet he composes no religious odes to nature such as we find in the Psalms (8; 19,1-7; 29; 104). We find in the words of Jesus no reflections and meditations on nature such as we find in the Indian Christian mystic, Sadhu Sundar Singh.[12]

Jesus' conception of nature, as of the whole of life, is purely religious. In all nature he sees only the hand and work of the Father:

"Behold the birds of the heaven, that they sow not, neither do they reap, nor gather into barns: and your heavenly Father feedeth them." (Matt. 6, 26a.)

"Consider the lilies of the field, how they grow; they toil not, neither do they spin: yet I say unto you, that even Solomon in all his glory was not arrayed like one of these. But if God doth so clothe the grass of the field, which to-day is, and to-morrow is cast into the oven, *shall he* not much more *clothe* you, O ye of little faith?" (Matt. 6,28b-30.)[13]

"He maketh his sun to rise on the evil and the good, and sendeth his rain on the just and the unjust." (Matt. 5,45b.)

---

[11]*Jesus*, p. 306.
[12]*Reality and Religion*, pp. 17, 31.
[13]*See also* Matt. 10, 29-31 quoted above for Jesus' word on the fallen sparrow and the hairs on human heads.

In these words on the birds of the heavens, the lilies of the field, the grass, the sunshine, the rain and the fallen sparrow, we do not have to do with an adoration of nature but of the Heavenly Father whom these simple facts reveal. These things have only a derived value and glory. It is the presence of God that enhances them in the faith of Jesus. All such words are simply direct reflections of his experience of God as a living, loving Father.

This presence of the Father in the natural world was real for Jesus, but it was only the key to a higher order of values, His presence in human life. All of these providences reveal a higher order of interest and love, God's fatherly love for men. Jesus finds the Father in closest touch with all the interests and concerns of men. The commonest mercies are the expressions of the divine thought and care. Fate and fortune, life and death are in the divine hand. The very hairs on human heads are all numbered; men can not by taking thought add or subtract a single cubit from their stature. Finer expressions of the simple human consciousness of dependence upon the Divine are not to be found than we meet here in Jesus' experience of God as Father.

The divine disposition is naturally, instinctively, infinitely kind. The Father will not give His son a stone for bread, a serpent for a fish, a scorpion for an egg. (Luke 11,11-13.) The Father of Jesus' experience is in such close contact with His children and their needs that He has no need of being informed; He knows the needs of men before they ask Him. (Matt. 6,8.) To the Father men may turn in complete confidence; they may bring to Him all the major and minor concerns of their life. The Father's care touches the whole cycle of

life, as we see in the *Lord's Prayer*. Men may pray for
the kingdom and its coming, for forgiveness of sins, for
protection in time of temptation and against the evil one.
They may even pray for their daily bread in the same
breath in which they petition His forgiveness.

Such a view of life that forbids anxiety concerning food
and drink and raiment, or concerning the morrow in
general, such an exalted estimate of human life as a great
boon, such a calm confidence in God are absolutely without parallel in human experience. Nevertheless, just
such is the religious faith of Jesus, his experience of God
as Father. Jesus felt nothing of the groaning of nature
and creation in travail that was so terrible for Paul,
nothing of Paul's inner war between flesh and spirit,
which resulted for him in a religious pessimism.

The matter-of-fact mind of to-day with its problems
and puzzles of a practical sort hears these words of Jesus
coming, it seems, from a far-off and wholly unattainable
order of things. In its world of fact, in its fatalism, this
mind feels that Jesus is wholly apart from the world as
it is, from life as it knows it. A drought or a deluge, a
frozen sparrow or a withered flower, a hungry family or
a naked orphan, it feels, refutes the whole of Jesus'
philosophy of Providence. But in all of its questionings
the modern mind only reveals that its faith has been submerged by fact. Jesus' faith is unjustifiable in the face
of fact, but real religious faith does not seek justification
in the world of fact. Sometimes it believes *because of* the
facts; again, it believes *in the midst of* facts both for and
against; but when faith rises to its native altitudes, it
ventures to maintain itself *in spite of* all the facts. The
prodigalities and cruelties of nature, the survival of the
fittest, and the struggle for existence created no problems

for the religious faith of Jesus. Jesus did not resort to faith in God as a man at bay in the world; he did not trudge along under the strain of existence as a man who makes the best of things. In spite of all the facts to the contrary, Jesus felt the thrill of living life in the uninterrupted presence of the Heavenly Father, and he lived his life as an experiment in faith, not as a compromise with fact.

Jesus' faith is naive; his experience of God as Father is childlike—two essential elements which personal piety must retain if it is to remain pure and a source of power. Jesus' faith is triumphant, an unfailing source of personal power that carried him to the conquest of the cross. God, the living and loving Father, is the heart of the religious experience of Jesus. Whether we like it or not, whether or not we can attain it, it is the faith that he lived and died by.

Before drawing our conclusions on Jesus' faith in God, we may survey its general relationship to the faith from which it came, the faith of Israel, and its bearing on the faith that followed it, the Christian faith.

The main content of Jesus' experience of God is not radically different from the best of the Old Testament faith. For Jesus, as for the whole of Israel, there was one great article of faith: Jehovah alone is God; there is none like unto Him; He is holy, eternal, faithful, good, gracious, infinitely merciful and kind. These elements, with a new emphasis in a fresh experience, become so commanding that the final form of his experience of God appears as something new. Jesus' contribution is not in new thoughts and new teachings about God; it comes rather in the form of his own fresh experience of God. As Bousset writes, "Never in the life of any man was God such a living reality as in the life of Jesus."[14]

God in the experience of Jesus was something more for him and is something more for us than anything that we find in the Old Testament. Some of the older and less worthy elements he allows to drop out simply by his neglect of them; other elements he deliberately rejects. But still other elements that lay on the periphery of Israel's faith Jesus brings to the very center of the experience of God. He strikes a balance in the unbalanced elements in Israel's faith. In the Old Testament the experience of God as holy so predominates that the Father falls into the remote and hardly visible background. In Jesus, however, the attitude of calm confidence and trust is fully as strong as the attitude of awe and reverence. In his preaching and praying God as Father acquires a meaning and importance that is new and different and that constitutes his real contribution to man's experience and knowledge of his Maker. The faith in God that came to Jesus by social inheritance he makes his very own in that the Holy One of Israel lays hold on the deepest sources of his personal life and in the crucible of his religious experience becomes the Heavenly Father. As Professor Otto writes on this point, "He did not teach and preach something that was self-evident, but his own personal discovery and revelation—that just this Holy One is the Heavenly Father."[15]

Jesus' experience of God is reflected in all his attitudes toward the religious past of his people. It was in the light of his own experience of God that he reproduced

---

[14]*Jesus*, p. 47.
[15]*Das Heilige*, p. 104.

and rejected, that he revised and recast, that he accepted and assimilated the religious traditions of his people. For Jesus religion is much more than accepted tradition of long standing; it is more than the authoritative voices of the past. As we see in Matthew 5,17 he had other authorities than sacred codes and precepts. A personal experience of God he sets high above the best of the past. His famous series of words on the law,

"Ye have heard it said of old . . . but I say unto you,"

reveals very clearly the nature of the sources of his certainty. His own experience of God he sets in open opposition to the highest religious authority of his people. Such an attitude on the part of a true son of Israel required an unparalleled conviction born of a unique experience of the meaning of God in an individual life.

Jesus' reactions to and appraisals of his contemporary religious environment are direct reflections of his experience of God. Such institutions as the synagogue and the temple presented themselves to him as recognized and necessary parts of the religious life of his people. The synagogue may have been an important factor in his religious education. Luke (4,16) tells us that it was his regular custom to attend the synagogue on the Sabbath, and we find the synagogue as one of the principal scenes of his activity in Galilee. Yet Jesus is neither an advocate nor a critic of the synagogue. He simply accepted it as it was; he did not break with it, nor did it break with him. But his mature experience of God was in no wise dependent upon the synagogue. With regard to the temple, Jesus shared the sentiment of Psalms 84 and 122 in his love for it. He goes directly to the temple upon his arrival in the Holy City; he becomes the champion of its purity; he cleanses it of its trade and traffic because it is the house of God, a place of worship and of prayer. (Matt. 21,13.) Yet for Jesus the temple is not the only dwelling-place of God; in his own personal experience he was convinced once for all that *a greater thing* than the temple is here. (Matt. 12,6.)

Toward the cult elements in the religion of his people Jesus shows his indifference by his neglect. It is reported that he sent the leper to the priest for the rite of cleansing (Mark 1,44) in keeping with the Levitical law. It is true that he drew an analogy from the religious act of offering a gift at the altar,* yet nowhere do we see him engaged in an external rite of cult-worship. Jesus seems to have felt no personal need for external and visible guarantees of God's existence in general or for His presence and power in particular such as we sense in the soul of the author of Psalms 42 and 43, where God is visibly present in the cult and ceremony of the temple. Jesus seems to have shared the prophetic skepticism regarding cult and its ability to bring man into the presence of the Holy One. He does not attack cult-worship as did Amos and others of the old prophets, but he does not advocate it as a part of the Holy Will nor as a source of religious assurance.

Jesus went up to Jerusalem at the time of the Passover; it was prepared for him, and on the last night of his life he celebrated this sacred feast in the closed company of his most intimate disciples. It was a festival of his people that he had anticipated with all the intensity of genuine Jewish sentiment,

---

*Matt. 5,23-24.

88   THE RELIGION OF JESUS

"With desire I have desired to eat this passover with you." (Luke 22,15.)

Yet it was a religious occasion that he interpreted in the light of his own experience of God, and into this most sacred of all his people's festivals he poured the very heart of his own personal religious faith.

Jesus' criticism of the contemporary practises of piety are also direct reflections of his experience of God. His pronouncement of woes on the scribes and Pharisees (Matt. 23,1-39) with their binding of heavy burdens, their titles of deference, their supposed monopoly on religion, proselyting, oath-taking, tithes, cleansings, memorials to the slain prophets, all describe in a negative way his experience of God and his worship of Him. Practically none of the things that were characteristic and central in later Judaism appears in Jesus' understanding of religion—circumcision, the Sabbath, fasting, tithes, food regulations, precepts of purification and so forth. Some of these things do not so much as claim his attention, and those that do figure in his thought, like the Sabbath, he judges and appraises in the light of his own experience of what God requires of men. In these matters Jesus was a non-conformist. But his failure to conform was not a striking course of conduct consciously chosen with a relish for conspicuousness and conflict; it was the natural expression of a sovereign freedom born of a rich experience of God that was all his own.

In this connection there is a group of words found only in Matthew which we may not neglect, for they reveal very clearly the nature of Jesus' religious experience over against the Pharisaic type of piety—his words on alms, prayer and fasting. We have no record to the effect that Jesus ever gave alms, but he does not forbid alms-giving:

"When therefore thou doest alms, sound not a trumpet before thee, as the hypocrites do in the synagogues and in the streets, that they may have glory of men. Verily I say unto you, They have received their reward. But when thou doest alms, let not thy left hand know what thy right hand doeth: that thine alms may be in secret: and thy Father who seeth in secret shall recompense thee." (Matt. 6,2-4.)

Jesus did not forbid prayer; he prayed as none before or after him. But he says:

"When ye pray, ye shall not be as the hypocrites: for they love to stand and pray in the synagogues and in the corners of the streets, that they may be seen of men. Verily I say unto you, They have received their reward. But thou, when thou prayest, enter into thine inner chamber, and having shut thy door, pray to thy Father who is in secret, and thy Father who seeth in secret shall recompense thee." (Matt. 6,5-6.)

Jesus did not fast, and it brought him into conflict with the religious sects of his day (Mark 2,18-22), yet he did not forbid fasting.* Concerning fasting he says:

"When ye fast, be not, as the hypocrites, of a sad countenance: for they disfigure their faces, that they

*The only notice to the effect that Jesus fasted is found in the account of the first wilderness retreat (Matt. 4,2 and Luke 4,2), and in this case it appears as a spontaneous personal practise rather than as the observance of a conventional religious custom.

may be seen of men to fast. Verily I say unto you, They have received their reward. But thou, when thou fastest, anoint thy head, and wash thy face; that thou be not seen of men to fast, but of thy Father who is in secret: and thy Father, who seeth in secret, shall recompense thee." (Matt. 6,16-18.)

In all of these things he sees more than conventional religious customs. For Jesus they are not matters of public parade, but intimately private and personal. They should be practises of the presence of God who looks within, not without. This emphasis on the inwardness of religion preached by Jesus is the organic expression of his own personal experience of where and how the Holy One and Heavenly Father is to be found and worshiped.

In his experience of God Jesus is, in general, true to the faith of his people. He neglects the legalistic and ritualistic elements, for he belongs to the prophets of Israel, not to its priests. He did not follow in the beaten track of tradition; he saw God in the past and sought to secure His presence in his own experience. But the sources of Jesus' knowledge of God and his faith in Him are less traditional and inherited, more personal and original. He does not imitate the past; he inherits from it, but his faith in God has always the freshness that can come only from individual experience. He does not constantly question himself as to whether this or that is in conformity with the faith of the past or the present. He speaks and acts, he feels and believes, at the direct dictation of his own experience of God. For Jesus, God's most certain revelation of himself is in human life and experience. The meaning of God in personal experience is for him the supreme source of religious authority. A faith in God must validate itself in individual experience. And it is exactly because he had validated certain elements in the religious faith of his people that he rejects and revolts against others and eliminates them from the essentials of religion. He accepted only those elements that made an unmistakable contribution to a personal knowledge of God as Holy Will and Heavenly Father.

When we come to consider the bearing of Jesus' experience of God and his faith in Him on the Christian faith we are struck at once by the great difference between the two. In its historical forms the Christian faith becomes fixed and formulated, systematically stated and logically defined. Calm confidence and implicit trust, both purely personal, are supplemented, even supplanted, by doctrine and dogma, creed and confession. In short, faith becomes belief, and the outstanding feature of the faith that followed Jesus is its intellectualism. Theology, Christology, and soteriology took the place that God and His kingdom held in the experience of Jesus.

Any student who turns to Jesus with the hope of discovering the intellectual foundations of his faith in God is doomed to disappointment. He offers no intellectual criticisms of the old, and he lays no intellectual foundations for the new. We possess really nothing from Jesus that we may properly call his reflections about God. Religious faith for Jesus was more than rational reflection, more than mystical meditation. The accrued attributes of God that begin in the Old Testament and mount to great numbers in Christian theology and philosophy have no counterpart in his simple religious language.

Christian rationalism ascribes to God pure being, absoluteness, intelligence, reason, purpose, good will, essential unity, consciousness and a whole host of technical attributes. But Jesus' experience of God did not come through the processes of rationalistic reasoning, and he does not express his faith in formal theological terminology. Wherever we meet an involved complexity in the Christian thought of God, we meet a corresponding and equally extreme simplicity in the faith of Jesus. He never seeks to reduce his faith in God to a system; rather he seeks to secure God as the commanding content of his personal experience. Instead of a systematic structure of reasoning, we find in the religious experience of Jesus the disparate and diverse ramifications of a soul in search of God. His faith in God is as unsystematic and spontaneous, as unformulated and organic as the unquestioning attitude of the child toward its father. Jesus questions his God; his God becomes problematic for him, but his questions and problems are not of the intellectual order.

There are no philosophical or theological tendencies in Jesus' thinking. He does not seek to demonstrate any of the ordinary tenets that a formal faith in God includes. It is true that he teaches Israel's ethical monotheism; he thought of God as one and good. But even here he does not use argument and dialectic. In the matters of religion, the only matters that appear as of vital importance in the experience of Jesus, we see that his mind was not geared to theoretical thinking. He announces no doctrine of the divine omnipotence, yet he accepts everything without exception as from God; no doctrine of the divine omniscience, yet he very simply confides to his contemporaries, "Your Father knoweth what things ye have need of, before ye ask him." (Matt. 6,8.)

There is nothing of the Christian philosopher, nothing of the Christian theologian in Jesus' religious constitution. For Jesus God is not a formal proposition in need of proof, and his faith in Him needed no supporting arguments of an intellectual sort. His experience of God, as is the case in all pure piety, carried its own proofs with it—those primitive proofs that are wholly remote from intellectualism, yet which possess a peculiar power to persuade and to sustain. When Jesus preached his faith to others, his faith in God as a living and loving Father, he did not call to hand any of the many stock arguments, but he struck straight at that native element in the human constitution that responds to spiritual stimulation and inspiration, not to convincement and logical proof.

The God of Christian rationalism is not the God of Jesus, nor is He the God of living personal piety. A rationalistic God may present a coherent concept that smoothes the way of intellectual difficulties, but He lacks the most essential elements that are present in Jesus' experience. Such a God is too consistent, too consequent, and there is left in Him none of those non-rational and paradoxical elements that are distinctive for the personal faith of Jesus. Jesus' experience of God is not philosophical but prophetic. By constitution he was instinctively sensitive to the fundamental realities and values which faith in God brings to the truly religious consciousness. His experience of God as Holy One and as Heavenly Father is paradoxical, and it is a paradox that can maintain itself only in a rich religious life that can stand the strain of contrary and conflicting forces. It is paradoxical because it is so intensely personal; and just because it is so intensely personal, springing from the sum total of his experience, it is powerful and possesses a warmth and glow that are illuminating, stimulating and life-giving.

Christian theologians have evolved elaborate soteriological systems, showing why and how and under what conditions God redeems men. From Paul down they have expounded the necessity of Jesus' death, the indispensability of the cross, and Jesus as the only mediator ⸺tween God and man. In the simpler faith of Jesus, however, man stands directly in the presence of his Maker, the child in the presence of his Father. In sharpest contrast with Paul's scheme of mediatorial salvation stands Jesus' childlike picture of God as the shepherd who goes into the wilderness and seeks till he finds the lost sheep, as the father who hastens to meet the lost son and welcomes him home. According to Jesus it is not a scheme that saves men, for it is not the will of the Father that any should perish. In his faith there is absolutely no theoretical scheme of salvation, because to his religious way of thinking God's children include all, the disobedient as well as the obedient.

In the religious thought of Jesus there are no difficult deductions, no intricate inductions. He gives no formal instructions on man's relation to his Maker and his hope of redemption by Him, but in a simple picture he settles this issue for ever,

"A certain man had two sons . . ." (Luke 15,11-32.)

Thus Jesus begins, and before he is done we know that he has pictured for ever the divine disposition toward men. Christian theology, philosophy and psychology have wrestled with the problem of prayer, with the possibility of man communicating with his Maker, but Jesus comes to us with another prosaic picture,

> "Two men went up into the temple to pray . . ."
> (Luke 18,9-14)

and before he has finished we know that men may or may not commune with the Holy One. The really important thing in all such pictures is not what they teach others, but what they reveal of Jesus' own experience of God. All are direct reflections of his own personal faith in Him.

The forging of Jesus' faith is not revealed to us by the Gospel writers. The dawn and development of his experience of God are shrouded in darkness. With regard to its history we can say little except that it seems to have been inherent in his religious genius. How he achieved his knowledge of God we can not say, for he did not choose to disclose such to others. He claims no special avenues of approach to the Divine that are unknown to ordinary men. In the Gospel story we see that he traverses the painful path that is open to all the children of men—prayer, the pursuit and performance of the divine will. He does not claim to know everything about God; he does not presume to have said all that there is to be said of Him. In all simplicity Jesus exposes his experience of God, what he has found Him to be and to mean. Yet it is his own personal experience that gives him authority for all that he has to say of God, for all that he does in behalf of His cause. In his experience of God Jesus had his great certainties, but he also had his uncertainties. For him God's great mysteries con-

tinue to exist.   God is infinitely more than man can know
or think.   In this respect Jesus remains rigidly religious.
There are many things that we would like to know, but
as long as we have a clear conception of the distinctive
elements in his faith in God nothing else matters greatly.
Jesus intended that his faith should be shared by his followers; it is ours to seek to share as he sought to share
it with all who have the necessary courage.

Jesus' faith and his experience of God are not easily
shared.   Both contain those non-rational elements that
are difficult of assimilation for a type of mind that has
been brought up in an atmosphere that is overcharged
with intellectualism, that looks upon religion as the entertainment of certain opinions rather than as an experience
of the Divine.   Jesus' experience of God is primitive in
its utter realism, in its passion and power; he could and
did dispense with the grounds of logic and the supports
of reason, and he even learned to know God in contradiction to both.   His ideal realm of faith often comes
into open conflict with the world of fact.   Such a faith is
difficult for a type of mind that has been taught that religion must always be rational, that faith must accom-
modate itself as best it can to fact.   And it is this very
thing that accounts for the powerlessness of our modern
Christianity.   We shall never experience the purging
power of Jesus' faith in God until our faith ventures to
trust itself as true and dares to dispense with all the rational excuses for its existence.   Then we may be in a
position to fashion fact according to faith and learn one
of the great lessons of religious experience—that faith
must overcome fact, that such is faith's necessary destiny, and that, in this constant conflict with fact, faith
freshens itself, enriches its life and augments its power.

We are convinced that we share Jesus' faith in God as Father. For us such is the simplest and richest address of the Divine. It was for Jesus. All but two of his seven prayers begin with *Father*, and their content corresponds to this intimate type of address. But we forget that God as Father was more than a concept, title or style of address in the religious experience of Jesus. It was the most compact single expression of what he had found God to be in the whole of his experience. But we apparently do not share this experience in all of its implications. If we do, it is not yet sufficiently commanding, for we have never drawn its inevitable consequences for the social structure of our human life.

The paradoxical character of Jesus' experience of God is not so easily assimilated as might be thought at first glance. It can not be assimilated except as it strikes the full range of our experience. It is a matter hopelessly foreign to a religion of pure reason—if there is such a thing. God as Father arouses our sympathetic emotions, but there is a reverse side to this faith. For Jesus, God is not just Father; He is just as truly the Holy and Sovereign Ruler of the universe who can "destroy both soul and body in hell." The God of Jesus is ethically exalted and holy, demanding of men character and conduct that correspond to His own. Jesus did think and teach of God in a spirit of startling frankness, but this frankness is always tempered by a feeling of awe in the presence of the Father's sublime majesty, of His unapproachable goodness, of His infinite love that must bestow gifts upon men who are not in a position to merit them, of the God who imparts himself to men who are utterly unworthy. Jesus never forgot for a moment that *the Father is in heaven*, high and holy, all that God can signify and be.

There is still another feature in Jesus' experience of God that renders it difficult of assimilation even for the modern Christian mind, accustomed as it is to look upon faith as a more or less impersonal body of religious subject-matter that is to be held. There is always a strong personal element in the faith of the great religious genius, and it is usually just this striking personal element that gives him that peculiar power and persuasion that is most convincing for others. The faïth of the great genius is not something that has come to him in an impersonal way, but he feels that he personally has been gripped by it. It is that type of religious conviction that Paul shared and described in Philippians 3,12:

"I press on, if so be that I may lay hold on that for which also I was laid hold on by Christ Jesus."

Jesus' faith in God was not something that he held, but something that held him. In his words and deeds, in all that we know of him, we get the clearest sort of impression that his faith reaches down into the deepest sources of his personal life. Certainly all that he is and hopes to be, he trusts to the fate of his faith. It is the grip that his experience of God has on the whole of his life that gives his faith a flash and a flare that sweeps everything before it. The faith of Jesus is a veritable fire. He himself said,

"I came to cast fire upon the earth," (Luke 12,49)

and this is more than a mere figure of speech. Jesus' faith in God was not something that was fixed and formulated for him. It is fresh and fervent; it kindles an ex-

alted enthusiasm in him; it is a source of seemingly limitless personal energy. Disappointment, despair, distress,
unanswered prayer could not tear him from his faith.
He confronts his God with a faith that is absolutely unflinching, unreservedly loyal. It is a faith that knows no
defeat; it has about it a deliberate and dazzling daring
that even death can not daunt. For Jesus, faith was a
source of power that makes the impossible possible:

"All things are possible to him that believeth."
(Mark 9,23.)
"Whosoever shall say unto this mountain, Be thou
taken up and cast into the sea; and shall not doubt in
his heart, but shall believe that what he saith cometh
to pass; he shall have it." (Mark 11,23.)

Such an estimate of faith in God is not just an exaggeration of speech. Just such a faith we see operating in the
religious life of Jesus. Both passages reflect his own
personal convictions concerning the power of religious
faith and both come straight from his own experience.
We keep the faith—impersonal; the faith does not keep
us—personal. This is the sorry plight of our Christian
religion over against that of Jesus.

The fervent faith of the religious genius has often led
to a fanaticism that has hindered the accomplishment of
the very thing that it points out to be accomplished. The
fanatic often resorts to the spectacular in a mistaken confidence in what God desires and does. The faith of
Jesus is a fire that consumes, but it is absolutely free from
fanaticism. There are evidences of fanatical faith in the
religious past of his people. Elijah was the great prophet
of the popular imagination even in Jesus' day. He had

called down fire from heaven (I Kings 18,25-40; II Kings 1,9-16), and the God of Elijah's faith was known as *the God that answereth by fire.* Even as late and sane a prophet as Isaiah challenges King Ahaz to demand a sign. (Isa. 7,10*f.*) This fanatical faith had its occasional outbursts within the circle of the twelve and to two of his disciples Jesus gave the surname, *Sons of Thunder.* (Mark 3,17.) These outbursts Jesus regularly meets with a word of suppression that brands such faith as irreligious. To James and John who would call down fire from heaven, "even as Elijah did," and consume the inhospitable Samaritan village, he says,

"Ye know not what manner of spirit ye are of, for the Son of man came not to destroy men's lives but to save them." (Luke 9,55 marg.)

Jesus did not share the spectacular piety of Elijah and others of his prophetic predecessors. He refuses to give a sign from heaven (Mark 8,11-12), but his rejection of this spectacular type of piety does not point to a lack of confidence in God. For Jesus, God and faith in Him operate elsewhere; they lay hold on the deepest sources of human life. His faith is fervent and fiery, but it is never fanatical and feverish. Nothing can be more refreshing and stimulating to the earnest religious imagination than that constantly calm confidence, that firmly fixed faith in God which Jesus always exhibits and which was at the same time the driving power of his life. The simple and clear consciousness that the Holy One was Heavenly Father seems to have been all the assurance and guarantee that Jesus needed to raise him above the common conflicts that so often bring upheaval and turmoil into the lives of the greatest of the saints who have had faith in God.

The intensity of Jesus' faith, free from fanaticism as it is, has its reverse side or contrary part. His experience of God is exceedingly simple, especially his experience of God as Father, and many speak of the mysticism of Jesus, or of Jesus the mystic. The preacher speaks of the mystical faith and personality of Jesus, and he has in mind Jesus' insistence upon true piety as inward and as a matter of the spirit. This is true to Jesus, but not to mysticism as it has appeared in great religious personalities which form a distinct type well known to the student of the psychology of religion.* There is nothing of real mysticism in him. Like the mystic, he trusted his own personal experience of God as true and as authoritative above all else—tradition, practise, custom and so forth. But this is not peculiar to mysticism; it appears in every great religious figure who has any freshness about him. In Jesus we see no *exercitia spiritualia,* no *via negativa,* no *scala paradisi,* no *unis mystica.* There is no ascetic mortification of the human equipment. All this he regards as God-given, as forces and factors for the construction of character and for the control of conduct. All of these human faculties must contribute to the richness and reality of the individual's experience of God. He gives us no mystical psychology of the human faculties; he regards every talent as a trust, every gift as a rigid and relentless responsibility. In Jesus we see nothing of the mystic who brands the world and self with a

---

*A characteristic scientific understanding of religious mysticism is that of Professor Leipoldt: "By mysticism I mean an emotional type of piety that seeks to secure the presence of God with man in a manner that alters, either totally or partially, the normal human self-consciousness." (*Das Gotteserlebnis Jesu,* p. 6.)

flat negation, and who seeks solely to sink away into the
impersonal All-One.   Mysticism's *summum bonum* is the
melting, mingling and merging of the one in the All, the
complete dissipation of the real in favor of the Ideal.
Even in his prayer-life, as we shall see in the next chapter,
where mystical communion is most likely to appear, Jesus
is not a mystic.   He did not go through the devotional
drill by which the mystic shuts himself off from the offense of the real world.   His problems in prayer were not
psychological as they are for the mystic.   Jesus' problems were so pressing that they consumed the whole
center of his consciousness and automatically excluded all
the distractions which handicap the mystic as he concen-
trates and contemplates.   "The childlike confidence of
Jesus toward God the Father always remains a personal
communion; it never has its issue in a mystical union."[16]

The whole temper of Jesus' personal piety is foreign
to the truly mystical personality.   His experience of God
is intimate, intense, simple, but in the main too prosaic
and practically personal to admit of true mysticism.
Jesus' goal of religious living was a consistent life constantly lived in the presence of God whose holy will is the
measure of character and conduct.

In conclusion on this first phase of Jesus' religious
faith, we may say that it remains a strict ethical monotheism, admitting of the intrusion of no other object of
worship, yet conceived and experienced with a personal
warmth and intimacy that makes his experience of God
as Father something new and distinctly different from the
traditional faith of Israel.   His religious faith is prophetic in depth of conviction and certainty.   God for

---

[16]Heiler, *Das Gebet*, p. 282.

Jesus is a matter of personal experience rather than a formal faith; for this reason his faith in God is not to be systematized. The very attempt to introduce a system will result in its devitalization. This does not mean that we are not to attempt to understand the faith of Jesus; in reality, this is our principal task. But we are to seek to understand it as it was, not as Christian prejudice might desire that it should be. Those who think of religious faith in terms of creed and confession, doctrine and dogma, theology and metaphysics will experience the greatest of disappointments in the religious faith of Jesus. To such Jesus has little to say. His faith is to be understood only as the spontaneous expression of his own personal experience of God. It is this purely personal source from which it sprang that renders it intelligible, as intelligible as it can be made. The problem of the intelligibility of Jesus' faith is not to be solved in the terms of an intellectual insight that will ferret out the last of a system of involved and intricate implications, for there is nothing involved and intricate in his faith in God. Its intelligibility will come in terms of the sum total of religious experience, by the personal ability to appreciate and appropriate, to sense and to share, to be inspired and to reproduce.

God as Holy Will and as Heavenly Father is the sum and substance of Jesus' experience of the Divine. It is this peculiar and paradoxical experience of God that gave the whole of his personality the single stamp of deep inner certainty, of complete confidence that left with his contemporaries, and that leaves with us to-day, the impression of religious authority. Jesus' contribution to humanity's faith is not to be found in new and original beliefs which he first formulated and expounded, nor is it to be sought in any novel and striking religious teachings. His contribution is less formal but more firm. In his experience of God he contributes a solid substance from which humanity may build its religious life with complete confidence. The God of Jesus is not new. The new thing is God in the experience of Jesus. There is no reason why we should ever fear to trust God for what Jesus in his own experience found Him to be.

JESUS' FAITH IN THE KINGDOM OF GOD

Thus far we have discussed only one element in the faith of Jesus, his experience of God, but we shall realize fully what God meant for Jesus personally only when we come to the next chapter to the discussion of his experience of God as Holy Will and to his quest of God in prayer. We now come to the second of the two principal elements in his faith, the kingdom of God, the meaning of God not only in his own personal experience but in all human experience. His faith in the kingdom has aspects, like his faith in God, that reach out beyond himself. The kingdom is what Jesus found the meaning of God to be in the formation and structure of human life and experience as a whole. Who and what is God for men? Jesus would answer: The kingdom of God. To be sure, God is to be Holy Will and Heavenly Father in the experience of men, but this experience has its natural issue in the kingdom.

As a problem of the life of Jesus the kingdom of God has been studied from an almost infinite number of angles, and each angle of approach conscientiously pursued has made at least some contribution to our understanding of him. An almost endless amount of scholarly material has been written on the kingdom of God as conceived and announced by Jesus. Our more humble task here is to seek to determine the rôle that the kingdom played in his own personal piety. From the point of view of our present study of Jesus as a religious subject, we shall discuss briefly the kingdom of God as his religious message, as the outlook of his personal religious faith, and as the religious cause chosen by him.

The Kingdom of God as the Religious Message of Jesus

The historical message of Jesus may be stated in a single sentence,

"The kingdom of God is at hand; repent ye." (Mark 1,15.)

In Mark and Luke we meet almost without exception the expression, *the kingdom of God*. In Matthew, however, this form is suppressed almost entirely by the expression, *the kingdom of heaven*. Matthew's form is very probably an early Jewish-Christian revision. In all probability Jesus himself used the term *the kingdom of God,* as Mark and Luke regularly represent. Jesus, himself a layman from the ranks of the common people, would naturally use the popular language. We do not find him in other matters using the professional and technical religious language of the clerical classes of his day, but the lay language of the plain people. Further, a prophet who spoke in such an intimate way about and to God as he did would hardly share Israel's traditional shyness in the use of the divine name, even when we keep in mind the deep awe and real reverence which

Jesus never failed to manifest toward man's Maker.

Upon his very first appearance in public Jesus announces the kingdom of God and its coming, and he continued to announce it to the very end. But never once does he stop to explain the term. He simply announces the kingdom as a thought quite familiar to his contemporaries, familiar enough at least to enable him to dispense with all definition and explanation. Moreover, Jesus' contemporaries do not ask him to define or to explain it. His disciples and others ask when and where it will appear, but they never ask him what the kingdom of God is.

The familiarity which Jesus assumes on the part of his contemporaries, and which they in turn show with the expression and what is meant by it, makes it clear that the term was not coined and used for the first time by him. However, this very fact creates for us a problem, for the historical background out of which this great thought and faith of Jesus came is by no means clear to us. Because of the meagerness of the literary expressions of Judaism's religious life that have come down to us from the first and second centuries before our Christian era, we can say little of the birth and development of the idea. The exact details of its origin and early history we do not know, but when Jesus appeared in public with the message of the kingdom of God, it was a well-understood and familiar element in the religious thinking of his contemporaries.

As a definite expression for a special idea and faith and in the full sense it has in the message of Jesus, the term, kingdom of God, is not found in the Old Testament, the later Apocrypha or Pseudepigrapha. The nearest approaches which we find to it as expression and as idea are in such passages as Psalms 22,28; Obadiah 21; Isaiah

24,23; 52,7; Micah 4,7; Zechariah 14,9; Wisdom of Solomon 3,8; Psalms of Solomon 17,3; Assumption of Moses 10,1. But in all such passages, the religious idea is that of the kingly rule, reign or régime of God rather than the purely religious entity, the society of God and men, announced by Jesus.

As an expression of religious reality and hope, the kingdom of God stands practically isolated on the lips of Jesus. But certain strains in the substance of his message of the kingdom, as well as the form in which he expects its arrival, reach back to the remote and immediate past in the history and development of Jewish religious thought. Both in substance and in form Jesus' message of the kingdom of God has its historical antecedents, in reality, a solid substratum reaching back through the religious life of later Judaism to the faith of the great sixth and eighth century prophets.

In substance of religious conception, the kingdom of God as preached by Jesus is prophetic. One of its root ideas goes back as far as Amos, the idea of an impending future originating with and to be accomplished by God. Amos took *the day of Jehovah* from the lips of his complacent contemporaries and painted it as a day of doom and darkness, not of light. This idea of an impending future is expanded and developed in the thought of the later prophets, increasingly clothed with a warm optimism, until it reaches its climax in the kingdom of universal and eternal peace as pictured by Second Isaiah. (40-66.)

Further, Jesus' thought of God as the God of history and human affairs, involved deeply as it is in the kingdom, also goes back to the earliest prophets, and it stands as one of the signal victories won by them. This idea began in a narrow nationalism that had not yet entirely disappeared in Jesus' day and that confined the divine interest to the fates and fortunes of Israel alone. But in the minds of Israel's great prophets it expanded to include not only the whole of mankind but all of living creation. We might point out other aspects of the kingdom of God that had their foundations in the prophetic past and without which their full fruition in the religious faith of Jesus would have been impossible.

In form of realization, the kingdom of God as preached by Jesus is eschatological or apocalyptic. Here the influence of the immediate past is much clearer and stronger than in the case of the term or the substance of the thought of the kingdom. It is only relatively recently that this fact, with rather extreme emphasis, has been called to the attention of students of the life of Jesus by men like Johannes Weiss, Albert Schweitzer and Alfred Loisy.[17] Jesus lived and worked in an apocalyptic atmosphere that had invigorated certain sections of Judaism's religious life for two centuries and which found literary expression in the book of Daniel within the Old Testament and in the apocalyptic writings of the Pseudepigrapha.

It is perfectly clear that the form of Jesus' message

---

[17]These men interpret Jesus almost exclusively in the light of what is now known among New Testament students as his eschatology. *Eschatology* is a technical word of simple meaning. The best understanding of its real meaning is not to be found in a dictionary but in the thirteenth chapter of Mark. In the discussion that follows *eschatology* means simply: Jesus' *religious view of the future with its spectacular scenery*—the collapse of the present world order and the appearance of a new supernatural order to be introduced by God's chosen agent, the Son of man—in short, the coming of the kingdom of God. Consult the eschatological or apocalyptic words of Jesus referred to in the following paragraph.

and faith in the kingdom of God came directly from this Jewish apocalyptic atmosphere which, in a modified form, lived on in the religious outlook of his followers as is evident in the earlier letters of Paul and in a book like Revelation. Jesus' message of the kingdom of God as an impending event, as a supernatural order that is to supplant the present order, is apocalyptic. Certain words seem to have been spoken by him under the conscious influence of Daniel 7,13-14 and similar passages in the Jewish apocalyptic writings. Numerous apocalyptic or eschatological words of Jesus might be cited, but a few outstanding instances will suffice: Matthew 10,23; Mark 9,1; the whole of his longest address in Mark 13; 14,62; Luke 22,18.

> "And then shall they see the Son of man coming in clouds with great power and glory. And then shall he send forth the angels, and shall gather together his elect from the four winds, from the uttermost part of the earth to the uttermost part of heaven." (Mark 13,26-27.)

In such passages Jesus stands for us almost unapproachable and inaccessible. This element in his message is so strange and foreign to our wholly different worldview that it is only by conscious and sustained effort that the historical imagination can find its way back to him. Nevertheless, it stands as an integral element of his religious thought. We can not and must not seek to explain it away, as some have sought to do, for it belongs to the real Jesus of history. It is rather the seeker's task to learn to see and to share something of the tremendous religious faith that surges behind and through this strange setting.

The kingdom of God in the message of Jesus is not just a social scheme or system; it is an actual society of God and men, the perfect performance and presence of the divine will on earth as in heaven. For Jesus, the kingdom of God is *eine durchaus religioese Groesse* (an exclusively religious entity and value).

The kingdom of God is the soul of all that Jesus has to say, and what he meant by the kingdom on earth and among men is clear to any one who can read and follow the simple yet profound thought of the *Lord's Prayer.* For the technical student Jesus' message of the kingdom of God involves historical, linguistic and other types of problems, but for the plainest Galilean peasant in his audience, as for the most unlearned lay reader of his words to-day, his message of the kingdom of God as the supreme religious value to be awaited, acquired or attained was and is as clear as crystal. Nothing is more characteristic of Jesus' presentation of his message than universal intelligibility.

Jesus presented his message in the greatest variety of forms. He projected the kingdom of God in parable and in paradox, by comparison and by contrast, often in short compact sentences, again in longer addresses. However, the longer discourses ascribed to him are usually collections of briefer and simpler statements. It is certainly characteristic of the address of Jesus that he did not speak at length but to the point. He presses his way at once to the very heart of the matter. In a simple statement, often in a single sentence, he sets forth in a complete picture, in an illuminating illustration with homely materials drawn from the familiar fields of human experience, what the kingdom of God is and what it is to mean in human life and living. Any one who ob-

serves merely the form in which he presented his great
message, the rich and attractive variety of graphic pictures which he projected, can not but marvel at the intellectual resourcefulness of Jesus, not to mention the deepest truths of religion which these pictures sent home to
the heart of the plainest hearer.

Jesus was a man with a single theme of thought, the
kingdom of God. Of a mind with a single theme, constantly presented, we might expect a certain monotony
of message, a mental and moral monotony as well, such
a dreary development as confronts us in certain sections
of the book of Ezekiel. But in the religious thinking of
Jesus our impression is the very opposite. The rich
variety of his method of presentation does not account
wholly for this lack of monotony. It is not due to sheer
intellectual resourcefulness. Back of Jesus' thought and
message of the kingdom of God is the infinite richness of
his own personal experience of religion, which kept him
free from monotony, always fresh in faith, vivid in
imagination, and impressive in presentation.

Compactness and clearness are certainly thoroughly
characteristic of Jesus' presentation of his great religious
message. However, nothing is more uncharacteristic of
his presentation of the kingdom of God than logical consistency. The kingdom is not a system of religious
thought logically developed and declared by Jesus.
There is no attempt at systematic statement of his thought
on this great theme. There is nothing in Jesus' teaching
that would suggest the systems of Christian doctrine
formulated by the earlier and later thinkers of the church.
He nowhere seems to aim at a methodical development,
at an orderly presentation of his thought that would result in a clear and coherent system. In fact, Jesus' pre-

sentations of the kingdom of God are often so different in
thought and conception that contradictions seem evident
on the very surface.

At times, Jesus presents the kingdom as the kingly
rule, reign or régime of God as is quite common in the
thought of the Old Testament prophets. This meaning
is bound up in the very term, the *kingdom* of God. The
kingdom is like "unto a certain king who made a mar-
riage feast for his son." (Matt. 22,1-14.) There is a
royal will to be obeyed. (Matt. 7,21.) There are
duties to be performed. (Matt. 25,31-46.) God may
arbitrarily give His kingdom to any or all independent
of any merit on the part of the recipients. (Matt.
20,1-16.) The kingdom as a reign or rule is perfectly
clear in a purely Jewish picture which Jesus projected
for the twelve (Matt. 19,28),

> "Ye who have followed me, in the regeneration
> when the Son of man shall sit on the throne of his
> glory, ye also shall sit upon twelve thrones, judging
> the twelve tribes of Israel."

At other times, Jesus presents the kingdom of God as
a realm with definite ways along which one may enter:

> "Enter ye in by the narrow gate: for wide is the
> gate, and broad is the way, that leadeth to destruction,
> and many are they that enter in thereby. For narrow
> is the gate, and straitened the way, that leadeth unto
> life, and few are they that find it." (Matt. 7,13-14.)

The kingdom is surrounded by borders and barriers
that may bar the way and exclude; one may be cast out
of the kingdom,

"Many shall come from the east and the west, and shall sit down with Abraham, and Isaac, and Jacob, in the kingdom of heaven: but the sons of the kingdom shall be cast forth into the outer darkness." (Matt. 8,11-12a.)

One may be near or far from the kingdom. To the Jerusalem scribe Jesus says (Mark 12,34),

"Thou art not far from the kingdom of God."

Again, the kingdom is a new world order, a supernatural entity that is to be awaited by men and which will come by divine intervention resulting in the complete collapse of the present order.

"There are some here of them that stand *by,* who shall in no wise taste of death, till they see the kingdom of God come with power." [18]

Still again, the kingdom of God is a community offering citizenship, a spiritual society requiring an attitude that is to be cultivated until it reaches perfection (Matt. 18,3) :

"Except ye turn, and become as little children, ye shall in no wise enter into the kingdom of heaven."

Finally, Jesus presents the kingdom of God, as the supreme value, the priceless treasure, the precious possession which the individual may aspire to and acquire for his own (Matt. 13,44-46) :

---

[18]Mark 9, 1; *see also* Mark 13, 24-27.

"The kingdom of heaven is like unto a treasure hidden in the field; which a man found, and hid; and in his joy he goeth and selleth all that he hath, and buyeth that field. Again, the kingdom of heaven is like unto a man that is a merchant seeking goodly pearls; and having found one pearl of great price, he went and sold all that he had, and bought it."

Jesus' thought that men may expect, await, approach, aspire to, attain, acquire the kingdom of God presents a complexity of passive and active human attitudes that defies the processes of logical reasoning, but that springs organically from the pure depths of a consecrated religious consciousness wholly concentrated upon its one great objective.

This lack of strict logical consistency is also apparent in Jesus' teaching concerning the time of the arrival or realization of the kingdom of God. In some words, the kingdom is to come in the immediate future. It is imminent, at hand, nigh, even at the doors; the sky is red with its dawning. To the twelve as he sends them out on their mission, Jesus says (Matt. 10,23):

"Ye shall not have gone through the cities of Israel, till the Son of man be come."

In other passages, the kingdom belongs to the remote future and its realization is to be the outcome of a process of gradual growth and development. (Mark 4,26-29.) Again, it has its roots struck in the present, but its perfection lies in the future. (Mark 4,30-32.) And in still other words, the kingdom appears as present, here and now. (Matt. 12,28; Luke 17,20-21.)

But straight through all of these variations runs Jesus' confidence and certainty that God *will* establish His kingdom. Such is the deeper unity that expresses the very essence of his message and faith. The early or late date of the kingdom's complete realization and perfection is a matter of secondary importance which, even for Jesus himself, lies hidden in the divine will. (Mark 13,32.)

Many students of the life of Jesus have taken these paradoxical elements with great seriousness. Some have sought to remove the contradictions by reconciling what are only apparently conflicts. Others have brought about consistency by an extreme emphasis on some one element to the exclusion of other equally evident elements. But neither is true to the temper of the genuinely religious consciousness in general, nor to the state of the facts in the thought and teaching of Jesus in particular. Both try to accomplish for Jesus a logical consistency for which he himself very clearly felt no need and in which he manifested no interest. He nowhere seems to think or to teach under the restraints of reason and logic. His thought is free from fallacy, but logic and reason seem to have had no command over him. And all this for the reason that Jesus did not deliver his message of the kingdom in the interest of clear thinking, but in the interest of the whole of human life and experience with the demands which religion places upon both. Further, it is thoroughly characteristic of the passionately religious personality that it can live and work, even thrive, in the very midst of those tensions in thought, those conflicts in conceptions, that are so distracting and disturbing to the strictly logical type of mind. For as life is more than logic, so is faith more than fact, and religion more than reason.

Such conflicts as do exist in Jesus' message and his presentation of it disappear only as the student of his life learns to see in his teaching concerning the kingdom of God something more than a system of thought. The student must learn to press back beyond the outer form to the single and solid religious life and experience of which they are expressions. Jesus, true to the Semitic mind and temper, thought and taught in pictures. He shared nothing of the academic inclination of the Western mind. In his thought and teaching concerning the kingdom of God, we do not meet and can not expect to find a fine and delicately membered argumentation, a careful articulation of all parts to the whole. In his message we meet rather a straightforward and simple presentation of one fundamental theme, a single great thought clearly and plainly pictured in a way intelligible to all. Such lack of logical consistency as appears is due to the fact that Jesus, as all truly great prophets who feel themselves called and commissioned to the cause of God in behalf of men, thought and spoke under the pressure of his own deepest convictions and faith.

The Kingdom of God as the Religious Outlook of Jesus

Every great message, religious or otherwise, that contributes worth and value to human life and living must spring organically and spontaneously from the personal faith and conviction of the one who announces it. We can not separate a man from his message, an error too often committed in the study of the great men of the past. Historical and biographical studies are often too

THE RELIGIOUS FAITH OF JESUS 117

objective. They give a systematic presentation of the thought and teaching of the great man in question as though the man's thought and teaching were quite separate from the man himself. In the study of great religious genius this has often been the case. We can read whole volumes on the thought, teaching and theology of Paul, Augustine, Luther and a host of others, and yet learn very little about the men who did the thinking, teaching and preaching. By this impersonal method of study a rupture is made in the life of a man whose life was a single solid substance of soul and who was never conscious of his message as a thing apart from himself, or of himself apart from his message. Not a few studies of the thought and teaching of Jesus have fallen into this grave error. They are treated objectively and impersonally as though neither was an organic part of Jesus himself. Such treatments are often very learned, but very lifeless.

A man must be in his message; he must throw himself into it. It is this launching of himself in his message that gives it weight and carrying power. There is a great difference between a man with a message and a message with a man. When the messenger is possessed by the message his own person is so absorbed in and by it that it in turn is filled with a fire and fervor that carries its own conviction. We may not separate Jesus from his message; they constitute such an organic unity that separation means the devitalization of both, and we have left only a heap of green branches cut from the mangled body from which they sprang and grew.

Jesus' message of the kingdom of God is simply the natural expression of his own personal religious faith. His words, parables and addresses on the kingdom tell us more of his own faith than they do of anything else. Here we find in rich deposits the pure metal of his own mind as it hoped, believed and aspired to God and His kingdom. As Professor Deissmann writes, "It is not his system, which one finds in his words, it is his soul."[19] Jesus' message has, then, an intensely personal source—his own experience of God. His utterances are never cold and formal on the question of the kingdom; they always have about them that personal warmth which betrays their origin from within. In fact, many of his words, a number of his most familiar teachings, are intelligible only in the terms of the personal religious life from which they come. Therefore, we may not treat as impersonal what for Jesus was intensely personal.

Jesus was more preacher than teacher, more prophet than pedagogue. His message is more an announcement and declaration of his own personal faith than an effort to impart religious instruction. In the whole of his public work Jesus' aim is less to win men to his message, more to communicate to them his faith. He did not go about teaching the kingdom of God and what it involves; rather he announced with all the fire of his spirit that the kingdom is coming and that soon. Too many studies have him preach the kingdom in a too impersonal manner and fail to see that the kingdom for Jesus was not a formal, but a deeply personal matter. Its announcement was by no means just his life-work and occupation; it was not just a public profession chosen by him. It was the one point where all of his religious conviction centered, where his faith and feeling focused.

Jesus is seized by the importance of the time in which

---

[19] *The Religion of Jesus and the Faith of Paul,* p. 44.

he lives. The conviction that the kingdom of God is coming is for him a consciousness not only of a new but of the final episode of Israel's religious life and history. For the whole world it is at the very doors. He feels the impact of the new age; he sees the dawning of God's great day. In a moment of exalted faith he tells his disciples:

"Blessed are your eyes, for they see; and your ears, for they hear. For verily I say unto you, that many prophets and righteous men desired to see the things which ye see, and saw them not; and to hear the things which ye hear and heard them not." (Matt. 13,16-17.)

Jesus feels that *something greater* is here than anything that has been in the glories of the past. In triumphant faith and exalted conviction he announces to his contemporaries:

"But I say unto you, that one greater than the temple is here.... The men of Nineveh shall stand up in the judgment with this generation, and shall condemn it: for they repented at the preaching of Jonah; and behold, a greater than Jonah is here. The queen of the south shall rise up in the judgment with this generation, and shall condemn it: for she came from the ends of the earth to hear the wisdom of Solomon; and behold, a greater than Solomon is here." (Matt. 12,6 41-42.)[20]

---

[20]The text of our American translators is non-committal, *one greater* or *a greater*. The best manuscripts read, *something greater, a greater thing, a greater matter*, which is the genuine thought of Jesus. The minority reading, *a greater one, some one greater*, presents the Christian point of view which centers upon the person of Jesus rather than Jesus' own point of view which centered upon God and His kingdom.

When Jesus announced his message (Mark 1,15),

> "The kingdom of God is at hand,"

when he sent his disciples out with the word (Matt. 10,23b),

> "Ye shall not have gone through the cities of Israel, till the Son of man be come,"

when he turned and said to his followers (Mark 9,1),

> "There are some here of them that stand *by,* who shall in no wise taste of death, till they see the kingdom of God come with power,"

he was announcing very simply yet very clearly his own personal faith and religious conviction. The immediate coming of the kingdom was his own fervent hope and expectation, the great goal of the near future. And on the last night of his life, when the kingdom had not yet come and when he stood face to face with his own fate, he tells his disciples that he may perish but the kingdom *will* come,

> "I shall not drink from henceforth of the fruit of the vine, until the kingdom of God shall come." (Luke 22,18.)

Thus from beginning to end, we see that he believed that God has a kingdom; he is convinced that it *will* come, and that soon. Jesus' faith in the kingdom of God and its coming is one of the most personal and reliable features

of him that has come down to us. This faith he holds
unflinchingly; it holds him, and he does not surrender it
even in the very face of his own personal fate.

All that Jesus says of the kingdom of God he himself
esteems it to be. When he presents it as the hidden
treasure which a man finds and as the pearl of great price
(Matt. 13,44-46), we see very clearly what the kingdom
is in his own estimate. In the kingdom of God he located
the highest of all values. It is something for which one
gladly, even enthusiastically, makes the greatest sacrifices
in order to possess it. Such a location of values belongs
to the very heart of any real religion. When he says,
"Seek ye first His kingdom," we see the goal of his own
faith and aspiration. Just such a quest of the kingdom
of God runs through all that we know of him. Such a
word is autobiographical, an extract from his very soul.
Life and food, body and raiment, are wholly unimportant
in comparison with the great concern of God that commands and consumes the whole of his life.

The quest of the kingdom that leaves all else in a
secondary place is born of the experience and conviction of
only the greatest souls whose personal courage equals
their consecration. The hunger and thirst of which Jesus
speaks in Matthew's beatitude (5,6) is a personal religious confession in a veiled form. But we do not realize
fully what it meant for Jesus personally until we hear
him pray for its coming. "Thy kingdom come," is the
very heart of the *Lord's Prayer*; all the other petitions
are simply elaborations and implications of this one
thought. In his prayer-life he put the kingdom of God
first, ahead of all other human needs and interests. The
primary place of the kingdom in this greatest of all
prayers is not due to conscious reflection on the part of

Jesus. Its place was first in his own thought, and it should be the chief of all Christian aspirations because it was primary in the scale of religious values personally held and sought by Jesus. We must not forget that the *Lord's Prayer* has the rich prayer-experience of Jesus behind it, of which it is the fine fruit.

Jesus' faith in the kingdom of God took on a strange form, one quite foreign to us to-day, yet as natural to him and his contemporaries as it is strange to us. The kingdom in the faith of Jesus is a supernatural order, a divine intervention that is about to come; it is to be introduced by a special divine agent, the Son of man, who is to come on the clouds of heaven in great power and glory, attended by the angelic hosts, as we see in such passages as Mark 13,26-27 and 14,62.

This peculiar form of Jesus' faith has given rise to extensive discussion and debate in the twentieth-century life-of-Jesus research. This controversy has waged about Jesus' view of the future, in more technical terms, about his eschatology. On the one hand, we have the eschatologists who, in milder or more extreme form, regard Jesus' view of the future as the key to the understanding of all that he said and did and was. The most prominent advocate of this view is Albert Schweitzer who reduces the whole of Jesus' life to a series of eschatological words, acts and sacraments; even Jesus' teaching is only a probationary ethics, *Interimsethik*.[21]   On the other hand, we find the anti-eschatologists, headed by Wilhelm Bousset,[22] with the claim that Jesus' view of the future

[21]*Die Geschichte der Leben-Jesu-Forschung*, pp. 222-235, 390-443. For a recent, exclusively eschatological life of Jesus, *see* J. Warschauer, *The Historical Life of Christ*.

[22]*Jesu Predigt in ihrem Gegensatz zum Judentum*. *See* Schweitzer, *Die Geschichte der Leben-Jesu-Forschung*, pp. 236-259.

is not eschatological, and that eschatology is not essential to the understanding of him. The eschatological passages in the Gospels are ingenuine, the product of a later age.

But, on turning to the first three Gospels, we find that eschatology is absolutely characteristic of the form of Jesus' faith in the kingdom of God and its coming. The eschatological passages are too numerous and extensive to be eliminated, too deeply set in the bed-rock of our best Gospel tradition to be uprooted without tearing him from his century. If Jesus did not express his faith in eschatological form, if these passages are not genuine, then we can not be sure that any words in the Gospels go back to him. Eschatology, that fantastic view of the future so foreign to our way of thinking, is thoroughly characteristic of the Jesus of history, and it is important in our approach to an adequate understanding of him. It stands as the great achievement of Albert Schweitzer in the field of New Testament criticism to have forced modern scholarship to face this long-neglected aspect of Jesus' thought and faith. As Professor Heiler writes, "The recognition of the eschatological character of Jesus' gospel is the Copernican achievement of modern theology."[23]

The eschatological form of Jesus' faith is an established fact of modern research, and it rests upon the solid foundation of all that the Gospels tell us of him. There is no natural reason why his faith should have expressed itself in any other form. His very historicity and our own historical judgment demand it. Back of him are two centuries of Judaism's faith, the predominant strain of which is eschatological. In our best records of him are

---

[23]*Der Katholizismus. Seine Idee und seine Erscheinung*, p. 3.

those eschatological passages that defy invention. They stand as unfulfilled words of Jesus, and the only possible motive for ascribing such statements to him would be the fact that he made them and believed them.

It was on the basis of his eschatological faith that the early Christian community founded its hope and expectation of Jesus' speedy return to inaugurate the new age. The first Christians, like Joseph of Arimathea, were looking for the kingdom of God. It was the fervent faith of Paul, as we see in I Thessalonians 4,15-18 where he cites the speedy return of the Lord Jesus as a chief source of Christian comfort and consolation. Such a hope had a solid basis in the thought and faith of his Master. "Piety for Jesus was an altogether eschatological matter."[24] The same is true of the faith and religion of the earliest Christians. The failure of Jesus to appear in cosmic triumph, the death of fellow believers in the face of Jesus' promise that the kingdom would come in his own generation, constituted a serious problem for the first Christians. It was a problem that Paul was forced to face as presented to him by his mission stations whose members were dying before the Lord Jesus came. The earliest Christian prayer addressed to Jesus was very probably,

"Marana tha—Our Lord, come."[25]

This eschatological faith survived Jesus, Paul and the first generation of Christians. It became the theme of a whole document like Revelation. It was surrendered by Christians generally only in the face of fact, but it was

---

[24]Heiler, *Der Katholizismus*, p. 23.
[25]I Cor. 16,22; Rev. 22,20; Did. 10,6.

not a complete capitulation of confidence in Jesus. The early Christian faith surrendered its form and that of Jesus, but it did not surrender the substance of Jesus' faith nor its own.

"Although we are not sure as to the exact character and extent of the eschatological hopes of Jesus' day, we do know that his picture of the future was not peculiar to himself, but a picture painted before him as early as Daniel 7,13-14 and that it was not shared by Jesus alone, but by many of his own people. That Jesus' view was a common view is clear from the fact that he finds it no more necessary to explain or define it than he does the notion of the kingdom of God. He simply refers to it as a well-known element in the religious acumen and atmosphere of his day. How widely this view was entertained by Jesus' national contemporaries can not be determined; the sources are too inadequate. But they do attest that when he spoke of the future in such glowing terms his teaching was not new and strange, but well enough understood to dispense with definition. It was a picture so vividly visualized by his disciples that they even engaged in a dispute as to their respective rôles in the future and requested reservations for prominent places. (Mark 10,35-41.) They had but two questions to ask: Where? (Luke 17,37), and when? (Mark 13,4.)"[26]

The eschatological form of his faith belongs to the very Jewishness of Jesus, and the modern student is forced to take a Jewish view of him in this respect. The

---

[26]Bundy, *The Psychic Health of Jesus*, p. 256f.

historical setting in which he appeared and worked, thought and taught, believed and hoped, makes any other view impossible. Jesus' genius and temperament were Oriental, Syrian, and they must be recognized as such in spite of the difficulty that the Western mind experiences in trying to find its way through this maze of eschatological thought, faith and hope so generally characteristic of the ancient East, and in spite of its failure to feel at home in such an atmosphere.

But the eschatological form of Jesus' religious outlook is only a secondary matter. The primary concern is that solid substance of religious faith expressed in this strange form. It is at this point that both the eschatologists and the anti-eschatologists have committed grave error. The weakness of the position that sees in his thought eschatology only is that it condemns Jesus hopelessly to his own century and leaves him anchored there without a clear word for us to-day. Anti-eschatology is even weaker: it strips his thought of its characteristic form, it leaves only shreds of his teaching, and it commits the gravest of historical errors by tearing Jesus from his own century. Eschatologists and anti-eschatologists alike miss, at least in theory, the tremendous religious faith of Jesus that expressed itself in this strange but natural form. Both have mistaken the characteristic for the essential; they have found the form and lost the content. Eschatology belongs simply to the upper strata of his faith in God and His kingdom. We may maintain it or reject it, and interpret Jesus accordingly, and yet in the end miss what it really has to offer.

To identify Jesus' eschatology entirely with his view of the future is a serious error, for it overlooks the real faith of Jesus. His eschatology stands out as clear as crystal for an immediate divine intervention, but his view of the future is essentially religious. The future, as he sees and believes in it, is God's. It is of and from God. It is God and men in perfect society. If Jesus' view of the future had been a mere dream, an unattainable Utopia, it would have perished with its failure to fulfill itself. It was the religious substance behind it, that expressed itself in and through it, that saved it for his first followers and for us.

We must remember that there is nothing sacred in the spectacular scenery of Jesus' religious outlook. It is thoroughly characteristic of him and it may not be stripped from him as an historical figure, but it is never primary. The essential element in Jesus' view of the future is his faith in the fact that God has a kingdom, that it can and will come, and that soon, and that it is the highest calling of men to be worthy of it as their divine destiny. Jesus' eschatology is permeated with his fiery faith for the future that belongs to God the Father and to men His children. This religious faith, announced with such great conviction and certainty, is the chief treasure that Jesus has in store for his followers. If we miss this, we have missed Jesus himself. Jesus was not committed unreservedly to the form of the future's realization, but to God who was to bring this future about. With all of his strange eschatology Jesus belongs in the ranks of the prophets rather than in the ranks of the apocalyptists, for whom only too often the spectacular scenery of the future constituted the principal substance of their faith.

"Eschatology has its evident elements of strength. It is conservative in its treatment of the sources. It leaves Jesus to live seriously and genuinely in his own day and time. It also offers what Strauss in his 1835 *Life of Jesus* called 'true and splendid elements' that are not to be underestimated. Finally, eschatology pays a tremendous tribute to Jesus himself in that it shows that primitive, and essential, Christianity was not committed to the formal fulfillment of any particular promise but to Jesus himself and the substance of his faith."[27]

The imminent kingdom of God stands at the very center of all of Jesus' thinking and teaching, at the very heart of his deepest feeling and faith. In the parables of the mustard seed and the leaven Jesus' mind is moved by a tremendous optimism. He does not mention, nor in his thinking does he reckon with any counter-forces, so confident is he of the final triumph of the kingdom. Both parables are organic expressions of his own personal faith: Independent of beginnings, the kingdom *will* triumph. It will come in his own generation. Mark 13,30 is an outburst of just such certainty,

"This generation shall not pass away, until all these things be accomplished."

The following word (Mark 13,31),

"Heaven and earth shall pass away: but my words shall not pass away,"

is a clear echo of the old prophetic consciousness and conviction. The kingdom of God is the great religious objective of Jesus; he works and prays for its coming; it is the great concern of his life.

---

[27]Bundy, *The Psychic Health of Jesus*, p. 219.

The Kingdom of God as the Religious Cause of Jesus

Every great faith must have its champion, and a faith is never really great until it finds its champion who is held by it and wholly consecrated to it. A truly great religious faith is not just held and advocated. On the contrary, it lays hold upon men and presses them into its service. A man of really great faith becomes active and aggressive. If his faith is religious, it becomes the cause of God which he champions. A great religious faith enlists men in its enterprise; they choose it as their cause; in it they invest their lives, everything.

Just such is the kingdom of God for Jesus. His faith in God's kingdom and its coming is so firm and fervent that he becomes its champion. It presses him actively and aggressively into its service. The personal piety of Jesus seems to have been more than all else the espousal of the divine cause. He is so absorbed in the kingdom and its coming that it amounts practically to an identification, to a loss of self-identity in the commanding conviction of a cause to be championed. For him it was at the very center of everything. Nothing else could command him except as it demonstrated its vital relationship to this one central concern; he consecrated himself to it with a perfect abandon.

"Ye can not serve God and mammon." (Matt. 6,24.)

In such a word we feel the intensity with which he threw himself into the cause of God among men.

Jesus possessed an unparalleled, an almost incredible personal power in the experience and expression of religion. And the secret of this personal power is to be sought in his utter devotion to his faith in the kingdom of God. It was this faith that forged his life into a single solid substance, and all else fell into the background or out of his life for ever. For the kingdom he is ready to sacrifice everything; he gives all, even life itself, in order to possess and present it. The world has never witnessed a greater quest of religious faith. For Jesus, the kingdom of God was much more than convincing; it was completely commanding. His faith in it created his character; it determined his conduct down to the least and last detail of his existence.

This cause of the kingdom of God was not chosen for him but by him. Jesus, as the prophets before him, did not regard his task as that of general public instruction in certain religio-moral, religio-ethical ideas and ideals. He was not just a teacher with a certain subject-matter at his command. He was a spokesman of God, a man whose faith gave him a task to accomplish. He was not a man who uttered pious precepts, a man ready to die for his opinions. It was the sheer weight of personal religious conviction that brought Jesus into the service of the kingdom of God. It was not tradition or custom, profession or precedent. He came from no school or sect; he represented no special tendency of religious thought, no shade of opinion. He did not posit and prove, neither did he debate and dispute. In the utter simplicity that belongs to the truly great, he declared his faith. When Jesus appeared in public he represented just one thing, a purely personal thing, his own faith in God and His kingdom.

It is true that for Jesus the kingdom was a supernatural thing; it was the work of God, not the work of men, and it was to be established by the divine agency. But in his conviction it is among men that the kingdom is to realize itself. It is to this kingdom, to this eternal enterprise that seeks the permanent society of God and men, that men are called. They may enter into it; they may attain it; they may acquire its chiefest treasures. For Jesus the kingdom of God is the goal toward which human history moves and in which it must find its culmination. It is the new, the final, the glorious order to be established by God with men. In brief, the kingdom of God is simply the divine cause in human life and history—"the practice of the presence of God." (Jeremy Taylor.)

In the faith of Jesus the kingdom of God is the one thing that can give permanent value and worth to human life and living. He presents it as the one great goal of all human ambition, aspiration and endeavor. The single and supreme interest of humankind should be to approach and to attain it. It is the pearl of great price to be sought and secured, and no sacrifice is too great on the part of the individual or group. Men can if they will, if they have faith. This is the very heart of Jesus' faith in humankind. And it was his faith in men as well as his faith in God that brought him into the public service of both.

There is a triumphant daring in this faith of Jesus that it is among men that the kingdom of God will realize itself. The daring lies in Jesus' limitless confidence in men. He had more confidence in men than they have ever manifested in themselves. He believed more of them, had more ambition for them, than they would dare ask or think for themselves. And men have never yet justified this tremendous confidence of Jesus in their ability to attain.

The great religious task to which Jesus felt himself

called and commissioned was to set before men the prospect of the kingdom of God, the way that leads to it, and to bring them to share in it. To show men the kingdom of God and to share with them his faith in it, this was the very essence of his mission in public. In its service he set every personal religious resource at his command.

In this connection we may not fail to inquire into the promoting factors that brought Jesus out of private life into public. If we turn to the Gospel writers for an answer, we find that Mark very clearly locates these in the three sketches he gives us prior to Jesus' first announcement of his message (1,14-15): the Baptist and his work (1,2-8), the vision and voice at the Jordan (1,9-11), and the period of seclusion and temptation in the wilderness (1,12-13). All of these experiences may have contributed to Jesus' determination upon a public career, although all three are presented by Mark more from the point of view of what they meant for the Christian faith of his readers than from the point of view of what they meant for Jesus personally. In just what sense and how they were significant for Jesus himself Mark does not make clear to us. But as historical students we are inclined to locate his decision upon a public career in something other and deeper than any one incident or series of incidents such as Mark arranges in his immediate prepublic life of Jesus. (1,2-13.) The grounds for Jesus' determination upon a public career seem rather to be found in Mark 1,14-15—in his conviction that God has a kingdom which is at hand and in his consciousness of being called and commissioned to preach as a public message this deep religious faith. It is the consciousness of possessing the message of the kingdom of God and the conviction of being chosen to make it his cause that explain best the nature of a public work and mission such as that in which Jesus engaged.

Mark's promoting factors—John the Baptist, the Jordan experience and the wilderness retreat—may have helped, but they do not account for all that Jesus represented. In every feature of the Gospel picture Jesus is characterized by the consciousness of high call and holy commission. It is this elusive element of high call and holy commission that has been present, without exception, in the person and work of all the great leaders of human history. And in the case of Jesus, it seems to have been the one force in his personality and public appearance that caused the common people to hear him gladly (Mark 12,37b) and that distinguished him and his message from the conventional and professional religious leaders of his day.

"The multitudes were astonished at his teaching: for he taught them as *one* having authority, and not as their scribes." (Matt. 7,28b-29.)

This impression of personal authority in matters of religion Jesus left with his hearers from the very first, and it continued to the end. Only some such powerful personal factor, emanating from an exalted consciousness of high call and holy commission, can account adequately for the constant thronging of the multitudes, the winning and retaining of permanent followers, the effecting of cures, and the bitter hatred of opponents.

When, where and how Jesus received the substance of this deep conviction we can not say. We have no record of any experience that would tell us when and where the substance of his message was imparted to him, no account of a personal call in which he received his commission to the particular work of the kingdom of God, such as we find in the experience of his great predecessors—Amos, Isaiah, Jeremiah, Ezekiel.

the prophet also

Jesus nowhere states the grounds for the faith that was in him, but we may be sure that they were not the product of rational reflection and reason. His reasons for this hope he does not reveal; the sources of this certainty he does not disclose. They do not seem to have been in the signs of the times—political, social or religious, matters which furnished some of his great predecessors with their convictions, or in turn confirmed them. Like Amos (3,8) Jesus seems to have responded to inner impulses. By prophetic intuition he feels that he and his contemporaries are living at the dawning of the new age, a situation that demands religious reconstruction of mind and life.

The sources of Jesus' faith in the kingdom of God and its coming are not clear to us. We must confess that we do not know, that such lies hidden for ever in the depths of his profoundly religious consciousness. The most that we can say with certainty is not a great deal, but we may say that Jesus possessed a genuine genius for sensing, seizing and sharing all that is highest and best in religion—an unfaltering faith in God and in His plans and purposes for men. And this faith in God and His kingdom was sufficiently strong to carry him through all disappointments and discouragements. In inner conflict and crisis, in severest personal stress and strain, the consciousness of the worth and right of his faith, the very greatness of the cause he had chosen, seems to have supported and sustained him.

But after surveying all the possibilities, we shall have

to say that above all else it was the kingdom of God as the object of his own personal faith, as the sum and substance of his deepest religious convictions, as the divine cause which he felt himself called to preach and commissioned to champion publicly, that brought Jesus out of private life in the little village of Nazareth into the engagement in a public career at the command of God and in behalf of men.

Jesus devoted himself with an exclusiveness and exhaustiveness to the cause of God in human life and history, to all that religion at its highest and best stands for, that is without parallel in our human history. Yet he did this without the fury of the fanatic, without the effervescent enthusiasm of the extremist. He did it with a sanity and seriousness that makes human life, with the kingdom of God in prospect, a supreme happiness and boon.

Jesus accepted what many might call an almost impossible cause, the kingdom of God among men. He did not live to see his cause accomplished; the kingdom did not come as he expected and announced. His own forecasts remained unfulfilled both for himself and for his followers. The twelve disciples returned from their mission in spite of the fact that he had told them that they should not go through the cities of Israel till the Son of man be come. (Matt. 10,23.) Jesus perished and his followers died after him in spite of the fact that he had promised that they should not taste of death till they should see the kingdom of God come with power (Mark 9,1) and that it should be accomplished in his own generation (Mark 13,30). In vain the disciples awaited the fulfillment of his word that he should not taste again of the fruit of the vine until he should drink it new with them in the kingdom of God. (Matt. 26,29.)

But it is just at this point that Jesus proves himself a prophet and not an apocalyptist. The prophets before him were relatively indifferent toward the fulfillment of their forecasts of the future. Jonah is the great exception among the prophets, and the chief point to his discipline is that the prophet is not a predictor of the future but the spokesman of his own great faith in God. The failure of their forecasts did not deter the great prophets from their work because their faith in God meant more to them than their own announcements of what the future would bring. The prophetic pictures of the future were always cast in moments of high inspiration and confidence; they were expressions of the prophetic faith at its best, and they served as such rather than as detailed predictions of future events. The prophetic attitude toward the fulfillment of forecasts was characteristically undogmatic. The great prophets were preaching the God of the past, the present and the future. All that they announced as to come was dependent upon the will of Him who is the Eternal Now.

Such was Jesus' own attitude toward the future and what it was to bring. The future was wholly dependent upon the divine will. In the work of Jonah he saw, not the failure of his forecast, but his message of repentance—Jonah's sign to his generation, and Jesus said that the sign of Jonah was the only sign that he would give to his own contemporaries. (Luke 11,29-30.)

Jesus' faith in the kingdom of God is the most vital and powerful venture of the religious spirit that human history knows. As Loisy writes, it is "the greatest manifestation of faith ever displayed on earth."[28] Its failure

---

[28] *The Gospel and the Church*, p. 123.

to realize itself in the form of his forecast is a thought
that will hardly cross the threshold of the religious consciousness that has felt the fire of Jesus' spirit and that
has launched itself in the quest of the kingdom that Jesus
announced and sought. It will be difficult, however, for
the modern mind to regain its relinquished hold on religion and to realize that *faith is never a failure* either
for its subjects or for its objects.

In conclusion on the kingdom of God, we may say that
Jesus, in keeping with the spiritual genius of his prophetic
predecessors, looks forward rather than backward. He
does not rehearse those outstanding instances when God
long ago proved himself the shepherd of his people, and
he does not preach the God who revealed himself in
ancient signs and wonders. He does not review God's
dealings in the past, rather he announces His purpose for
the future and His demands on the present in the light of
this future. For Jesus the best is yet to come; the golden
age lies just ahead; it presses upon the doors; it is as
near as the summer when the fig tree's branches become
tender and shoot forth their leaves. (Mark 13,28-29.)
In the religious literature of his people the kingdom
of God is not more than a rare piece of religious terminology, but in the religious experience of Jesus himself it
becomes the central issue for God and for men, and into
it Jesus poured the entire wealth of his own religious
mind. His contribution to the history of the conception of
the kingdom of God was the central and exclusive place
which he gave it, not only in the divine plan but in human
experience. Jesus sets it as the highest possible goal for
human aspiration and attainment. Men are to participate
in this kingdom; it is among men that God will realize

His plans and purposes, that He will realize himself. The important thing for Jesus and his work is what the kingdom and its coming are to mean in human life and history. It is to mean everything that religion at its best can mean in the realm of human experience—God Himself.

In the thought of Jesus the kingdom of God is not a system of religious philosophy. In his message of the kingdom Jesus was not a philosopher but a prophet. His faith in its coming is not based on any historical calculations or grounds of reason, but on an intense inner conviction that dared fly in the face of fact and logic. He presents the kingdom very plainly, even prosaically, for the most part, in parables. He appealed to the imagination of his hearers rather than to their power to reason. His own thinking concerning the kingdom is plain picture-thinking. For Jesus, the kingdom of God was "a simple idea," better doubtless, "a simple reality."[29] And yet it was as full of paradox, contrast and contradiction as life itself, for it sprang from an intensely personal religious faith that in its expressions must reflect something of the "ebb and flow of a great inner life."[30]

The kingdom of God does not exhaust the religious significance of Jesus, but it comes to us as our one great heritage from him. As all the great spiritual values of mankind, the kingdom of God comes to us from the very depths of a unique religious nature.

Jesus appeared in public preaching an exclusively religious message, a prophet possessed by a deeply religious faith, consecrating himself to and consuming himself in the championship of the greatest of all religious causes—

[29]Loisy, *The Gospel and the Church*, p. 124.
[30]Deissmann, *Evangelium und Urchristentum*, p. 90.

the kingdom of God on earth and among men. The kingdom of God stands as the most adequate single expression of Jesus' own personal piety and religion. It constitutes his greatest contribution to the religious faith of mankind, for God and His kingdom with all that both signify and imply in the religious experience of Jesus are not only Christianity's but religion's chiefest treasure and possession. But the puzzling thing in the history of Christianity is that this kingdom of God, believed in and preached by Jesus, this cause which he championed and for which he died, this greatest of all his contributions to religious faith, has never found official expression in any Christian creed—creeds which pretend to crystallize in succinct statements the essential elements of a religion that names itself after him.

In this chapter we have sought to delineate the religious faith of Jesus, and we are struck at once by the marked contrast between the religion of Jesus and Christianity. Christianity has always been *Christocentric*—its faith focusing on the person of Jesus. The faith of Jesus, however, his own personal piety, centered upon God and His kingdom—it was *theocentric*. His faith was nothing more, nothing less, than the issue of his own personal religious experience, his experience of God as holy and as loving Father. In keeping with the psychology of religious genius, Jesus trusted his own experience of God as true; upon the basis of this experience he lived his life and performed his work. In the light of it he believed and felt, thought and taught, preached and prayed. His personal faith in God and His kingdom gave the whole of his life a unique quality. His certainties and convictions grew out of the nature of these objects of his faith and

his experience of them as the highest religious values.
His faith in God was not for his personal protection, to
preserve him from a tragic death. In fact, it was this
faith that brought him to and through his end.

All that Jesus had to say of God and His kingdom
came straight from his own breast. The goals and religious objects which he set for others were first of all
his own. What he himself had sensed, sought and secured, he in turn sought to show and to share with
others.

Jesus' faith in God and His kingdom presents itself
to us in the terms of the sum total of a vital religious
experience that wholly possesses an individual in his quest
of the Divine, in his pursuit of the divine presence as the
permanent possession in human life and history. His
great faith did not come to him by rational processes, nor
was it his merely by social inheritance as elements from
the religious past and present. It became his very own
by that more painful process of personal religious conviction. As such it laid hold of the deepest sources of
his life, and it was the firm grip of this great faith upon
his whole person that forced him out of private into
public life as the commissioned champion of the cause of
God among men. The religious faith of Jesus functioned
as the most vital and powerful thing in his life. It was
the driving force of his existence, for "religion is not an
intellectual abstraction but a power to live by."[31]

[31]Hauer, *Die Religionen—Ihr Werden, ihr Sinn, ihre Wahrheit.* Erstes
Buch: *Das religioese Erlebnis auf den unteren Stufen,* p. x.

CHAPTER III

The Religious Consciousness of Jesus

THE religious consciousness is peculiar to human experience. It springs from a genuine sense of native and natural limitation. Without a startling sense of serious limitation the religious consciousness would be an impossibility. It appears in both primitive and cultured religion. This sense of limitation is strongest in primitive man and it manifests itself in practically every item of his life. The whole of his existence is a puzzling problem far beyond his capacity and comprehension. Often he feels himself hopelessly helpless in the presence of the mysterious powers about him. In deep depression and desperation he turns to his gods. Cultured man is more reserved in expressing his sense of limitation because in his experience it takes on a finer form. He feels himself more at home in the world, for he has a richer experience and a fuller understanding of the order of existence that surrounds him. He masters it and makes it serve him and his ends, and he prides himself in his mastery. He feels that he knows things, that he can accomplish things, and that he himself possesses worth. But, sooner or later, cultured man finds himself confronted by his own limitations. He comes to the end of his knowledge; he meets powers stronger than his own, things that are beyond him; and finally he reaches a place where he ceases to trust in his own merit and where he begins to hope for mercy.

Thus human experience always ends in a strong sense of limitation which in turn has its issue in the religious

141

consciousness. Man feels himself in need of supplementation, of a help that is higher and more than human.
Fortune and fate, life and death are in hands more
powerful than his, a feeling that has its classic expression
in the ninetieth Psalm. The religious consciousness of
man with its sense of limitation has expressed itself in a
series of antitheses: profane and Sacred, natural and
Supernatural, human and Divine, finite and Infinite, man
and Maker, creature and Creator. "Man has religion
because he is not wholly identical with God."[1]

In the preceding chapters we have seen that the genius
of Jesus is really and essentially religious, that his experience of God is religious in the finest sense, resulting in
his personal faith in God and His kingdom. In the
present chapter we come to the very heart of our study
of Jesus as a religious subject. Did Jesus manifest a
truly religious consciousness? Did he feel those native
and natural human limitations universally characteristic
of the religious consciousness?

Christian thought has always made a great deal of the
humanity of Jesus. With pride it has pointed to those
sporadic details in the Gospels that supposedly establish
his genuine kinship with us, his fellowship in our finite
experience: the fact that he wept over Jerusalem (Luke
19,41), that he was hungry (Mark 11,12), and that he
was tired and thirsty (John 4,6-7). But none of these
scattered notices really demonstrates the humanity of
Jesus. Christian interest in these minor items has overlooked that solid substratum that supports all that we
know about him and upon which he stands as an historical
and human figure—his clear and profound sense of seri-

---

[1] *The Meaning of God in Human Experience*, by W. E. Hocking,
p. 153. Courtesy of Yale University Press.

ous limitation. The humanity of Jesus goes deeper than superficial detail; it rests upon the fundamental religiousness of the whole of his personality. The whole of his experience is to be described as religious—therefore, genuinely human.

The sense of native and natural human limitation runs through the whole of the Gospel story. It is an inextricable golden strand that belongs to the very warp and woof of the Gospel picture. And it is one of the chief glories of the Gospel writers that they have preserved this for us.

In the first three Gospels Jesus very frankly confesses that there are things that he does not know; he is limited in knowledge, a genuine human limitation. In his famous address on the last things, Mark 13, he announces with great certainty (Mark 13,30),

> "This generation shall not pass away, until all these things be accomplished,"

and at the height of prophetic conviction he declares that heaven and earth may pass away, but his own words shall not pass away. (Mark 13,31.) But at exactly this high point Jesus' thought and feeling reverse into a consciousness of self-limitation that is deeply religious,

> "But of that day or that hour knoweth no one, not even the angels in heaven, neither the Son, but the Father." (Mark 13,32.)

This word is cast in a Christian form; the language and style are of Christian origin, but the thought expressed is a genuine thought of Jesus. As Johannes Weiss writes,

"This word belongs to the most genuine matter that we possess from him," although "the language is that of early Christian theology."[2] This limitation of knowledge preserved itself even in the early Christian picture of Jesus, a feature that stood in open conflict with the rapidly developing Christian claims. We find it ascribed even to the Risen Lord,

> "It is not for you to know the times or seasons, which the Father hath set within his own authority." (Acts 1,7.)

The only possible motive for the rise of such a thought in the early Christian faith would be the fact that such was the actual attitude of the historical Jesus. It was only later that faith submerged such prosaic and plain fact from his life.

Jesus was also conscious of limitations of power. There were things that he could not do. On the fatal journey to Jerusalem when the faith of the disciples had reached a high point of enthusiasm, two of the twelve came to him with the request,

> "Grant unto us that we may sit, one on thy right hand, and one on thy left hand, in thy glory." (Mark 10,37.)

But in his reply Jesus tempered this enthusiastic outburst with a word from the depths of his own religious consciousness, an expression of his own sense of profound limitation,

---

[2]*Die Schriften des Neuen Testaments*, I, p. 197.

"The cup that I drink ye shall drink; and with the baptism that I am baptized withal shall ye be baptized: but to sit on my right hand or on *my* left hand is not mine to give; but *it is for them* for whom it hath been prepared."   (Mark 10,39b-40.)

Jesus preached the imminent kingdom with prophetic conviction and certainty, but it involved things that were not in his power to give, even to his most faithful followers.

Jesus was also conscious of limitations of personal worth. When the rich young ruler came to him with the question,

"Good teacher, what shall I do that I may inherit eternal life?"   (Mark 10,17)

his reply is as quick as a flash, an instinctive revolt:

"Why callest thou me good? none is good save one, *even* God."   (Mark 10,18.)

This is one of the most splendid of all of Jesus' words. The really religious person is always driven to the confession, "None is good save one, even God."   And the purer the piety, the more necessary and deeper is this confession.

In the three passages quoted above, it is perfectly clear that Jesus took a religious view of his own person. He is clearly conscious of the natural human limitations of knowledge, power and personal worth. All three words spring from the very depths of his religious consciousness and afford us one of our finest insights into his religious life. Such are clear confessions of dependence upon God, and in them Jesus places himself on the side of humanity for ever. Such are genuine human features that reach to the very core of his being. In the experience of Jesus we see that same sense of distance that separates man from his Maker, creature from Creator, that same sense of limitation that characterizes religion in all of its historical forms and appearances and that gives it its primitive power and strength.

Universally the religious consciousness expresses itself in corresponding attitudes, aspirations and acts. These expressions, both in form and in content, are conditioned by the stage of man's general development. In the lower stages they are often crude, primitive and naive. But in the higher stages they are of a superior order and represent our human experience in its best form and in its richest content. If the consciousness of Jesus is genuinely religious, we shall find these expressions, and they will appear not only as characteristic of him but as absolutely essential to the understanding of his personality. Therefore, we shall take up in order the religious attitudes, aspirations and acts of Jesus.

THE RELIGIOUS ATTITUDES OF JESUS

The religious consciousness in its attitudes toward its deity includes two elements that are fundamental to personal piety in its higher forms: a feeling of dependence and a feeling of confidence. Both of these we see in Jesus, and both are the issue of his experience of God as holy and as loving Father. With all of his certainty concerning the close relationship that actually exists between

God and man, in the light of which he himself lived and loved, Jesus never forgot his own condition or that of God. His attitude toward God is regularly and without exception that of deep reverence. Any other attitude on the part of the historical Jesus is inconceivable. The long-standing ethical monotheism, the great religious heritage from the prophets for whom any other faith than that in the one and only true God of Israel was apostasy and idolatry, was too deeply ingrained in his soul to permit of any other attitude. His reserve about going into detail concerning the Divine, his failure to describe the divine predicates, are really a witness to the actual awe which he felt toward his own God and that of his people. Jesus never presumed on God, never exalted himself, but had in God a living, loving Father whose will he, as the rest of men, must learn to know and to do.

Jesus was conscious of close personal relationship with the Father; he was on the most intimate terms with the Infinite, but this relationship is always religious. In his experience God remains a religious object because he himself is an experient of God, a religious subject. Christian theology and Christology have gone into all sorts of intricate and involved speculations concerning the relation of the Son to the Father, but none of these things claimed the thought of Jesus. He assumed no other relationship toward God than a religious relationship. His attitude toward God, free and frank as it was, was always the attitude of purest personal piety. Between himself and God Jesus draws that line which the truly religious consciousness always draws between itself and its deity.

All of the deepest emotions known in the experience

of religion that has reached a moral and ethical level, some of them reaching back to the unstudied piety of primitive man, are found in the picture of Jesus in the first three Gospels. These feelings of pure piety, when confronted with the Divine and the Holy, belong to the innermost precincts of his religious life, and they spring forth spontaneously, with an unmistakable genuineness. Jesus taught men that they should worship God, fear God, love and serve Him. But all of these things are more than just teachings. They express his own personal religious attitudes. In God Jesus believed; God he worshiped; God he feared; God he loved and served— all attitudes that emerge from the very soul of the really religious subject.

The religious attitudes of Jesus, as is characteristic of profound personal piety, are full of paradox. On the one hand are feelings of awe, fear, dread, wonder, amazement and reverence. On the other hand are feelings of implicit trust, fervent faith, complete confidence, deep love and longing. As we saw in the preceding chapter, these emotions are the issue of his experience of God as holy and as living, loving Father. This ebb and flow of religious emotion is inherent in the very genius of the personality that is completely consecrated to the Divine and its cause. Of the religious emotions of Jesus we may say with certainty that he was never their victim. His soul was raised to the highest heights of exultation and expectancy. His feeling often ran high, but never to the clouding of his clear religious consciousness nor to the impairment of his self-control. He had his times of depression; he must search and struggle for clearness and certainty concerning the Divine. But whether exalted or depressed in soul, the issue is always the same—unremitting loyalty to his experience of God. Always he ranges himself within the divine dictates; the sense of finite subordination never leaves him. Moments of elation do not destroy the compass and scope of his reflection, nor do they deflect him from the rigid régime to which he has submitted himself. Depression does not develop into despondency and despair. In his darkest hour he does not desert God, but asks why God has deserted him.[3] The religious emotions of Jesus are only the shifting states of his experience of God, which fact is clear in every word and work in the first three Gospels. Professor Wernle describes this paradox in Jesus' religious attitudes as those of the "child that feels itself at a distance from the Father and yet always bridges over this distance with confidence and trust."[4]

The whole underpinning of the known life of Jesus is a sense of complete dependence upon the Divine. He did possess a clear consciousness of high call and holy commission; he spoke and acted with the confidence and certainty of the chosen spokesman of God. But beneath this assurance that marks his every act and attitude there is that foundation stone of a sublime and reverent humility—a deep dependence upon God whom he worships, loves and serves. This devout feeling reaches into every item of his existence. Food and clothing, life and body are the gifts of an all-pervading Providence in which both he and his followers must have unfailing trust. When he tells his disciples that they can not make one hair white or black (Matt. 5,36), that they can not by taking thought add or subtract a single cubit from the measure of life (Matt. 6,27), he is simply stating his own sense

---

[3]*See* Bundy, *The Psychic Health of Jesus,* p. 246.
[4]*Jesus,* p. 199.

of dependence such as belongs at the very center of even
the primitive religious consciousness. The *Lord's Prayer*
is the supreme expression of Jesus' own sense of personal
dependence upon the Father. The items of this prayer
touch upon the entire cycle of life—things spiritual and
things material. Daily bread, forgiveness, deliverance
from temptation and the evil one, the kingdom itself—
all come from the Divine. It is the Father who sustains
the whole of man's life, his own as well as that of his
disciples. As we shall see when we come to his prayer-
life, the need of the divine help and support is a constant
element in the religious experience of Jesus. It is this
feeling of dependence that leads him to the highest goal
of religious aspiration—unreserved self-surrender.

Jesus' attitude toward the kingdom of God is religious. It calls forth his awe, wonder, marvel and reverence. There is for him about the kingdom that holy, that
numinous, unintelligible, non-rational element that we
discovered in his experience of God. He speaks of "the
mystery of the kingdom of God." (Mark 4,11.) It is
the *mysterium tremendum.*[5] The kingdom is not the
work of man, nor is it Jesus' own work. It is the work
of God; in its coming and in its culmination God himself
is the aggressor. Like the man in the parables of the
tares (Matt. 13,24-30) and of the seed growing of itself
(Mark 4,26-29), Jesus can not interfere, he can not in-
tervene and hasten its accomplishment. All men can do
is to prepare and show themselves worthy. They can

---

[5]"Das 'Reich' aber ist . . . die *Wundergroesse* schlechthin, das allem
Jetzigen und Hiesigen Entgegengesetzte, 'Ganz andere' 'Himmlische,'
umdaemmert und umwoben von allen echtesten Motiven 'religioeser Scheu,'
das 'Furchtbare' und das 'Reizende' und das 'Erlauchte' des Mysterioesen
selber." Otto, *Das Heilige*, p. 102*f.*

only work, watch and wait. But the kingdom in all its details, development and dénouement is the work of the Divine alone.

The very thought of the kingdom calls forth a consciousness of limitation within Jesus. In a parable like that of Mark 4,26-29 we have a clear reflection of his own sense of insufficiency over against the divine cause and its realization. Like the man in the parable he sows the seeds and sleeps and rises night and day. Jesus feels himself limited both in knowledge and in power; consciously he here sets limits for his own task and ability. He sows the seeds; they "spring up and grow, he knoweth not how"; for "the earth beareth fruit of herself." All he himself can do is to work, watch and wait in the quiet confidence that the kingdom will come, for it is God's. Thus Jesus feels purely religious restrictions set for his own life and work.

As we saw in the preceding chapter, Jesus' view as to *when* the kingdom will come has been one of the much-debated problems in the life-of-Jesus research. Some have attempted to establish a progressive postponement of the kingdom in his thought and teaching. He appears in public announcing that the kingdom is at hand. (Mark 1,15.) Later he sends out his disciples, never expecting to see them again in this world; the arrival of the kingdom is only a matter of days or weeks; they shall not compass the cities of Israel till the Son of man shall come. (Matt. 10,23.) Still later, however, the kingdom seems to be a matter of years; his contemporaries are to be witnesses; they shall not taste of death until the kingdom come with power. (Mark 9,1.) But during the last week of his life he tells his disciples that no man knows when the kingdom will come, "not even the angels in heaven, neither the Son, but the Father." (Mark 13,32.)

Further, a number of his words teach that the kingdom tarrieth; it delayeth its coming. Some students find that the delay of the kingdom constituted a great personal disappointment for Jesus. They find that he was driven from one expectation to another with each succeeding disappointment. It may be that the failure of the kingdom to come as he had announced it brought him face to face with a serious problem, as it did the early Christians. But if Jesus did experience disappointment in the delay of the kingdom, such was only superficial and did not disturb the foundations of his faith in it. As we saw in the preceding chapter, Jesus was not committed to the fulfillment of his forecasts, nor was his faith defeated by their failure.[6] Jesus was a prophet with a faith, not an apocalyptist with a forecast. He did not attempt any disclosures of the secret scenes of the future; he set no signs and times; he manipulated no magical names and numbers such as we find in the book of Revelation.

The many ingenious attempts to harmonize Jesus' diverse statements as to the *when* of the kingdom and its coming are quite aside from the centers of his faith, and they neglect entirely his unbroken religious attitude. Back of these apparent conflicts concerning the time of the kingdom is his fervent faith that God has a kingdom

---

[6]"Fuer die grossen Profeten ist gerade die fast ueberraschende Tatsache kennzeichnend, dass die zeitliche Fizierung des Eintritts einer Weissagung ihnen verhaeltnismaessig wenig bedeutet; immer wieder wird die Erfuellung der Weissagung fuer die allernaechste Zukunft angekuendigt und, wenn der Termin verstreicht, unbekuemmert weiter hinausgeschoben. Das innere Erlebnis selbst hat fuer den Profeten so viel Ueberzeugungskraft in sich, dass ihn auch das Verstreichen des zuerst erwarteten Zeitpunktes nicht irre machen kann." Hoelscher, *Die Profeten*: *Untersuchungen zur Religionsgeschichte Israels*, p. 75.

and that it *will* come. And this fine faith has cast about it a wondrously religious atmosphere—the kingdom will come according as God wills that it should come. Any conflicts disappear when we see that all the forecasts of Jesus are outbursts of a faith that remains fine and firm even when the forecasts fail of fulfillment. What the kingdom is to be and to bring, just when and where and how it is to perfect itself, are all, for the thought of Jesus, matters of the divine way and will. His expectation of the kingdom is unfailing and unfaltering, yet with regard to the time of its coming we see in his faith that tentative element that is fundamental to the genuinely religious consciousness—the future is God's; soon or late, it will be according as He wills.

Albert Schweitzer is probably correct when he represents Jesus' view of the coming of the kingdom as undergoing alterations and revisions. There was very probably a progressive postponement in the fulfillment of his faith; the kingdom did not come as he had hoped. But fact did not defeat the faith of Jesus. His religious attitude is constant—the kingdom is wholly a matter of the divine will. To any delays he adjusts his thought and conduct; his duty is patience and persistence; in any event, it is the divine will into which Jesus seeks to fit himself. The kingdom, all that it implies and involves, lies hidden in the divine plan and purpose. Whether soon or late, Jesus feels his faith as a task that demands that he work, watch and wait. He and his contemporaries may perish, but the kingdom *will* come as God himself may will—an attitude that is not only essentially but exclusively religious.

Jesus took a religious attitude toward his cures. They

are not his own work; they are the work of God through him. It is "by the Spirit of God" that he casts out demons. He did not entertain a low view of his power to heal and cure, nor did the Gospel writers. In his cures both Jesus and the Gospel writers see the dawn of the kingdom of God; here and now God through him is breaking down the power of Satan. That he brought his ministry of healing into organic connection with the coming of the kingdom is clear in Matthew 12,28:

"If I by the Spirit of God cast out demons, then is the kingdom of God come upon you."

His woes on the Galilean cities are based upon their failure to repent in the presence of the mighty works they have witnessed. (Matt. 11,21-24.)

Jesus did not ascribe his cures to himself and his own personal powers, but to God. In Mark 9,23 he rests the hope of cure upon the power of faith in God. The cure of the Gerasene demoniac he ascribes to God; in his parting word to the cured man he says,

"Go to thy house unto thy friends, and tell them how great things the Lord hath done for thee, and *how* he had mercy on thee."

This same view of his power to heal and cure has survived in the book of Acts (2,22),

"Jesus of Nazareth, a man approved of God unto you by mighty works and wonders and signs which God did by him in the midst of you, even as ye yourselves know. "

This attitude of Jesus appears in other great religious personalities who have effected cures. We see it to-day in our Christian contemporary, Sadhu Sundar Singh, who is credited with cures quite like those of Jesus. The Sadhu confesses, as pure piety dictates, "There is no power in these hands."[7]

Jesus' approach to the whole of his life and work is religious. It is in the name of God and in behalf of His cause among men that he appears in public, that he preaches, that he cures, that he works. The whole of his mission he approaches in a religious attitude; all of life's responsibilities he accepts religiously.

THE RELIGIOUS ASPIRATIONS OF JESUS

The quest for the divine will, to learn to know it and to perform it, is the loftiest aspiration of the religious consciousness. Human experience may not be described as really religious unless it includes this quest. That such an aspiration is fundamental in religious experience is clear from the fact that it is characteristic of the religious consciousness wherever and however it appears. The really religious man, primitive or highly cultured, holds the knowledge and performance of the will of God as his highest aim and ambition; it is his chief task in life. The religious group, as in the case of the Hebrew people, feels that it must know the divine will for itself; its performance is the law of land and people.

The quest of the divine will has often been very crude on the part of the primitive man. He had his seers who read the stars, the movements of the entrails of freshly slaughtered animals, the flight of birds, and all sorts of

---

[7]*Sadhu Sundar Singh*, by Mrs. Arthur Parker, p. 169. Courtesy of Fleming H. Revell Company.

signs and oracles. But in such cases religious experience has not yet reached the level of intelligence and is still on the plane of superstition. On a higher level the quest turns from without in, and the divine will is discovered in the supposed disclosures of mental states. Such a quest of the divine will is prominent in the Old Testament, but in the later prophets we see a growing lack of faith in dreams and trances and more of an inclination to trust visions and ecstatic states for the revelation of the divine will and way. Visions and ecstatic states are regarded as disclosures of the Divine down to this very day.[8] Throughout the history of Christianity there have always been those sects that have insisted that the genuineness of religious experience is to be tested by the ability to participate in a certain type of striking visionary experience.

What the divine will has required has varied as much as the means of quest and discovery. For primitive man the divine will requires certain acts which must be carefully and punctiliously executed. The usual issue is a system of religious cult and ceremony that contains a prominent element of *taboo* and that is quite far below the level of morality. On a higher level, the divine will is conceived in terms of ethical character and moral conduct. The Divine comes to lay hold on the deeper sources of individual and group life. Cult and ceremony are subordinated, even rejected, in favor of righteous living. (Mic. 6,6-8.) Such was the great contribution of the eighth and sixth century prophets to the history of re-

---

[8] The freshest source-book on such experiences, by one of our contemporary Christians, is that of Sadhu Sundar Singh, *Visions of the Spiritual World*. It is confessional and autobiographical, and it is specially interesting because the author and experient takes his visions with full seriousness.

ligion, and this conception of the divine will persists in the experience of Jesus and it is the heart of all that he has to say on this important subject.

In its highest form the performance of the divine will becomes intensely individual and personal. The religious subject comes face to face with his God, and he feels the deep inner pressure of pursuing and performing the divine will for himself. The general requirements for religious living hold for him as for all, but over and above this he must live his life personally in the sight of God and face all of its issues in the light of the divine plan and purpose for himself in particular. The meeting of the divine will for himself may require the greatest personal sacrifices; it may lead him into conflict with his contemporaries; it may bring about his own destruction. Yet quite independent of the issue of his own personal fates and fortunes his supreme aspiration is to meet the divine requirements which he feels placed heavily upon him. To fail in meeting the divine will in this purely personal sense becomes, for the religious subject who feels it, pure apostasy—a denial of his personal faith in God. The divine will, when felt as a personal pressure and conceived as highly individual, results in a complete self-surrender on the part of the religious subject. As Professor Heiler writes, "The greatest of all offerings that the religious man brings to his God is the surrender of his own will in complete obedience."[9]

In turning to Jesus we find that he interpreted religious living wholly in terms of the divine will. It is the sum and substance of his understanding of the religious life both for himself and for his disciples. The discovery

---

[9] *Der Katholizismus*, p. 450.

and performance of the will of the Father is the highest
goal of human endeavor. It is the very essence of discipleship. (Matt. 7,21-23.) It is the bond that binds
him to his disciples and them to him. (Mark 3,35.)
Jesus' understanding of the divine will is prophetic, and
it brought him into conflict with the religious leaders of
his day. In this respect Jesus was a dissenter. He rejected cult with its tithes, alms, fasting, periodic prayers,
offerings and holy days; in short, he rejected organized
religion in favor of a personal pursuit and performance
of the will of God.

But the divine will was something more for Jesus than
the essence of religion for others. It was something intensely personal for himself. In Jesus we see the definite
and deliberate orientation of the whole of life about the
will of the Father. The quest of the divine will, its discovery and performance, was the supreme passion of his
life. It is the one goal that he sought to attain from
first to last. He seeks above all else to bring himself into
accord with this will even at the greatest personal cost.
In his fates and fortunes he hears the voice of God and
he accepts both as the divine will for himself. Among
the sons of men who have sought the will of God, none
has sought it so sincerely, so seriously, and yet so sanely
as Jesus sought.

Jesus' quest of the divine will ends in the complete surrender of self, as is clear in his prayer of submission in
Gethsemane. Jeremiah and the Psalmist submit to the
divine will as something to be borne, a cross. But Jesus
in his quest of the Father's will completely forgets himself and presses toward it as something that represents
the highest religious goal that is to be attained. What
the attainment costs he gladly gives that he may attain.

Self-surrender in the personal piety of Jesus, however, is
not mystical, but moral. It would be difficult to find a
sharper contrast in religious faith than that which exists
between the submission prayers of the great mystics and
that of Jesus in Gethsemane.

The divine will was not always perfectly clear for
Jesus. As close as was his contact with the Father, His
will was not always self-evident in his experience. He
must struggle long and hard for clearness and certainty,
and once he has attained this he must struggle for the personal power to perform this will for himself. In chapter
one we spoke of Jesus' natural genius, of his native endowment in the field of religious experience. But his
personal piety is not just pure genius, not just something
given. It is primarily the actual attainment and accomplishment of Jesus himself. The firmness of his faith,
the completeness of his consecration, the depth of his devotion, the certainty of his convictions are all accomplishments that cost him the most intense struggles of soul,
as is perfectly clear in the Gospel picture. In Jesus we
do not witness those dramatic flashes and outbursts that
are unassociated with painful and persistent quest. In
his religious experience we see none of those intense, in-
stantaneous illuminations which the religious subject
often regards as completely isolated from the general
content of his experience. Such Jesus does not exhibit or
claim for himself. His native religious genius stands as
an integral, inextricable element in the Gospel picture,
but it did not give him unsought-for clearness and certainty. It did not dispense with pressing personal problems. His unique genius for religion did not supersede
the need of his own personal effort, enterprise and endeavor in learning to know and to perform. His native

religious genius included an almost infinite capacity for strain and stress of soul, a tremendous expenditure of personal energy in attainment and accomplishment. When Jesus said,

"Agonize to enter in by the narrow door," (Luke 13,24)

he was, as always, speaking straight from his own personal experience of what it means to be engaged in the quest of the divine will.

Historical Christianity has with right made a great deal of the sinlessness of Jesus, but historical Christianity has never done Jesus full personal justice in this respect. The sinlessness of Jesus is much more than the theological theories have been able to make of it. First of all, it is neither theological nor theoretical as Christian thought has always treated it. It is an actual religious attainment of Jesus accomplished by traversing that painful path that leads through the depths of personal religious struggle to triumph. The most impressive enhancement of Jesus' personality does not come from his native religious genius but from his genius in action.

Jesus was one of those rare souls who work out their own salvation with fear and trembling. (Phil. 2,12.) His personal piety was prosaic and moral rather than poetic and mystical. We never find it expressing itself in poetical form such as appears in Psalms 34 or in the mystical language of the Apostle Paul. Those who have seen in Jesus only a sage uttering words of religious wisdom have done him and the Gospel picture great injustice. Jesus was a religious subject struggling with his God. As Professor Wernle writes, "The greatest of all of

Jesus' struggles was not the struggle with his opponents but a struggle with himself and his God."[10]

In this element of intense personal struggle Jesus is true to the type, true to the psychology of religious genius. Like the great religious genius Jesus had his great religious certainties, crystal-clear convictions that were so strong and warm that they never came into that colder atmosphere of doubt or skepticism. These certainties and convictions are so powerful that they carry their subject along and they are never seriously called in question. Such was Jesus' conviction concerning the kingdom of God and his certainty concerning its coming. Doubt upon this central element of his faith seems never to have crossed his mind. But the great religious genius has his personal uncertainties as well as his certainties, and the psychological law seems to be: the greater the genius, the greater the strain and stress of soul; the stronger the central convictions, the severer the personal struggle through which he must find his way to triumph.

These struggles are usually of an intense, almost distracting nature. They rage within, often wholly concealed from the general public to whom the prophet of God preaches his message with unmistakable certainty and conviction. Just such appears in Jesus. In the very midst of his strongest convictions and certainties we find harassing uncertainties, pressing personal problems that submit him to the most severe tests as he moves toward triumph. Jesus lived and worked under an intense inner pressure. He faced the most puzzling and perplexing problems of personal piety. From beginning to end of his public life he struggles with his God in quest of His

---

[10]*Jesus*, p. 151.

holy will for himself. The events and experiences of his
first day in public (Mark 1,21-38) bring him under a psychic tension from which he is never again free. Henceforth to his latest breath struggle of soul is his portion in
life. He dies, wrestling with his God. (Mark 15,34.)

Jesus' quest and accomplishment of the divine will
seems to have been a twofold struggle that runs through
the whole of his public life. In the first phase, he must
strive to learn to know the divine will for himself, a
struggle for clearness and certainty. However, these
personal problems that force themselves upon Jesus as he
comes into the full swinging stride of his public work remain more in the background of his mind. In the foreground of his thought and work is his message and mission as the called and commissioned prophet of God and
His kingdom. His thought is almost entirely objective
and he goes through the major part of his Galilean work
in the presence of a large public announcing his message
in the greatest variety of forms. But all the while we
know that personal problems are pressing persistently
upon him, and toward the end the problems that earlier
were in the background of his thought come to the front.
The Galilean period, before it closes, sees important
changes in Jesus himself. His thought becomes increasingly introspective, although there is no abating in the
conviction with which he announces God's kingdom. But
Jesus seems to have found at least relative clearness and
certainty concerning the divine will for himself. At least
he is clear enough to act with precision Then the second
phase of the struggle begins—to accomplish the divine
will concerning which he is clear enough for action. His
personal problems now become intense conflicts of soul;
they are clearer than ever. This second phase reaches

its climax in Gethsemane, in his prayer of complete submission to the divine will that points to the cross.

Thus we see that Jesus' personal problems, his struggles of soul, are the deepest and most characteristic problems of personal piety, problems that appear without exception in one form or another whenever and wherever religion becomes intensely personal and is taken seriously—the quest of the divine will and the endeavor to perform it.[11]

THE RELIGIOUS ACTS OF JESUS

The religious consciousness manifests certain attitudes and aspirations that correspond to its content, but it also expresses itself in certain acts. These acts are the natural issue of the religious experience from which they come, and they are absolutely indispensable to its life, continued health and vigor.

The religious acts of mankind exhibit the widest possible range: from the simple act of extending a cup of cold water to an elaborate festival requiring days, even weeks, for its celebration; from the crude, half-crazed conduct of the savage to the dignified and majestic religious service of cultured man who makes his act of worship the supreme expression of his artistic genius; from the grossest acts that outrage the ethical conscience to the noblest deeds of which man at his best is capable. In their best form religious acts are the organic issue of the individual's experience of religion. These acts are purely personal, wholly spontaneous, springing from an intense state of soul that demands outlet in appropriate expression. All religious acts in their purity have their source

---

[11]An adequate discussion of *The Personal Problems of Jesus* would require too much space and is reserved for special study. Cf. p. xi.

in personal piety seeking issue in conduct that corresponds to its content of experience.

But when a particular religion becomes the common property of the community, when it becomes organized and official, then religious acts take on the form of a system of cult and ceremony. Participation in these religious acts becomes for the individual a matter of convention. The religious celebration passes by him as something formal and impersonal; it is quite foreign to himself; it proceeds independent of his own state of faith and feeling; he may or may not possess a corresponding content of experience. In their organized and official forms religious acts can and usually do result in the partial, or even total, depersonalization of religion. Their execution calls forth no corresponding state of emotion within the participant. Thus there comes a complete divorcement between religious experience and its expression. The result is a ritual without religion, a state of religious degeneration against which the prophets from Amos down protested,

"Come to Bethel, and transgress; to Gilgal, *and* multiply transgression." (Amos 4,4.)

The natural tendency of religious acts that are regularly repeated is a wide departure and finally a complete severance from their original personal source. It is only by conscious and sustained effort that an organized religion maintains its connection with the personal religious experience of which its acts originally were the spontaneous expression. The great problem that confronts the participant in what has become a conventional religious act is that of sensing and sharing something of the relig-

ious experience in which the act had its birth and apart
from which it has no spiritual significance.

Upon turning to our sources for religious acts of
Jesus, we find that they are numerous and varied enough.
However, the religious acts of Jesus are never conventional; they are always personal. The conventional religious acts of his day he neglected for himself and for his
followers, or he even combated them openly as practised.
He preached and practised only personal religious acts.
The conventional religious observances of his day did
not appeal to him, and by some of them he felt restricted
and hindered; some of them he openly violated. Against
the Pharisaic practises of piety he exercised the most
cutting criticism. The almsgiving, praying and fasting of
his day had become conventional religious acts of the re-
ligious-by-vocation, unattended for the most part by a
corresponding content of experience.

Jesus regularly insisted on religion as a matter of inner
content and showed little interest in outward religious
acts as such. We never see him engaged in a formal and
impersonal act of worship. As a pious Galilean he goes
directly to the temple upon his arrival in Jerusalem, but
he participates in no cult and we have no record of his
bringing an offering. About the only allusion which
Jesus makes to the temple cult[12] is his word in Matthew
5,23-24:

"If therefore thou art offering thy gift at the altar,
and there rememberest that thy brother hath aught
against thee, leave there thy gift before the altar, and

---

[12]Cf. Mark 1,40-45; Luke 17,11-19.

go thy way, first be reconciled to thy brother, and then come and offer thy gift."

But even here the principal point is the emphasis on the inner content of consciousness.

Every act of Jesus may be described as religious, for there is a conscious religious control that reaches down to the last detail of his conduct. Upon his first personal appearance in the Gospel of Mark (1,9-11) we see Jesus taking a religious step, his coming to John for baptism.[13] The Gospel account of the baptism of Jesus is presented from the point of view of what it meant for the early Christian faith rather than from the point of view of what it meant for Jesus personally. The thing that must have been most significant for Jesus himself, his baptism at the hands of John, is passed over with a mere mention and without detail by the Gospel writers whose interest centers on the voice and its declaration. The experience of being baptized must have been the central thing for Jesus, otherwise he would not have come to John at all. The Gospel writers tell us nothing of the motives and impulses that brought him to John's baptism. But we may say with certainty, since the act is essentially religious, that he must have been moved by the deepest religious motives and impulses. Jesus came to the Baptist with no theological questions in his mind, with no personal scruples about the propriety of his participating in this distinctive religious rite. His act on this occasion is fundamentally religious, the response of his own pure personal piety to the prophetic religion represented by the Baptist. For Jesus, the Baptist was a great prophet

---

[13]*See* the author's article, "The Meaning of Jesus' Baptism," *Journal of Religion*, VII (January, 1927), pp. 56-71, from which this paragraph and the following are taken.

and preacher who championed the cause of God in Israel; to such a man with such a message Jesus responds, and such a cause he joins.

There is no reason to suppose that Jesus reflected over the fact as to whether he needed the baptism of John. A man of such centrally religious consciousness as Jesus betrays in Mark 10,18 would feel no reluctance in responding to the call of the Baptist. Matthew's representation (3,14-15) that Jesus participated in a religious rite for which he felt no need but to which he submitted for the sake of appearance contradicts the genuineness of the religious motives which everywhere characterize him. Matthew's representation of this act as an accommodation is harder to accept than the plain fact that Jesus, without reservation of any kind, was baptized by John. In Matthew this act loses its distinctly religious character; Matthew robs Jesus of the deep religious impulses that must have moved him on this occasion and that must have brought him to this step. For Jesus his participation in this religious rite can not have been perfunctory and superficial, for these are the very things in religion that he condemns most severely. His baptism can not have been a mere compromise, for it is just in the field of personal piety, where the genuineness of motives and the sincerity of acts are at stake, that Jesus knows and makes no compromises.

For Jesus personally, judging from his high estimate of the Baptist and his mission, John's baptism was a sacred religious rite. When Jesus threw his Jerusalem enemies into that fatal dilemma (Mark 11,30),

"The baptism of John, was it from heaven, or from men?"

he revealed very clearly his own conviction concerning John's baptism as a heaven-sent and God-given religious rite. For Jesus, his baptism must have been an act of religious consecration to all that the Baptist represented and he participated in it, actuated by deep inner impulses that sprang from his own personal piety. The religious character of his act is clearest in Luke 3,21, which represents Jesus as praying as he participates in this rite.

Thus one might go through the whole of the Gospel accounts, singling out the distinctive religious acts of Jesus. His cures are religious acts performed in response to human need, in the presence of unreserved faith, toward which he took a religious attitude. His journey to the north (Mark 7,24-30) is a religious act, a more remote retreat, a more extended stay in solitude.

The feeding of the five thousand is an incident that has caused theologians untold embarrassment in their effort to retain it as a wonder-work, but it is simply a religious act of Jesus, one of the most impressive that has come down to us. Even in the account of Mark (6,35-44), a writer who has a special relish for the wonder-works of Jesus, the miraculous element falls entirely into the background. The incident is not followed by astonishment on the part of the witnesses, by a command for silence, by a further spread of fame—the usual aftermath to Jesus' wonder-works. The miraculous element seems later and acquired; in the account itself all emphasis falls upon the blessing, breaking and giving of the food. It seems to have the force of a sacrament for all concerned. The very quiet with which the scene closes shows that it is a devotional occasion. Johannes Weiss calls it "the first

Lord's Supper."[14]   In such an account we have to do, not
with a case of miraculous multiplication but of devotional
division.

Whether we regard the journey to Jerusalem as a pilgrimage to the Passover, as a journey to death, or as a
shift in the scene of Jesus' work, it stands as a religious
act in obedience to deep and genuine religious impulses.
The cleansing of the temple is a religious act, the outstanding feature of which is its religious character.   As
Professor Weinel writes, "Jesus' zeal for the temple is
not in behalf of a center of cult but a place of prayer."[15]
On the last night of his life Jesus celebrated the most
sacred feast of his people, but it was not a formal and
impersonal religious act; into it he poured the whole substance of his own personal faith:

> "With great desire have I desired to eat this pass-
> over with you before I suffer: for I say unto you, I
> shall not eat it, until it be fulfilled in the kingdom of
> God.   And he received a cup, and when he had given
> thanks, he said, Take this, and divide it among your-
> selves: for I say unto you, I shall not drink from
> henceforth of the fruit of the vine, until the kingdom
> of God shall come."   (Luke 22,15-18.)

But the supreme of all religious acts of Jesus, the
highest and finest of all the expressions of religious experience, is to be found in his prayers and practise of prayer.
To this we turn, for nowhere is the genuineness of his
religious consciousness more clear.

---

[14]*Das Aelteste Evangelium*, p. 217.
[15]*Biblische Theologie des Neuen Testaments*, p. 75.

The Prayer-Act

Prayer is the most distinctive feature of that human attitude which we call religion. It is the practise and principle of prayer, the quest of God involved in it, that distinguishes religion from other systems of thought and observed codes of conduct that sometimes, quite erroneously, are looked upon as religion. Without prayer, in one form or another, the great religions would not have arisen nor could they have survived. We shall never be able to estimate the contribution which prayer in all its forms has made to the religious life of mankind.[16] Feuerbach, one of the most radical critics of Christianity, who saw in all religion only a dreary delusion of the human spirit, wrote: "The deepest essence of religion is revealed in its simplest act—prayer."[17] Professor Deissmann writes: "Religion, wherever it is vital in human life, is primarily prayer."[18] From Professor Heiler: "Prayer is the heart and soul of religion. Not in dogmas and institutions, not in rites and ethical ideals, but in prayer we

---

[16]The finest of all studies on the history, psychology and essence of prayer is that of Professor Heiler, of the University of Marburg: *Das Gebet. Eine religionsgeschichtliche und religionspsychologische Untersuchung*. See also Professor Heiler's little book, *Die Buddhistische Versenkung*, which closes with a brief comparison: *Buddha, der Meister der Versenkung—Jesus, der Meister des Gebets* (pp. 61-67). An especially fine picture of Jesus' prayer-life is given by Professor Deissmann in his *The Religion of Jesus and the Faith of Paul*. This enlarged English edition had its earlier form in German: *Evangelium und Urchristentum. Beitraege zur Weiterentwicklung der christlichen Religion*. Both had their origin in an article which appeared in the *Christliche Welt* (XIII, 1899, cols. 701ff.), "Der Beter Jesus. Ein vergessenes Kapitel der neutestamentlichen Theologie." On prayer in the Old Testament, *see* Greiff, *Das Gebet im Alten Testament*; on prayer in primitive Christianity, *see* von der Goltz, *Das Gebet in der Aeltesten Christenheit*.

[17]*Das Wesen des Christentums*, VII, p. 184.

[18]*Evangelium und Urchristentum*, p. 95.

come face to face with the religious life. In its utterance
in prayer we apprehend the deepest and most intimate
impulses of the pious soul."[19]   The practise, principles
and place of prayer may in all justice be made touch-
stones for determining upon the essence of any particular
religious faith.   "The distinctions and differences between particular religions and religious personalities
reveal themselves with special sharpness in prayer."[20]

Prayer is the life-breath and pulse of personal piety.
No one can state fully what prayer has meant for those
who have really practised and experienced it. The great
men of prayer speak of it as an irrepressible inner necessity. Luther wrote: "He who does not pray, neither calls
upon God in time of need, certainly does not regard Him
as God and does not accord Him His divine honor."[21]
Prayer is the source-spring of authority and power in the
personal religious life. Professor Streeter quotes Sadhu
Sundar Singh: "The man of prayer is the only one whose
opinion is worth having in regard to religion."[22] Again
from Professor Heiler: "Prayer is certainly the freest
and most personal expression of piety; the original creative power of the outstanding religious genius reveals
itself with great clearness exactly in prayer."[23]

A history of prayer would amount to a history of religion, for in the prayers of mankind we have the most
reliable reflection of religious experience in all of its
stages of development, the lowest as well as the highest.
The prayers of men reflect their hopes and fears, their
ambitions and aspirations, their moods and tempers, their

---

[19]*Das Gebet*, p. 2.
[20]Heiler, *Die Buddhistische Versenkung*, p. 61.
[21]Quoted by Heiler, *Das Gebet*, p. 1.
[22]*The Message of Sadhu Sundar Singh*, by B. H. Streeter, p. 145.
Courtesy of The Macmillan Company.
[23]*Das Gebet*, p. 235.

cherished longings and deepest desires. It is generally true of the psychology of prayer that the *prayer*[24] brings into his prayers the things that matter most in his life. Thus prayer in all its forms exhibits the scale of values in the life from which it comes.

The values sought in the history of prayer range from the highest to the lowest. Primitive man prayed more frequently, more passionately and more persistently than does cultured man. This seems to be due to the fact that the prayer-process is one of the non-rational elements in religion; it is essentially naive, and neither in principle nor in practise did it create a problem for the primitive man who practised it. The cultured mind is rationalistic and reflective, and both things tend to compromise the purity and to weaken the power of prayer. The greatest prayers of history, however, have not come from primitive man but from cultured man. In these great prayers the *prayer* does not reason; he does not stop to reflect, but as primitive man he pours forth the deepest distress and desires of his heart in the presence of his Maker.

Primitive man poured out in his prayers every concern, major and minor, of his life. Nothing was too trivial or matter-of-fact to bring into the presence of his god or gods. If a thing concerned him in any way, it also concerned his deity, and he did not hesitate to confront his deity with his desire or need. In a most unhindered and unhampered fashion his praying released his emotions of fear and anxiety, his feeling of awe and wonder, expressed his faith and confidence, his sense of need as well as his momentary wish or whim, and often gave vent to

[24]*Prayer* is printed in italics to indicate *the one who prays.*

his vexation and displeasure with his god or gods.   In prayer, at times, he did not even hesitate to threaten and intimidate his gods.   Primitive man prayed to his gods for sunshine and rain, clothing and food and shelter, for increase in family and field and flock, for his own personal safety and prosperity.   Such were the central concerns of his life, and their abundance or shortage he linked up with his gods and their doings.   Consequently his prayers poured forth with all of his native primitive passion.

The prayers of cultured man often manifest a decrease in passion.   He excludes the more unworthy emotions that caused primitive man to find fault with his gods.   The chief progress in prayer from its lower to its higher forms is to be found in its scale of values.   Cultured man disdains to burden his prayers and his God with his every personal whim and notion.   His conception of the prayer-process is much higher, and he excludes from it all that is unworthy and trivial.   Like primitive man, his passion bursts forth in prayer when he is faced with the major issues of life and death, but the minor matters he seeks to face more on his own account because he realizes that they are minor and because he lives consciously on a higher religious plane.   Even the material necessities of life fall into the background of his prayers. He must have food, clothing and shelter, but he does not storm high heaven for their possession.   He looks upon them as the provisions of a gracious Providence, but still they remain values of a secondary order.   Prayer in its highest forms includes these things, but the *prayer* seeks of the Divine rather the light and strength necessary to the securing of the highest values.   The cultured man prays for spiritual values: moral content and solidity of

character, ethical control of conduct, religious restraint
of natural impulses, social good will and brotherhood, the
forgiveness of sins, triumph over evil in every form, and
finally for the society of the Divine itself.

Prayer represents both a personal and a social religious value. It is practised both by the individual and by
the group. But prayer at its best is personal, intensely
personal. The group may have its prayers and pray them
with genuine passion. But the group can but rarely pour
forth its emotions in a single expression; its sense of need
is seldom so intense, its concentration is never so spontaneous and involuntary as that of the individual. The religious emotions of the individual find an immediate focus
and even before he has time to reflect they have burst
forth into their natural expression. This immediacy, so
fundamental in the prayer-experience, is never quite accessible to the group. No matter how vital the bond that
brings the group together, a focus of feeling must be
sought and reflection is required to find its appropriate
expression, and this delays the prayer-process. The great
prayers of the collect are never really its own, for they
were first prayed by some great soul in its quest of God.
About the most that the group can attain in prayer-experience is the discovery of the prayer of some great *prayer*
for which the group finds verification in its own religious experience. Common prayers and praying face the
danger that confronts all religious acts that have come to
be observed by repetition—that they will become formal
and impersonal, leaving the individual participant without a corresponding content of experience.

Prayer may never become an institution and remain
true to itself, for at its best prayer is instinctive. It is
private and personal to a degree that the common cult

can never attain. And the student who would learn to know the heart of prayer will not turn to a prayer-book, but to the prayed prayers of some struggling soul. The twenty-third Psalm will never mean for us what it meant for the one from whose inner experience it sprang, for it comes to us as a composition. At its birth-hour and birthplace it was a communion with the Divine, a bursting-forth of faith and confidence in the God of Israel. The twenty-third Psalm becomes our very own only when we find ourselves in the identical situation of the original *prayer* and can pour into it the whole substance of our religious faith and feeling. "In its original form prayer is a spontaneous discharge of emotion, a free and full outpouring of the heart."[25]

Prayer may be made in public, it may be whispered in solitude with God alone as witness, it may be an unintelligible cry devoid of coherent expression, or it may be an unutterable longing of the innermost soul, but it is always, if it retains any measure of its native genius, a communion with the Divine. In its form it is spontaneous and extemporaneous, the free and involuntary improvisation of the moment.

The Prayer-Heritage of Jesus

Jesus came from a praying people. The practise of passionate prayer runs through the religion of the Old Testament like an unbroken golden strand. It survived all the fates and fortunes of Israel's colorful history, and exactly in times of crisis, even in the midst of catastrophe, we witness an intensification of Israel's prayer-life. In

[25]Heiler, *Das Gebet*, p. 150.

its prayer-experience Israel stands unique in the history of religion. No nation perhaps passed through a more tragic career, and, except for the solid substance of its religious life, this people would certainly have lost all confidence and faith in its God. Yet the pious souls of Israel, whether in time of defeat and death or in time of peace and prosperity, turned to their God in reverent petition, protest and praise. The God of Israel was a God who always heard and answered prayer, a religious confidence that was built into the very nerve and fiber of its personal and social life and without which such an array of prayer-literature as the Old Testament presents would have been impossible (Psalms 116,1-2) :

> "I love Jehovah, because he heareth my voice and my supplications. Because he hath inclined his ear unto me, therefore will I call *upon him* as long as I live."

The great heroes of Israel were all men of prayer— patriarchs, princes, prophets and priests. Prayer reaches back into the earliest traditions of this people. The Old Testament story opens with the first man walking and talking with his Maker. The story itself is naive and of relatively late origin, but it reflects an ancient conviction of Israel to the effect that man in his ideal state was in constant communion, in immediate and intimate intercourse with God. (Gen. 3.) The first great prayer-scene is Jacob's night of wrestling with the angel. (Gen. 32,22-32.) This is really a picture from Israel's prayer-life, a reflection of its persistent pursuit of its God,

> "I will not let thee go, except thou bless me,"

and in it is deposited Israel's sense of triumph in prayer,

"I have seen God face to face."

Moses appears as the great intercessor between God and His people, and his figure towers to its loftiest heights when he seeks out the solitude of the holy mount and prays for his people. (Deut. 9.)   In I Samuel 2,1-10 we meet Hannah's prayer of praise.   Samuel prayed all night for Saul. (I Sam. 15,11.)   David is Israel's prince of prayer, and with his name most of its prayer-literature was linked up.   Solomon's prayer has come down to us as a great classic. (I Kings 3,6-9.)   Even down to the last literary echoes of Israel's history we have great *prayers*: Manasses, Esther, Daniel, Judith, Tobit and so forth.   Throughout its history the great and small of Israel—prince and peasant, man and woman, rich and poor, young and old—turn with equal confidence to God in prayer.

But the high point in Israel's prayer-life—in its practise, principles and values prayed for—comes with the great prophets of the sixth and eighth centuries.   Almost without exception they are men who are in constant contact with the Divine, and their prayers appear and reappear in their writings.   The prayer-life of some of the prophets is more prominent than that of others, a difference due to individual temperament, but the common picture of the great prophet is that of a man praising, petitioning or protesting to his God in behalf of himself or his people.   From the first to the last they are men of vital prayer-experience.   Of Amos, Hoelscher writes: "It was in the experience of prayer that Amos became a prophet."[26]   Of Jeremiah, the most sensitive of the

---

[26]*Die Profeten*, p. 195. *See* Amos' prayers in 7,2-3; 7,5-6.

Surely not!

prophets, Wellhausen says: "Jeremiah is the father of prayer."[27] The prayers of the prophets are too numerous to be cited here,[28] and their importance is not due to their frequency but to the fineness of their spirit and the richness of their content. The prayer-life of Israel swung upward with the rising tide of the prophetic religion which brought to Israel's religious experience a moral and ethical content unattained by any other ancient people. Personal and private prayer of a high order is the product of prophetic piety, especially of a religious experience like that of Jeremiah. The prophets enriched the content of Israel's prayer-life, ennobled its principle and practise, and directed it toward the highest religious values. Such a development was necessary in view of the very nature of the prophetic type of religious experience; in it there was deeply imbedded a keen sense of social and personal need, a sense which must find an outlet in prayer, in prayer under inner pressure.

But the prayer-life of Israel did not remain on this high level. With the national downfall, all that Israel had left was its religious faith. And this was saved only because it became encased in a system of cult and ceremony. The priest supplanted the prophet as the religious authority, and the effect on Israel's prayer-life was only natural. "Law-loving Judaism preferred the formulated prayer of daily duty to the formless prayer of spontaneous expression."[29] Prayer became a prescribed practise of the faithful. There seems to have been, even at an

Is this an accurate statement?

---

[27]Quoted by Heiler, *Die Buddistische Versenkung*, p. 64.
[28]Cf. Hos. 6,1ff.; 10,12; 14,1ff.; Isa. 28,16; 30,15; 38,10-20; 40,26-31; 42,5ff.; 45,6ff.; 48,12; 63,6-64,11; Jer. 10,23ff.; 14,1ff.; 15,11; 15,16; 17,18; 18,20-23; 20,7 11 12; Ezra 9,5-15; Neh. 1,5-11; 9,5ff; Hab. 1,2-4; 1,12-17; Jon. 2,2-10; Zech. 13,9.
[29]Heiler, *Das Gebet*, p. 236.

early date, a system of daily prayer.[30] Praying became a religious good-work. Not only was praying prescribed, but the *prayer* was provided with prayers. Instead of pouring out his own heartfelt need in his own free fashion, there were prayers prepared for him for almost every occasion and emergency. Prayer became a cult and a ceremony, and the prayers were impersonal, formal, liturgical and ritualistic rather than free spontaneous releases of elemental religious emotions. The *prayer* became a participant in a religious celebration. Every religious festival had its appropriate prayers and psalms, and the pious soul was provided with the famous eighteen-petition prayer for rehearsal three times daily and sufficient to cover all the ordinary religious needs.[31]

But no religious system is sufficient to supply the prayer-needs of the individual and, even when the priest and his cult were supreme, the religion of the individual did not die out and become extinct. This we see in the collection of the Psalms where the conventional hymns of the congregation, the prayer-compositions of the temple and its festival cult, stand side by side with the passionate personal prayers of the individual who utters his own special petition, praise or protest. More than half of the Psalms are the individual and personal prayers of the layman.

No finer collection of prayer-literature is to be found than in the Psalms of the Old Testament, and they bear abundant testimony to the richness of Israel's prayer-

---

[30]Cf. Psalms 57,17; Dan. 6,10; Acts 3,1.

[31]*See* full text of this prayer in Schuerer, *Geschichte des juedischen Volkes im Zeitalter Jesu Christi*, II, pp. 384*f*.

life.[32] In them we see Israel praying in public as a people, and we hear the Israelite praying in private for himself and his people. As Greiff writes of the people of Israel, "The whole of their life is a prayer; everything they do is always with an upward look to God, and they undertake nothing without Him."[33] Every occasion, major or minor, personal or national, began and ended with prayer.

The prayers of the Psalter include everything that the Israelite regarded as desirous and worth while for himself and his people. He prays for personal and social values: prosperity and posterity in family and nation, for immunity in time of epidemic, for food in time of famine, for help against personal and national oppressors, for personal and national power and victory, for signs and wonders to demonstrate the majesty of God to unbelievers, for rain and harvest, for recovery from illness, for protection from evil, for clean hands and pure heart, for forgiveness of personal and national sin, for divine council and comfort and guidance, for spiritual and physical welfare of self and others, for deliverance from sins of tongue, pride, passion and inner lust, for the wisdom and fear and knowledge of God, and finally for the real presence of God with himself and people.

It was a feeling of deep reverence and gratitude that caused the Israelite to lift his face to heaven. In the midst of all the vicissitudes of life, when failure felled

---

[32]For an especially fine study of the Psalms as prayer-life and literature, *see* Professor Staerk's commentary in *Die Schriften des Alten Testaments*, 3te Abteilung, Band I. In his preface to this second edition Professor Staerk says that his revision was occasioned chiefly by Professor Heiler's masterpiece, *Das Gebet*.

[33]*Das Gebet im Alten Testament*, p. 119.

him or fortune favored him, the pious soul of Israel poured forth his petitions, praises and protests with all the intensity and passion of elemental emotion. The Israelite felt that his God was with him as he faced all the issues of life. The Psalter is a "wondrous expression of an unbreakable confidence in God."[34]

It was his sense of need that brought the Israelite to his knees: an augmented feeling of dependence, fear, awe, wonder, a deep consciousness of sin, increased need of forgiveness, deplorable inability and weakness in coping with the forces of evil. Psalm 51,9-15 is the great *Miserere* of the Psalter. In his prayers the Israelite expressed his highest hopes and aspirations. He manifested the greatest confidence in the prayer-process. He felt that it was a source of personal and social power, a positive reinforcement. It resulted for him in inner mobilization, refreshment and peace of soul, a clarification of puzzling situations and perplexing circumstances; in short, the prayer-act brought him all that he understood as religious light and strength. It gave him clearness and certainty concerning the divine will and, above all, the sense of the divine presence.

The failure of the prayer-act did not diminish his praying; on the contrary, he prayed with increased fervor and passion. His reaction to his praying was always a subordination of self, subjection and surrender. He began his prayer with assurance, and it ended with his reassurance. Often a passionate petition is followed by a prayer of praise and thanksgiving. In the religious experience of Israel prayer had the most definite kind of disciplinary and pedagogical function. It had its concrete issues in

---

[34]A. Bertholet, quoted by Greiff, *Das Gebet im Alten Testament*, p. 102.

moral character, ethical conduct, and in the fear and love of God. The greatest prayers of the Psalter are those private intimate prayers of Israel's great religious personalities. They mark mile-stones in the path of personal piety's progress to its goal. They exhibit a remarkable maturity of religious experience, a power, a purity and a rich religiousness that spring from a courage that grapples with all the problems that confront the religious consciousness and that forces them out into that awful arena where man stands alone with his Maker.

It is against this background that the praying and prayers of Jesus are to be understood. Behind him for centuries there reaches a rich heritage of prayer-life and literature. Prayer came to him by social inheritance, but for Jesus it was much more than a practise that came to him from a praying people. It was not social imitation that caused him to pray. Jesus was steeped in the prayer-literature of his people, but he kept up the spirit rather than the letter of Israel's prayer traditions. The conventional, ritualistic and liturgical prayers of the past and present did not satisfy his religious instincts. In that incomparable collection of prayers, the Hebrew Psalter, Jesus remained true to himself: He turned to those intimate personal prayers of the pious layman. In his prayer-life and prayer-experience Jesus was not the priest, but the prophet. Like Jeremiah before him, he poured forth his innermost soul to God.

In coming to the prayer-life of Jesus we strike upon the very pulse of his personal piety. In no feature of the Gospel picture is the real religiousness of Jesus clearer than in his teaching on prayer, in his practise of prayer, and in his prayers themselves. We shall approach his prayer-experience from these three angles, all of which are very clear in our best sources, the first three Gospels. We do not aim at an exhaustive study of his prayer-life, but we desire to know its full significance for our approach to Jesus as a religious subject. We are interested in it here only so far as it reveals his religious consciousness as unmistakably real and as thoroughly genuine.

Extracts from Jesus' Prayer-Experience

The first important step in the study of the prayer-experience of Jesus is the full realization of the fact that he felt no problem in prayer and praying. There is not the faintest shadow of doubt in his mind concerning the prayer-process. He offers no prayer apologetics, no defense or justification for its practise. The theoretical difficulties and the practical doubts of the modern mind connected with the practise and value of prayer never occurred to Jesus. Like all the great religious geniuses, the very passion of his personal piety threw him out beyond these. That prayer may be only an autosuggestive process by which the individual prods himself along the prosaic path of piety, a release of pent-up feeling resulting in the relief of inner tension, a devotional delusion with an imaginary rather than a real influence—such possibilities which harass the reflective type of mind seem never to have disturbed him. Jesus approaches prayer with a childlike unaffectedness and simplicity. He has no psychology, no philosophy, no theology of prayer such as the modern mind seems to require.[35] In his experience prayer is an instinctive process, the one great recourse of the religious consciousness. He is driven to prayer out of a deep sense of native and natural need, and all his teaching on prayer and his praying are expressions of just such need.

In his teaching Jesus attempts no definition of prayer. His approach to prayer is just as untheoretical as is his approach to all the elements that go to make up religious experience. His approach is naive and unreflective, and for this reason prayer appears in the religious life of Jesus in its primitive purity and power. The modern mind with all its reflections and reservations concerning prayer is seldom, if ever, able really to pray. Reflection chills and inhibits the prayer-process. Only as its sense of need completely overwhelms all its rational reflection can the modern mind really pray again.

Jesus presented prayer as a principal religious value. His words on prayer are simple and plain enough, and need no special exposition. All prayer is to be directed to God. Into the prayer-act men may pour the whole of their feeling and faith; in it they may express their deepest desires and most vital needs. He gave his disciples no prayer-precepts, no fixed prayer-text, no prayer-cult or prayer-rites, no stipulations as to time and posture, in short, no prayer-system. It stands as a high mark in the religious genius of Jesus that he left man alone with his Maker. He gave no formal instruction with regard to prayer; rather he sought to impart inspiration to true

[35]For characteristic academic approaches to prayer, *see:* Coe, *The Psychology of Religion*, chapter XVIII; Pratt, *The Religious Consciousness*, chapter XV; Selbie, *The Psychology of Religion*, chapter XI; Hocking, *The Meaning of God in Human Experience*, chapter XXIX; Streeter, *Concerning Prayer—Its Nature, Its Difficulties, and Its Values.*

prayer. From his many words on prayer we single out those which are most characteristic and distinctive of his own prayer-experience.

Jesus teaches that prayer is private and purely personal, an inner precinct in which man stands alone with his Maker where no curious eye may look on. Prayer as a religious good-work, prayer on public parade, he rejects as a distorted devotion to a true religious value:

"And when ye pray, ye shall not be as the hypocrites: for they love to stand and pray in the synagogues and in the corners of the streets, that they may be seen of men. Verily I say unto you, They have received their reward. But thou, when thou prayest, enter into thine inner chamber, and having shut thy door, pray to thy Father who is in secret, and thy Father who seeth in secret shall recompense thee." (Matt. 6,5-6.)

Jesus teaches that true prayer is brief and to the point. There is no reason for a recital of needs, no reason for a rehearsal of all the details of the situation in which the *prayer* finds himself:

"And in praying use not vain repetitions, as the Gentiles do: for they think that they shall be heard for their much speaking. Be not therefore like unto them: for your Father knoweth what things ye have need of, before ye ask him." (Matt. 6,7-8.)

Over against this calm assurance of answer to prayer are two perturbing parables of Jesus teaching prayer as a persistent pursuit, introducing that permanent paradox which is puzzling but real because it springs fresh and strong from actual prayer-experience:

"Which of you shall have a friend, and shall go unto him at midnight, and say unto him, Friend, lend me three loaves; for a friend of mine is come to me from a journey, and I have nothing to set before him; and he from within shall answer and say, Trouble me not: the door is now shut, and my children are with me in bed; I cannot rise and give thee?   I say unto you, Though he will not rise and give him because he is his friend, yet because of his importunity he will arise and give him as many as he needeth."   (Luke 11,5-8.)

"There was in a city a judge, who feared not God, and regarded not man: and there was a widow in that city; and she came oft unto him, saying, Avenge me of mine adversary.   And he would not for a while: but afterward he said within himself, Though I fear not God, nor regard man; yet because this widow troubleth me, I will avenge her, lest she wear me out by her continual coming."   (Luke 18,2-5.) [36]

Concerning the attitude of the *prayer* Jesus gives us two priceless prayer-pictures in what for me personally is the greatest of all his parables.   Prayer must be devoid of all personal pride; it defeats itself if it becomes a recital of virtues.   In the presence of God man can be conscious of only one thing, his sinfulness; he can pray first only for mercy and forgiveness for himself:

"Two men went up into the temple to pray; the one a Pharisee, and the other a publican.   The Pharisee stood and prayed thus with himself, God, I thank thee, that I am not as the rest of men, extortioners, unjust,

---

[36]These two parables, now widely separated, may have been spoken together originally by Jesus as a parable pair.

adulterers, or even as this publican. I fast twice in the week; I give tithes of all that I get. But the publican, standing afar off, would not lift up so much as his eyes unto heaven, but smote his breast, saying, God, be thou merciful to me a sinner. I say unto you, This man went down to his house justified rather than the other." (Luke 18,10-14a.)

Such are the characteristic and most distinctive words of Jesus on prayer. But all of them are more than mere teaching. All are autobiographical and confessional, springing fresh and strong from his own prayer-life. In all of these words Jesus is introducing us to the secrets of his own prayer-experience. "In the prayer-ideal which the great *prayers* have projected they have given to us a picture of their own praying . . . In his brief and scattered words on true and false praying Jesus has characterized himself."[37] When he hurls his sharp criticisms at the hypocrites who pray in public and at the Gentiles who think they will be heard for their much speaking, he gives us an insight into his own manner of praying: apart with God as the only witness, compact and to the point. His recommendation for retreat to the inner chamber is direct to us from his own personal practise. It reflects the reticence that surrounds the whole of his own prayer-life; it is a word that was born at his own soul-shrine. It is the privacy which Jesus preserved for himself. To expose the prayer-act to a curious public is to destroy its purity and power. Secrecy and seclusion afford a compact concentration of the whole personality in the prayer-act.

When Jesus says, "Your Father knoweth," he speaks

---

[37]Heiler, *Das Gebet*, p. 34.

straight from his own inner conviction and confidence won on his knees. When he says that the asker receiveth, that the seeker findeth, that to the one who knocks it shall be opened, he is simply expressing his own personal faith in the prayer-process. When he says that the father will not give his son a stone for bread, a serpent for a fish, he is openly confessing his deep personal faith in the Father who can not but answer the prayers of His children. When he gives us the picture of the friend who storms his neighbor's door at midnight, or of the widow who presses her case before the unjust judge, he discloses to us that relentless quest and pursuit in which he himself was engaged on his way to clearness and certainty.

This puzzling paradox in Jesus' words on prayer—on the one hand, quiet converse; on the other, stormy supplication—is the reflection of the paradox that existed in his own prayer-experience. Sometimes the pulse of Jesus' prayer-life exhibits a boisterous beat; again its action is slow, undisturbed, composed and confident. There is an attitude of complete confidence running through the whole of his teaching on prayer, also through his prayers. But when he is confronted with a pressing personal problem, we see him storming the heart of the Father for His mind, for his own personal assurance. Jesus' words on prayer, then, are the fine and full fruit of his own prayer-experience. What he has to say about prayer reveals what its practise has meant for him—an asking and a receiving, a seeking and a finding, a knocking at and an opening of closed doors.

Jesus' teaching on prayer is not impersonal, but intensely personal. It is not formal, yet it does contain a reflective element. His teaching on prayer is not the finest flower of his prayer-life. This we shall find in his own prayed prayers. His estimate of the place and value of prayer in the religious life is to be sought beyond his teaching on this subject—in his retreats to solitude, in his own personal petitions, praises and protests. It is only as we press back beyond teaching to practise and beyond his practise of prayer to his actual prayers that we realize fully what prayer meant for Jesus. Here we shall meet an intensification of feeling that, because of the very nature of the case, could not find its way into his teaching on prayer.

Jesus' Retreats for Prayer

The Gospel notices to the effect that Jesus prayed or that he retreated for prayer are relatively numerous. They are sporadic and appear with an irregularity which shows that they are not a planned part of the Gospel writers' program. In some sections of the Gospel story these notices are few and far apart; in other sections they become frequent and pile up. This very fact gives the historical student a large measure of confidence in the Gospel picture of Jesus' practise of prayer: His retreats for prayer increase when portentous events and experiences are heaviest upon him. The first three Gospels report nine notices of

	Jesus' Retreats for Prayer	Matthew	Mark	Luke
(1)	At the baptism			3,21
(2)	Apart from Simon's house		1,35-38	
(3)	After the cleansing of the leper			5,16
(4)	Before the choosing of the twelve			6,12
(5)	After feeding the five thousand	14,23	6,46	
(6)	At Cæsarea Philippi			9,18
(7)	At the transfiguration			9,28-29
(8)	At the giving of the *Lord's Prayer*			11,1
(9)	In Gethsemane	26,36-44	14,32-42	22,40-46

Besides these retreats for prayer, there are other notices that Jesus prayed as he blessed the bread and the fish at the feeding of the five thousand[38] and the four thousand,[39] also at the last supper[40] in connection with the offering of the bread and the wine. Luke 24,30 and 35 would lead us to suppose that Jesus had a peculiar way of blessing bread which made him known to the Emmaus disciples. These notices have to do with prayers of thanksgiving and with the consecration of food. In Matthew 19,13 Jesus appears almost as a popular holy man whose benediction and blessing is sought by all. Mark's notice in 7,34—"And looking up to heaven, he sighed"—may be a prayer (*Gebetsseufzer*).[41]

In the nine retreats for prayer listed above it is interesting to note that the first seven are Galilean retreats. Matthew has only one Galilean retreat, and Mark has two. The notices that Jesus prayed, or retreated for prayer, are most numerous in Luke who gives special attention to the devotional life of Jesus and has him engaging in prayer at critical junctures throughout his public career. (3,21; 6,12; 9,18   28-29.) All three report that greatest of all his retreats, in Gethsemane.

Such are the Gospel materials on Jesus' retreats for prayer. In the concrete they do not tell us a great deal. In only one of the nine is a prayer reported, in Gethsemane. Usually we have simply the uncommunicative notice that Jesus prayed. The immediate experiences and the impending events that drove him apart for prayer

---

[38]Matt. 14,19b; Mark 6,41; Luke 9,16.
[39]Matt. 15,36; Mark 8,6b.
[40]Matt. 26,26; Mark 14,22; Luke 22,17   19-20.
[41]There are other notices of Jesus' retreating to solitude in which prayer is not mentioned: Mark 1,45; 6,30-31; Luke 4,42-43.

are seldom given. However, it seems that crises in character and conduct, important junctures and turning points in his fates and fortunes, brought Jesus to his knees. In the second retreat (Mark 1,35-38) it is clear enough that the experiences of this Sabbath (1,21-34) bring him apart for prayer early the following morning. The Gethsemane retreat is occasioned by the pressure of impending events. Otherwise, his retreats for prayer come at important junctures in his public life—at the baptism, the choosing of the twelve, at Cæsarea Philippi and at the transfiguration. "For Luke the decisions and choices of Jesus at great moments and junctures in his public career are the result of prayer and petition."[42] Sometimes these retreats precede, again they follow, and still again fall upon critical moments in his experience. The decisions and choices to which these retreats for prayer bring him, the results in his subsequent conduct are not always clear. But in spite of this unclearness in detail, the general fact remains that Jesus retreated for prayer and did pray.

As we noted earlier, there is no regularity in these retreats. They are in no sense a part of a prayer-system. For Jesus prayer was not a traditional religious institution to be engaged in and observed at certain set hours, but the spontaneous impromptu practise of an intense personal piety. Prayer in the practise of Jesus seems to have been the exception rather than the rule, dictated by consciousness of need rather than by imitation of a traditional custom of his people. Some of his retreats seem to have been occasioned by a pressing popularity and the thronging of the multitudes, as well as by the inner need

---

[42]Bundy, *The Psychic Health of Jesus*, p. 190.

he felt for communion with God.   His word to the twelve upon their return from their mission (Mark 6,31a),

"Come ye yourselves apart into a desert place, and rest awhile,"

is probably a reflection of the need for retirement and rest which he himself felt at times. His word in Gethsemane (Mark 14,38b),

"The spirit is willing, but the flesh is weak,"

is probably the expression of his own need of prayer.

Retreat, retirement and rest are necessary for any man who is always at his best and who is working under high pressure in the realm of the spirit.   Jesus felt a deep native need of prayer.   Than this there is not a finer expression of the real religiousness of his personality.   With all of his natural and native resourcefulness in the realm of religion, Jesus nowhere manifests a sense of self-sufficiency that enabled him to dispense with that primary religious practise—prayer to God.   In hours of direst distress he takes his flight to solitude and there seeks a refuge in prayer.   All that passed through the soul of Jesus on these occasions we shall never know.   But that he did pray and continue to pray, that he died in prayer, is all that we are in need of knowing.

The religious experience of our great Christian contemporary, Sadhu Sundar Singh, throws an important light on these retreats of Jesus.   Mrs. Parker writes of the Sadhu:

"In South India in 1918 nobody seemed to realize

that he was ever exhausted or needed rest, and the long unbroken toil in an atmosphere as foreign as the languages of the people, wore down his spirit. He longed not only for the rest of body but for those periods of quiet meditation and prayer which are the very breath of his existence and source of his power. . . . He loves the open air by night and the open spaces by day, where without any eye to watch he can be alone with his Lord. In such an atmosphere he lives and gathers to himself those reserves of strength and peace which characterize him."[43]

Apart from such a personal parallel, it is sufficiently clear in the Gospel picture that Jesus' retreats for prayer were creative moments in his religious experience, and we may add, in the religious experience of all humankind.

Jesus' retreats for prayer seem for the most part to have been at night. In Mark 1,35 he rises "a great while before day"; according to Luke 6,12 he spent the whole night in prayer to God before choosing the twelve; according to Luke 9,28 and 37 Jesus is all night on the mountain with the three disciples; Gethsemane is a nocturnal retreat. This habit of retreat accords with his instruction on the proper place for prayer as apart and in private. (Matt. 6,6.) "For him praying was a holy thing, so holy that the world might not witness, so serious that too-much-speaking is of the evil one."[44] "Out of a sense of shyness genuine personal praying conceals itself from profane eyes and ears. . . . The personal prayer-life of the great religious geniuses has its scene in solitude and seclusion."[45] In Jesus' retreats to solitude

---

[43]*Sadhu Sundar Singh*, p. 163, 165*f*.
[44]Deissmann, *Evangelium und Urchristentum*, p. 103.
[45]Heiler, *Das Gebet*, p. 26.

we witness a survival of the spirit of Elijah who sought Jehovah in the desolation of the desert, in the loneliness of Mount Horeb. For the really great religious personality, silence has always been a sacrament; Jesus seems to have loved it as such. He knew the value of solitude and seclusion.

In these periods of prayer engaged in by Jesus there is nothing to suggest the typical temper of the mystic. There are no indications of mystical mannerisms and methods, no seeking for a severing of self, no attempt at the dissolution of the ego, no effort to effect a mystical merging with the object of prayer. In fact, Jesus' retreats seem to have been the very opposite—an intensification of self-consciousness that sought a moral harmony with the divine will. No ecstatic elements, no visionary visitations seem to have invaded these retreats. Luke alone (22,43) has an angel appear to strengthen him in Gethsemane, but this is a later legendary addition not found in Matthew and Mark, or in the best manuscripts of Luke.

These retreats seem to have resulted for Jesus in a rallying of personal resources and to have been a source of strong self-possession. They seem to have been times of complete detachment, of compact concentration upon certain central issues, resulting in a state of mind and soul that was undivided and undistracted. Few men in history have attained unto this pinnacle of prayer-experience. Still fewer are the instances in which others have beheld them at this high point, but in these rare instances the experience for the witness has left an indelible impression. Of George Fox, William Penn wrote: "The

most awful, living, reverent frame I ever beheld or felt,
I must say was his in prayer."[46]

The great men with great calls and commissions who
have made permanent contributions to our human progress upward have passed through times—hours, days,
months, even years—when their deepest convictions were
submitted to the most terrible and trying tests. Often
even the validity of their cause and the genuineness of
their personal consecration to it were at stake. These tremendous conflicts they have been forced to face and fight
out alone, and in many cases, before God. At such times
such men know themselves to be immediately in the presence of their Maker, and they pour out the naked substance of their souls. It is in the solitude of such prayer
that the world's great religions have been born.

It was in the desolation of the Galilean deserts, in the
heavy solitude and seclusion of its nights that Jesus struck
deep into the richest source-springs of personal religious
experience that our human history knows. Solitude,
seclusion and silence filled with his supplications were the
things that made Jesus the One he was and always will be.
"To go up into the mountain and to come back as an am-
bassador to the world, has ever been the method of humanity's best friends."[47]

The Prayers of Jesus

We now turn to the prayers of Jesus, for in them we
feel that we come closest to his very soul. Only a few of
his prayers have come down to us, a total of seven in the
first three Gospels. That we have so few of his prayers

---

[46]Penney, *The Journal of George Fox*, p. xix.
[47]Evelyn Underhill, quoted by Heiler, *Der Katholizismus*, p. 513.

is, of course, due to the very nature of his practise of prayer. In protected privacy, in solitude and seclusion, he prayed to his God. In the language of Plotinus, Jesus' retreats are a φυγὴ μόνου πρὸς μόνον—(the flight of the the lonely one to the Only One). We may be grateful that even seven have come down to us. In the first three Gospels we have the following

	Reported Prayers of Jesus	Matthew	Mark	Luke
(1)	"Our Father, who art"	6,9-13	....	11,1-4
(2)	"I thank thee, O Father"	11,25-26	....	10,21
(3)	"Simon, Simon . . . I made"	....	....	22,31-32
(4)	"Abba, Father, all things"	26,39-42	14,36	22,42
(5)	"Father, forgive them"	....	....	23,34
(6)	"My God, my God, why"	27,46	15,34	....
(7)	"Father, into thy hands"	....	....	23,46

Mark reports only two prayers of Jesus, in Gethsemane and on the cross, both in the last hours of his life when stress and strain were heaviest upon his soul. Matthew reports both of Mark's prayers and adds two, the prayer of praise (11,25-26) and the *Lord's Prayer* (6,9-13), both of which were without doubt Galilean prayers. Luke again shows the greatest interest in the devotional life of Jesus by reporting six prayers, all of those reported by Matthew and Mark except the cry on the cross, and by adding an allusion to a prayer for Simon (22,31-32) and two prayers on the cross (23,34 46). Five of the seven prayers fall within the last twenty-four hours of Jesus' life, and three of them were uttered from the cross.

In a survey of Jesus' prayers the first thing that impresses the student is their utter, unadorned simplicity. In this respect they stand in sharp contrast with the typical prayers of mankind. "The most profound disposition of vital religion is to clothe its objects of faith with the highest predicates of honor."[48] It is to God alone that Jesus prays, in no name, and for no sake. All of those admonitions to pray "in his name" or "for his sake" are of later Christian origin. They do not go back to Jesus' own prayer-life, for such would contradict his constant religious attitude and would result in a complete collapse of his religious consciousness. In his prayers Jesus follows no pious program, no mechanical method, no tedious technique, no fixed formulas, no heaping-high of the deity's titles and predicates. Five of the seven prayers begin with the simple and intimate address, *Father*. We have only the substance of his prayer for Simon (Luke 22,31-32), and we do not know the address of the prayer itself. However, such an intimate supplication could hardly have had any other address. His cry on the cross is verbatim from Psalms 22,1; it begins with the address, *My God, my God!* In such a cry Jesus' experience of God as high and holy, as inscrutable and unfathomable, predominates over his experience of God as Father. In it we see a distressed human being laying bare the substance of his soul—mere man in the terrible presence of his mighty Maker. In his prayer of commitment (Luke 23,46) he supplies to the Old Testament text (Psalms 31,5a) the affectionate appellation, *Father*. There is a specially intimate feature preserved in Mark's text of the Gethsemane prayer (14,36); its address is in Jesus' native provincial dialect, *Abba, my Father*. The most elaborate address is in his prayer of praise, *O Father, Lord of heaven and earth,* where a fuller form is only natural. Jesus' prayers are all models for his own

---

[48]Mundle, *Das religioese Leben des Apostels Paulus*, p. 54.

word, "In praying use not vain repetitions." (Matt. 6,7.) The simplicity of his prayers is only a natural counterpart to the simplicity of the whole of his religious faith. He does not throw himself in the dust after the manner of his own East, but in the prayer-act he lifts his voice and his soul in simple yet complete confidence. On his knees he feels himself, as always, a child in the presence of his loving Father. It is on this quiet but sublime level that the prayers of Jesus move, always a reverent and confident converse, whether in praise, petition or protest. "In his praying the urphenomenon of prayer, the filial relationship to the Father-God, bursts forth in all its primitive purity and power."[49]

The second thing that impresses the student of Jesus' prayers is their striking brevity. The longest is the *Lord's Prayer*, a half-dozen simple sentences. The prayer of eighteen petitions repeated thrice daily by the pious Jew of Jesus' day was ten times as long as the longest of his prayers. With the exception of the *Lord's Prayer*, all others are sentence-prayers. Within a single simple sentence he pressed the substance of his supplications. Each of his prayers is compact and to the point, terse utterances with not a word to spare. The very brevity of his prayers is the chief guarantee of their genuineness. This remarkable brevity is the product of something deeper, the fine fruit of his general conception of the whole of religious experience, according to which every excess, every too-much, compromises its sincerity and purity. These pointed prayers are the perfect pattern of his own

---

[49]*Das Gebet*, p. 239. Professor Heiler further describes the praying of Jesus as "eine lebendige Zwiesprache mit einem Du, ein realer Umgang, ein dramatischer Verkehr mit dem persoenlichen Gott." (*Die Buddistische Versenkung*, p. 63.)

word to the effect that men are not heard for "their much speaking." (Matt. 6,7.) The prayers of Jesus may be characterized, as William Penn characterized the prayers of George Fox, "by the fewness and fulness of his words."[50] In this respect Jesus is true to prayer in its best form. Long prayer loses its free and fresh flow, its spontaneity, because it demands too much reflection and thought. Even when the period of prayer lengthens in the experience of Jesus, the prayer itself remains brief, as in Gethsemane where he repeats three times the same brief petition as the only adequate expression for the hurt of his soul.

A third thing that impresses the student of Jesus' prayers is their elemental character. Without exception they strike down into the very rudiments of religion; in them we see the first principles of piety. The whole ebb and flow of the emotional life finds expression in the prayers of Jesus. They reflect all the varying moods of the religious consciousness in its quest of God. All of those types of prayer most characteristic of genuine personal piety fall from his lips—prayers of praise, petition and protest. In moments of sublime exultation and complete confidence, in times of deepest need, in hours of greatest humiliation and direst distress, Jesus praises, petitions and protests to his God. The pendulum swings from one emotional extreme to the other. The two extreme poles of his prayer-experience are to be found in his prayer of praise—highest joy—and in his prayer of protest—deepest distress of soul and body. It is this strong emotional element that accounts for the utter simplicity and brevity of his prayers. They are terse because

---

[50]Penney, *The Journal of George Fox*, p. xix.

they are tense; his words are few because they are full.
His prayers are spontaneous outbursts, intense outpour-
ings of his innermost soul. Each is a release of an inner
tension. They spring vitally and organically from a subjective state which, in turn, finds free expression. Jesus,
as is natural to the strongly religious consciousness, prayed
under personal pressure, and his prayers are charged
with emotions of high intensity—joy, native human need
and distress. They are primitive in that they are born of
the need of the moment, out of a fulness of heart, unrestrained by any degree of rational reflection. In the study
of such praying as that of Jesus, theology can not help
us. The introduction of a dogma will only obscure our
vision. Here we have to do with the solid substance of
a sublime soul that launches out into the deep and stakes
its all in the quest of God.

A fourth thing that impresses the student of Jesus'
prayers is the fact that they are all prayed prayers. His
praying was not from habit. He prays out of deep inner
impulse. In his hours of need he does not require to be
taught how or what to pray. His words betray no reflection, no conscious effort at composition; they are involuntary unpremeditated utterances of a soul in search
of satisfaction for its deepest desires. Jesus' prayers are
never professional; they are the prayers of the pious layman—always personal, never impersonal; always informal, never formal. They are abrupt and broken with no
attempt at rhetorical finish or stylistic smoothness. This
is due to the fact that Jesus' prayers are always private
and personal; they are never public prayers, even though
witnesses are present. Public prayer by its very nature
and the demands placed upon it can never be pure. The
prayer must think of what he is saying because others are

listening. This destroys the spontaneity of the prayer-act at its best. Jesus was forced to pray in public, on the cross, but his prayers are not public, for he is alone with his God. In the prayer-act his attention is undivided; the concentration of his consciousness is complete, undisturbed. Witnesses may be present, yet he has but one Auditor. We have no instances of prosaic prayers from Jesus, prayers that were prayed in response to the general conviction that prayer is a religious duty, a practise that should be observed faithfully. The prayers of Jesus that have come down to us arise out of some unusual situation, and they usually reflect the special situation in which he found himself and which determined their content. For this reason they are always prayed prayers.

A fifth thing that impresses the student of Jesus' prayers is the complete lack of detail. In none of his prayers does Jesus catalogue his needs; he does not rehearse the situation in which he finds himself; he does not elaborate upon all that is involved for himself. He includes in his prayers no promises, no pledges; there is no bargaining with the deity for a favorable hearing and answering such as prayer on a lower level almost always exhibits. In many of the Psalms the petitioner goes into great detail, acquainting the deity with all the items as though such were necessary in the prayer-process. The twenty-second Psalm is a good example of such minute delineation. In his darkest hour Jesus quotes the first sentence of this Psalm, but his confidence in the Father dispenses with all need of elaboration. In Gethsemane he does not say that death is just ahead of him, that his enemies are upon him, that one of his trusted few has betrayed him into their hands, that another is about to deny him, and that all are on the point of deserting him.

In such a situation a single simple statement suffices to express his need, and it says all that prayer can or needs to say.

"Your Father knoweth what things ye have need of, before ye ask him." (Matt. 6,8.)

Such is the clear crystallization of this phase of Jesus' prayer-experience. And all this rests upon something deeper, his unreserved faith in God. It is this that gives the prayers of Jesus their solid substance. His disinclination to dwell on detail is the most profound confession of his personal faith in the divine omniscience, omnipotence and omnipresence.

A sixth thing that impresses the student of Jesus' prayers is the richness of their content, the high order of values sought in prayer. It is in prayer, as we saw, that the religious subject expresses the sentiments that are strongest, the desires that are deepest, the values that he holds highest and seeks to acquire. In the experience of primitive man the bare necessities of physical existence and survival were of great importance and consequently they occupy the foreground in his prayer-outlook. The exigencies of existence loom up large on the horizon of Old Testament prayers. Jesus' prayers are primitive in the elemental strength of emotion from which they spring and which carries them along. But in the scale of values sought in prayer he is heaven-high above primitive man. Over against many Old Testament prayers those of Jesus manifest a narrowing of the horizon of things prayed for. His objects of desire in prayer are the noblest; he seeks the highest values of human conception. He is really radical in his exclusion of thoughts and things from the prayer-process. His selection of goods constitutes one of his chief contributions to the history and practise of prayer. The *Lord's Prayer* is positively unique in the choice of things prayed for. The needs of human existence find expression, "Give us this day our daily bread," for Jesus regards all the concerns of human life, outer and inner, as under the divine providence and direction. But these things fall into the background, or at best they win only a secondary recognition. Jesus prays for the great spiritual values. In his prayers the pressure of outer circumstance, no matter how strong and severe, recedes in favor of an inner pressure of soul which occupies the whole foreground. More intense than the physical pain of crucifixion is the feeling of being forsaken of God.

A seventh thing that impresses the student of Jesus' prayers is the sublimity of their purpose. The goal toward which he strives is the highest which the history of prayer and its practise presents: In prayer he seeks the divine will into which he would fit himself. As we saw earlier in this chapter, the divine will was not always clear for Jesus. He must search to learn it and struggle to perform it. With all of his natural religious genius, Jesus nevertheless belongs to that plodding prosaic type of piety that must battle every step of the way, and prayer is the path which he pursues. In prayer he seeks the harmonization of self, of the whole of his life, with the plan and purpose of God.[51] For Jesus, religion in its highest attainment is the perfect cooperation of the human with the Divine, of man with his Maker. This attainment of religious experience involves one of the

---

[51]Sadhu Sundar Singh writes: "We cannot *alter* the will of God, but the man of prayer can discover the will of God with regard to himself." *At the Master's Feet*, p. 42. Courtesy of Fleming H. Revell Company.

principal paradoxes of personal piety: exaltation through submission and self-surrender. Professor Coe states this paradox in its psychological phases: "The prayer-life may be said to be . . . the organization into the self of the very things that threaten to disorganize it."[52] In Jesus' own word it is put:

> "Every one that exalteth himself shall be humbled; but he that humbleth himself shall be exalted." (Luke 18,14b.)

This aspect of Jesus' prayer-life, in fact, this supreme goal of the whole of his religious experience, reaches its climax in the Gethsemane submission. Through self-surrender he lifts himself to the exalted plane of the divine will. This goal he regards as the highest open to attainment for the religious subject. He himself attempts and attains it. His goal is not a mystical union with the Divine, but a moral harmony of life with the divine will. Here the prayer-practise and experience attains its height, and here again we strike upon one of Jesus' greatest contributions to the religious enterprise of mankind. "Prayer that climaxes in complete self-surrender is the creation of Jesus."[53]

In an earlier connection we noted that prayer was in no sense a psychological problem for Jesus. There is not a hint in the Gospels to the effect that he in any wise questioned the prayer-process and its power to produce, or that prayer was in any way problematic for him. The only difficulties with which he deals are of a practical and personal nature, and they concern the *prayer* rather than

[52] *The Psychology of Religion*, p. 316.
[53] Heiler, *Das Gebet*, p. 385.

the prayer-process as such.   Any real skepticism regarding prayer—that it is only a monologue of the *prayer* with himself—seems never to have crossed his mind. The prayer-experience of a critical temperament like Alfred Loisy has no parallel in that of Jesus.   "For a long time I have not found it possible to pray to God as one beseeches an individual from whom some favor is anticipated.   My prayers consist of retiring into the depths of my own consciousness and there gathering my best impulses together to determine what for me is right and lawful."[54]   The very volume of Jesus' experience of God as living, loving Father threw him out beyond such rational reflection.

The great *prayers* of history are unanimous in the conviction that prayer is a producing process, and many of them like St. Teresa have left warm testimonials of their prayer-experience.   Some of them are really remarkable in their psychological insight and critical care in self-analysis.   The scientific psychologist who bases his findings on concrete data fresh from the prayer-life of great and small souls must reckon with prayer as a primary power in the religious life at its best.   The following statement of Professor Coe is careful and true to the facts:

"It is a way of getting one's self together, of mobilizing and concentrating one's dispersed capacities, of begetting the confidence that tends toward victory over difficulties.   It produces in a distracted mind the repose that is power.   It freshens a mind deadened by routine. It reveals new truth, because the mind is made more elastic and more capable of sustained attention.   Thus

---

[54] *My Duel with the Vatican,* by Alfred Loisy, p. 275.   Courtesy of E. P. Dutton & Co., Inc.

does it remove mountains in the individual, and through him in the world beyond."[55]

A highly conscientious man of prayer like Sadhu Sundar Singh writes: "The man who prays is himself changed."[56]

Prayer is a producing process only when it has its roots struck deep in the basal needs keenly felt by the strongly religious consciousness. The *prayer* must find in prayer a personal recourse and resort. It is the practise of the pressed soul. In its best form, then, the results of prayer for the *prayer* are: a discharge of soul, a release of inner tension, the quieting of turbulent emotions, the restoration of inner repose, a fresh sense of unity of self, a reinforcement of personal resources, a strength of will supplanting its former weakness, a virtue as well as a volume of volition, an ability to choose rightly where the ways were once hopelessly crossed, a full development of decision, a deepening of inner determination, a coming of certainty to displace confusion, a dawning of clearness, a full illumination, an intensification of impulse, and finally an enveloping inspiration that carries the *prayer* through to triumph.

Jesus has left us no first-hand testimonials of his prayer-experience such as Paul supplies in II Corinthians 12,8-9a:

"Concerning this thing I besought the Lord thrice, that it might depart from me. And he hath said unto me, My grace is sufficient for thee: for *my* power is made perfect in weakness."

However, it is quite clear that prayer was a religious re-

----

[55]*The Psychology of Religion*, p. 315.
[56]*Reality and Religion*, p. 6.

course and resort of Jesus and that he prayed in response
to elemental needs. On one occasion the need of prayer
escapes his lips, in Gethsemane,

"My soul is exceeding sorrowful even unto death:
abide ye here, and watch." (Mark 14,34.)

Professor Wernle writes: "Jesus was the most powerful
prayer of history because he did not rely on his own
power."[57] He manifested no sense of self-sufficiency; he
felt the need of powerful supplementation, and he experienced prayer as a producing process.

Just what and all that prayer meant for Jesus we shall
never know. The results of his prayers for himself are
not so clearly indicated as we might wish and we must
draw our conclusions from scattered straws that point,
however, quite unmistakably in one direction. His
prayer-experience seems to have brought him all that the
great *prayers* understand as religious light and strength.
Our glimpses into his prayer-life on one or two occasions
show us quite clearly what an important place prayer occupied in his religious experience. The first retreat, in
Mark (1,35-38), seems to have resulted in clearness and
certainty concerning the essence of his mission. His prayer
of praise is a discharge of soul. (Luke 10,21.) His
Gethsemane prayer strips the last shred of uncertainty
from his mind, and it results in an assembly of volitional
powers which bring him through the harassing scenes
before the Jewish and Roman authorities with a calm
and courage that are more than heroic. His cry of distress (Mark 15,34) is a release of inner tension which
reverses into a composure and confidence of soul (Luke
23,46).

---

[57] *Jesus*, p. 57.

On the whole, we may say that prayer for Jesus meant an expression of need, a release of soul, a relief of inner pressure, conquest over severe subjective struggle, an elevation and enrichment of mind, a reinforcement and refreshment of spirit, a clarifying of vision, a freshened functioning of faith, a whetting of will, discovery and illumination, restoration of confidence and courage, increased consecration and devotion, adjustment and orientation, a mobilization of personal powers to perform, in short, the energy and power by which to live and work. Even with an increase of clearness and certainty and of personal power to perform, we do not see a diminishing but an intensification of Jesus' prayer-life. His life ends with an almost awful climax—the cry to God *de profundis*.

In Jesus' practise of prayer we get an insight into the nature and sources of his personal power. His praying brought to him clearness and certainty concerning the divine will for himself; in his retreats he came to important decisions and determined upon the course and code of his conduct. In prayer to God he found that marvelous source of strength that enabled him to perform the divine will even to the cup that was his to drink. Not in visions and voices, but in prayer and communion with God— purely religious sources of light and strength—Jesus learned the divine will and found the personal power to perform it.

In the history of prayer Jesus marks much more than an advance or development. Jesus was the perfect *prayer*. His prayer-experience is an enrichment and enhancement of all that humanity may expect and hope from prayer, of all that man understands as his relation to his Maker. In short, he brought the prayer-act to its perfection.

In his practise of prayer and in his prayers we have preserved to us the deepest grounds of Jesus' religious consciousness. On the basis of his praying alone we may answer the question, Who was Jesus? The very virtue and volume of his prayer-life settles the issue for ever. In such a state of the facts theology can not help us, for we are not dealing with dull and dreary lifelessness but with a living personality whose whole existence centered exclusively upon God. The historical Jesus was a religious subject, an experient of religion. In his very humanness the religious experience of mankind attains its finest form.

In the first three Gospels the religious consciousness of Jesus is constant. It runs clear, straight and strong through the Synoptic picture, the principal force and factor that supports and sustains him. Without exception, his attitudes, aspirations and acts are religious. In every feature of his personality we witness a sense of deep dependence upon the Divine and an equally deep and determined devotion. In Jesus the religious consciousness appears in its purity.

CHAPTER IV

The Religious Demands of Jesus

Down to this point we have sought to indicate the sources of Jesus' religious experience, the objects of his religious faith, and the solid substance of his religious consciousness, in brief, the commanding and controlling elements of his religious experience. We now come to that more practical problem of determining the issues of Jesus' religious experience as they concern his followers. The issue of his religious experience for himself is clear enough. His personal experience of religion made him what he was. It accounts for all that he was able to say, to be and to do as a religious personality and character. But his followers feel that he has laid a task upon them, that he meant to do so, and they feel that they face the direct responsibility of realizing for themselves and for others the things that he himself sought and, in turn, sought to share with them and with all. What did Jesus demand of his disciples? What did he require in the way of religious living? What did he seek to do for his closest companions, for all of his contemporaries? What did he expect of his followers? What did he desire that they should do for others? These are the questions of practical piety, and the answers to these questions are of the greatest importance for us to-day.

As we have tried to show from the outset, Jesus belongs to that type of mind which, for want of a better name, we call religious genius. The great religious geniuses of history, without exception, have objectified the central content of their religious experience. Inherent in the very nature of religious genius is the clear conviction that personal religious experience makes a difference in the whole life of the experient, in the lives of others, even in the life of the whole world. In fact, it is this difference in the character of the whole of our human life that the great religious genius seeks as the ultimate goal of his accomplishment. He is convinced that the subjective experience of religion has its objective issues and that men and the world in general must become other than they are. He experiences religion as a producing process. Consequently, the great religious genius makes his very definite demands. The whole of life, personal and social, must reconstruct itself to correspond to the essential content of his religious experience; it must become the full and free expression of the meaning of God within.

Behind this fundamental conviction of the religious genius is a sound psychological law that operates in all fields of human experience: The commanding and controlling elements of experience demand expression and seek realization. The predominating convictions and aspirations seek to create a corresponding personal character and to establish corresponding codes and controls of social conduct. In personal character and in social conduct the serious individual strives to become the living expression of his experience. He seeks to convert his experience into a life that realizes his deepest convictions and his most fervent faith. Fervent and firmly founded faith must seek realization if it is to maintain itself. If it does not find such expression, it soon dies or, if it survives at all, becomes a mere theoretical concept that is entertained rather than an actual truth by which the subject lives.

This is especially true in the field of religious experience. The only hope for the continued life of a religious conviction is that it seek to mold character and conduct. A religious aspiration can live only as it seeks to realize itself. Faith must function, or it atrophies. Religious experience seeks to impress the whole of life with its essential and distinctive content. Religion in all its forms makes its demands upon the individual and the group. It requires a difference in the lives of men, personal and social. It lays its responsibilities and obligations upon the very heart of the individual and his community. It establishes principles for personal character, codes and controls for social conduct that correspond to the commanding elements of the religious experience from which they come.

The demands of religion, then, bear an organic relationship to the content of man's religious experience and they reflect the stages in the development and expansion of that experience. When his religious experience is limited, more or less impoverished, the religious requirements felt by himself and his group are correspondingly limited and poor. In its more primitive forms religious experience finds only a limited expression. Primitive man's sense of religious obligation exhausted itself in seeking the divine favor or in appeasing the divine anger. His religious life confined itself to more or less impersonal acts of worship, and his religious virtue consisted chiefly in the care and regularity with which he appeared before his gods. In some instances the performance of religious acts consumed a great deal of primitive man's time. In some of the lowest forms of religion we meet some of the most elaborate systems of cult and ceremony with numerous feasts and festivals extending over days and weeks. In general, it is true of primitive man's ex-

perience that he felt but a single religious relationship
and obligation, that of man to his Maker. The right
offering, at the right time, in the right place, prepared
and presented in the right way, satisfied his sense of religious responsibility. On such a level the religious life
exhausts itself in correctness of conduct in an hour of
worship. Although he lived under a conscious superstitious fear, the rest of his existence he led in a care-free
fashion, purely egocentric, feeling no requirements for
his personal character and social conduct.

One of the most remarkable phenomena of human history is the development and expansion of man's religious
experience. Its elevation and enrichment is one of the
most edifying chapters in the human story, and it is edifying because it has been accompanied by a corresponding
refinement of religious requirements. The movement has
been from the more elaborate to the more simple, from
complex cult and ceremony to plain principles and practises of living. The religious requirements of primitive
man were carefully stipulated down to the last detail; in
his worship he was guided step by step. But religious
experience in its higher forms leaves greater latitude to
the worshiper. This latitude is in no sense a laxity, but
grows out of a greater faith in the Divine and in man's
capacity to perceive and to perform the divine demands.

The expansion of man's religious experience comes to
include a second relationship. Man's relation to his fellow-man is raised to a plane that is on a par with his
relation to his Maker. An excellent example of this expansion of the religious consciousness is to be found in the
Old Testament decalogues of Exodus 20 and Deuteronomy 5, where seven of the ten commandments deal with
man's relation to his fellow-man over against the more

primitive code of Exodus 34,17-26 which comes from a religious experience that was conscious only of the relation of man to his Maker. In its highest form religion strikes the whole of life; religious obligation invades every detail of human existence, and man is never free from its requirements. The movement is from without in, from the punctilious performance of cult and ceremony to the perfection of individual and group life. This process of the purification of piety renders the requirements of religion easy of comprehension but difficult of performance, for they reach down and take a firm hold on the very source-springs of personal and social life. The chief danger that confronts religion in its higher forms is that the best elements of its experience will become theoretical and cease to be actual commanding forces which create corresponding character and control corresponding conduct.

The expansion, elevation and enrichment of man's religious experience is the work of the prophet, and it is the resourcefulness of the prophetic type of piety that has brought about the refinement of religious requirements. It belongs to the very genius of the prophet to simplify, to sift out the wheat from the chaff, to reject the elaborate and to insist on the essential, to depart from detail, to leave latitude in the comprehension and performance of religious duty, to widen the horizon of the religious outlook, to rise from the minor matters to the major issues, to discover principle rather than to dictate particular precept, to concentrate, to condense and to crystallize the commanding elements of religious experience. An excellent example of a product of such prophetic piety is to be found in that classic passage of Micah 6,6-8:

"Wherewith shall I come before Jehovah, and bow myself before the high God? Shall I come before him with burnt-offerings, with calves a year old?

"Will Jehovah be pleased with thousands of rams, *or* with ten thousand rivers of oil? Shall I give my first-born for my transgression, the fruit of my body for the sin of my soul?

"He hath showed thee, O man, what is good; and what doth Jehovah require of thee, but to do justly, and to love kindness, and to walk humbly with thy God?"

In such a passage the prophet is dealing directly with the divine demands, "What doth Jehovah require of thee?" Here we meet a departure from the elaborate in favor of the essential, a desertion of cult and ceremony in favor of plain principles and practises of living. The divine demands are brought down to a single simple statement. Such a passage can come from only a remarkably rich religious experience which expands to include character and conduct and which raises the divine demands to the moral and ethical plane. The rich religious experience back of Micah 6,6-8 does not dwell on detail. The requirements are cast in only the roughest relief. There is left to the individual and the group an almost loose latitude in the learning and living of religion. "To do justly," "to love kindness," "to walk humbly with God," are only most general principles. Prophet-like, Micah leaves to his contemporaries the correct interpretation and concrete application. The simplicity of such a statement is almost deceptive. The ease with which it is comprehended, its immediate appeal to better judgment, the subtle swing of sentiment which carries it straight to the moral conscience, obscure for the moment the drastic character of such a demand. It is only as the full weight of such a statement settles down upon the moral will of the individual and the group that its difficulty of performance is realized.

As we pointed out in chapter one, Jesus belongs to the prophetic type of religious personality. His religious experience is of the prophetic pattern and we may expect from him only the prophetic type of demand. Jesus is the prince of humanity's prophets, and his follower is religiously convinced that the progressive expansion, elevation and enrichment of man's religious experience reaches its climax in Jesus. In him we meet religious experience in its pristine purity and power. Of an experience so rich and deep we may expect only the highest order of religious demand, requirements that cover every human interest and relationship, that move on the most exalted plane of human conception, that allow a large latitude in interpretation and application, that are as simple of comprehension as they are difficult of performance because they reach down to the very roots of personal and social life. Of him we may not expect too much in the way of detail. The modern demand for detail meets with disappointment in Jesus. In his religious requirements we meet more often with general implications than with specific instructions. He projects for men only the major outlines of the religious outlook; he provides only the skeleton of the social structure leaving to them the task of building in the detail; the fundamental elements of man's religious life he casts only in the roughest relief.

The religious demands of Jesus, as is characteristic of the religious genius, correspond to the controlling ele-

ments of his religious experience, the experience of God
as high and holy, as living and loving Father, the quest of
His kingdom and will. These, for Jesus, are the fundamental elements of religious experience and enterprise.
Man's religion includes two inseparable elements: reverence and righteousness. These are the two great poles
of Jesus' own personal piety; they are the things that
matter most in the sight of God and in the lives of men.
With the same emphasis and energy that he preached
reverence for God he preached righteousness among men.
It is at this point that Jesus brings and welds together the
two most exalted heights of Old Testament piety:

"Thou shalt love the Lord thy God with all thy
heart, and with all thy soul, and with all thy mind, and
with all thy strength. . . . Thou shalt love thy neighbor as thyself. There is none other commandment
greater than these."   (Mark 12,30-31.)

Both commandments are the product of Israel's prophetic piety, but in the Old Testament they stand as lofty,
isolated peaks that tower high above the dead level of
Israel's religion.   (Deut. 6,4-5; Lev. 19,18.)   Jesus,
however, strikes his line from one peak to the other as
the high elevation on which the religious life is to move.
This is clearest in that greatest of all words of Jesus, the
Lord's Prayer, which moves from reverence to righteousness. (Matt. 6,9-13.)

At the very heart of human life Jesus places the experience of God. Men are to live a God-centered existence.
This experience of God is not something intangible and
theoretical but the actually commanding element in the

human consciousness; it is to reach down into the last and least details of man's existence—into his thought, feeling and conduct. The whole of his life man must live consciously in the presence of his Maker. This consciousness of being for ever in the divine presence is to be the creative and commanding force in his living. It must determine all that he is and aspires to be, all that he does and hopes to accomplish. Human life is a divine gift; as such it is to be accepted and lived. At the center of man's life is his Maker, toward whom he is to maintain an unbroken attitude of reverence. All about him are his human fellows, with whom he is to live on the principle and practise of righteousness.

THE CHILD MIND

Religion as Elemental Experience

The scene in which Jesus takes the little children in his arms and blesses them has always appealed to the Christian imagination as one of the most intimate and human touches in the Gospel picture. (Mark 10,13-16.) This it is, but in Jesus' word, which is the real heart of the incident, we have something more deeply human and elemental, for he is here laying the very groundwork for all religious experience.

"Suffer little children to come unto me; forbid them not: for to such belongeth the kingdom of God." (Mark 10,14b.)
"Except ye turn, and become as little children, ye shall in no wise enter into the kingdom of heaven." (Matt. 18,3.)

Just what elements in the child constitution appealed to Jesus we are not in a position to say, but to the child mind he promises the highest religious value—the kingdom of God. It is certainly clear that he is not setting up immaturity as a desirable state or virtue. Maturity as the goal of the religious life is too prominent in the thought of Jesus to permit this conclusion. In many of his words he speaks of seed-time and sowing, of small starts and beginnings, but these very words climax in the ripened grain and harvest, in large outcomes and issues. Growth and increase are a prominent theme in his message. The seed sown in good ground brings forth, some thirty, some sixty, some a hundredfold. The thought of development is equally prominent in his religious outlook. The smallest of all seeds springs up and becomes the greatest of herbs. Jesus regards the religious life as a becoming of something other than we are. There is continuity, but there is change. Men remain the same, yet they at the same time become something new and different. Life assumes new forms; its content is enriched; there appear new capacities, powers and capabilities. Jesus, then, can not be recommending the undeveloped state of the child mind. He seems to have in mind no special trait; rather he lays at the very base of religious experience the whole of the child's outlook and approach to life. He regards the child mind as indispensable in the relationship of man to his Maker. It is the very heart of his conception of men as the children of God.

Jesus gives us no analysis of the child mind as a basis for religious experience, but we may undertake this in the light of psychology and at the same time feel that we are pursuing the right path, particularly when the elements of the child mind have exact counterparts in the religious experience of Jesus himself. We may be sure that they are the marks of the mind that would sense and share the highest religious values. As we shall see at once, they are all native and natural endowments which we bring into the world and which we must retain even in full maturity if we are to remain religious in the sense of Jesus. All of these features are primitive and naive, but they are not marks of immaturity. They are elemental and essential to genuine religiousness, and our most careful psychology recognizes them as indispensable in the highest forms of religious experience.

In the child there is a native and natural simplicity in the whole of his approach to life that enables him to discover the wonder in the world. He is sensitive to the mysteries of his existence. This wonder-world is an elemental part of all genuine religious experience. The student of the history of religion finds it in the most primitive as well as in the highest forms of religion. It is the fundamental mystery of man's existence, the fact that he is surrounded by powers other and greater than his own, that calls forth the attitude of religious fear, awe, wonder and reverence. This has an exact counterpart in the experience of Jesus, who has his wonder-world which calls forth the deepest of religious emotions. A finer example of this elemental response to the mystery of man's existence, to this awareness of living in the presence of powers beyond man's control, than comes direct and fresh from Jesus' own religious experience would be difficult to find:

"So is the kingdom of God, as if a man should cast seed upon the earth; and should sleep and rise night

and day, and the seed should spring up and grow, he
knoweth not how. The earth beareth fruit of herself;
first the blade, then the ear, then the full corn in the
ear. But when the fruit is ripe, straightway he putteth
forth the sickle, because the harvest is come." (Mark
4,26-29.)

In the child there is an intense sensitivity and susceptibility to all that experience offers for apprehension and
assimilation. The child in his immaturity peoples his
world with imaginary beings; his fertile imagination
transforms the most prosaic objects into wondrous creatures that do wondrous things; inanimate objects take on
life; they are endowed with human and more-than-human
faculties; they converse with him, and reveal the hidden
secrets of his and their existence. The uncritical and uncontrolled imagination of immaturity becomes in the mature religious mind the faculty for the discovery of the
Divine. This also has its exact counterpart in the religious experience of Jesus. He shows himself intensely sensitive and susceptible to all that experience offers. What
for most men is plain and prosaic, dull and drab and
dreary, in our existence became for him infinitely suggestive. His world is plain at no point, for in every item it
is charged with the presence of the Divine. In the most
prosaic facts and pursuits of human life he learns lessons
of the Divine. A sower sowing his seed, a woman mixing
dough, a patched garment, a bursted wine-skin, a lamp on
a stand, cast-off salt on a rubbish heap—all suggest to
Jesus the ways and workings of God and His kingdom.
In the child there is a clear consciousness of dependence. It is the organic issue of his sense of the wonder-
world that surrounds him. He does not rely on his own

resources; he feels the need of powerful supplementation from without. He takes his refuge with those who understand better and who are stronger than himself. This, too, is fundamental to religious experience at its best. The forms in which this consciousness of dependence expresses itself may vary; they may be of a high or low order depending upon the stage of man's general development, but it is an absolutely indispensable state and condition apart from which genuine religious experience is impossible. The religious man never trusts exclusively in his own resources. He feels the need of powerful supplementation as he faces all the items and issues of his existence. He finds a refuge and resort only in a religious approach to all that experience offers. This, too, has its counterpart in the religious life of Jesus; it is a fundamental element in his experience of God. It is this consciousness of dependence, this sense of need for powerful supplementation, that is behind the whole of his prayer-life and that expresses itself in and through it. To his disciples he says that this sense of dependence must reach down to the last detail of life. Even a pious pledge may not be undertaken on the basis of one's own resources.

"Swear not at all; neither by the heaven, for it is the throne of God; nor by the earth, for it is the footstool of his feet; nor by Jerusalem, for it is the city of the great king. Neither shalt thou swear by thy head, for thou canst not make one hair white or black." (Matt. 5,34-36.)

"Which of you by being anxious can add one cubit unto the measure of his life?"   (Matt. 6,27.)

In the child there is an unreserved trust and confidence. He approaches life with an instinctive trust; in others he has an implicit confidence. The whole order of things works with him, and he gives himself wholly to it. He feels that he is in the midst of an order that looks out just for him and that has his care at heart. His fervent faith in the fundamental goodness of his world bears him over any momentary disturbances and disappointments. The very flood of his faith carries him along. In Jesus we see this same trust and confidence. He does not feel that he is thrown into the midst of an order that is careless and heartless. In the world about him he discovers the provisions of Providence. Back of all that experience offers he sees the holy and helpful heart of the impartial Father who

"maketh his sun to rise on the evil and the good, and who sendeth his rain on the just and the unjust." (Matt. 5,45.)

Jesus is fully conscious of the exigencies of human existence, yet the very force of his faith issues in a simple statement of trust and confidence that staggers us:

"Behold the birds of the heaven, that they sow not, neither do they reap, nor gather into barns; and your heavenly Father feedeth them. . . . Consider the lilies of the field, how they grow; they toil not, neither do they spin: yet I say unto you, that even Solomon in all his glory was not arrayed like one of these. But if God doth so clothe the grass of the field, which to-day is, and to-morrow is cast into the oven, *shall he* not much more *clothe* you, O ye of little faith? Be not therefore anxious, saying, What shall we eat? or, What shall we drink? or, Wherewithal shall we be clothed? For after all these things do the Gentiles seek; for your heavenly Father knoweth that ye have need of all these things." (Matt. 6,26-32.)

In the child there is a sense of absolute security. There is no skepticism that invades his mind and that inhibits the free flow of his life. There are no disturbing doubts; there are no dogmatic denials that hinder him in the unrestrained living of his life. There are no morbid fears that possess him. He is out of harm's way. He feels secure in his life-situation. This sense of security permeates the whole of the religious experience of Jesus. Uncertainty may throw him into struggle of soul; personal distress may bring cries of need from his lips. But his distress never develops into a permanent despondency and despair. He is never the victim of circumstances and the emotional reactions they may call forth. In his hardest hour he may feel himself deserted of the Divine, but it is into the Father's hands that he commits his spirit. This sense of security Jesus sets as one of the foundation stones of religious experience. In view of it he tells his disciples that they may feel that they possess real value in the sight of the Divine:

"Are not two sparrows sold for a penny? and not one of them shall fall on the ground without your Father: but the very hairs of your head are all numbered. Fear not therefore: ye are of more value than many sparrows." (Matt. 10,29-31.)

In the child there is a wholesome and sunny optimism. The entire substance of his experience conspires in the creation of this frame of mind. His relation to his world is happy and he confronts it with an irrepressible and irresistible cheerfulness. A passing disturbance only serves to augment his joy. He feels that life is a boon, not a burden. He goes to meet it in exuberant spirit, unshakably certain that it has much good in store for him. The golden days lie just ahead, and he is expectant and hopeful. The golden days may delay their coming, his joyous prospect may be postponed, but this fact can not daunt the enthusiasm he feels with life's whole outlook before him. This attitude with which the child confronts life has its exact counterpart in the religious experience of Jesus. He is never pessimistic in his piety. Even in his sharpest denunciations the element of hope is never missing. He meets the pressure of the present in the light of the future. The future is good because it is God's, who has great and good things in store for men. From beginning to end Jesus is expectant. The kingdom is at hand; it is about to appear; it is pressing upon the very doors. The kingdom may delay its coming, it may be postponed, but it *will* come. This fundamental optimism has its expression in Matthew 6,34:

"Be not therefore anxious for the morrow: for the morrow will be anxious for itself. Sufficient unto the day is the evil thereof."

This is not a strain of other-worldliness, an impossible idealism that neglects the world of fact, but a naive and childlike approach to the problem of the living of life religiously. It is an optimism that belongs to the higher ranges of religious experience, and it is absolutely necessary if we are to face human life and find in it more than a dull and dreary existence. Like the child, the mature religious mind must confront the world of fact with a faith that bids defiance to all that is contrary to it.

A final feature in the child mind is a singular lack of pretense and self-consciousness. The child is openly and frankly what he is. He speaks and acts under no artificial restraints; his thoughts and feelings find free and spontaneous expression. He is uncramped by custom and convention; he has not yet felt the pressure of social expectation and technique. In public and in private he is simply what he thinks and feels. His self is not yet submerged in a social system; he has not yet learned the suppression of public opinion. This lack of pretense and self-consciousness has its exact counterpart in the thought and conduct of Jesus. It is a religion of pretense that he condemns most severely. It is at the very heart of all that he has to say to the religious-by-profession of his day. The Pharisee was keenly conscious of his religious virtues and merits. Reputation was a strong motive in his religious life. He undertook his practises of piety in public—his fasting, almsgiving and praying. Social approval was often the end that he sought, decided deference to himself from others rather than depth of inner devotion. The religious-by-profession of Jesus' day lived a self-conscious existence. The Pharisee must be constantly on his guard; he was not allowed to forget himself for a moment. He must know exactly with whom he talked and walked, under whose roof he entered, exactly what was set before him to eat and how it was prepared. He lived his life under the constant and conscious danger of defilement. A fine reflection of this self-consciousness is preserved by Luke in his account of the penitent act of a sinful woman in the form of a reflection

of Simon the Pharisee at whose table Jesus is a guest.   As
Jesus' host observes the character of the woman and
Jesus' approval of her act, he questions the genuineness
of Jesus as a prophet (7,39b) :

"This man, if he were a prophet, would have perceived who and what manner of woman this is that
toucheth him, that she is a sinner."

Jesus' classic condemnation of a religion of pretense
we find in one of his major addresses:

"Beware of the scribes, who desire to walk in long
robes, and *to have* salutations in the marketplaces, and
chief seats in the synagogue, and chief seats at feasts:
they that devour widows' houses, and for a pretense
make long prayers; these shall receive greater condemnation."   (Mark 12,38-40.)
"But all their works they do to be seen of men: for
they make broad their phylacteries, and enlarge the
borders *of their garments* . . . and love . . . to be
called of men, Rabbi."   (Matt. 23,5-7.)

Jesus' classic picture of exaggerated self-consciousness
in religion is found in his parable of the two men who
went up into the temple to pray, the one a Pharisee, the
other a publican (Luke 18, 10-13) :

"The Pharisee stood and prayed thus with himself,
God I thank thee, that I am not as the rest of men,
extortioners, unjust, adulterers, or even as this publican. I fast twice in the week; I give tithes of all that
I get."

Over against this he sets the contrasting picture of the publican who, without pretense of any kind, conscious only of his need, utters a tense, terse supplication.

"But the publican, standing afar off, would not lift up so much as his eyes to heaven, but smote his breast, saying, God, be thou merciful to me a sinner."

According to Jesus, there were two sinners who went up to the temple to pray, and the one went down justified rather than the other.

One of the most refreshing features in the Gospel picture of Jesus is this singular lack of pretense and self-consciousness. A religious profession never crosses his lips; he never recites a single religious virtue that he himself possesses. And yet he made the most imposing impression as a religious personality. The people say, "What manner of man is this?" (Matt. 8,27.) "We have seen strange things to-day." (Luke 5,26.) "We never saw it on this fashion." (Mark 2,12.) "Certainly this was a righteous man." (Luke 23,47.) Jesus is unrestrained even by religious custom and convention. He follows his religious instincts even if they bring him to trespass upon sacred and long-standing tradition. He heals on the Sabbath and his disciples pluck grain; he does not observe the religious custom of fasting; he goes through no ceremonial washings before meals; he associates almost preferably with publicans and sinners. To these social and religious outcasts he feels himself strongly drawn,

"They that are whole have no need of a physician, but they that are sick: I came not to call the righteous, but sinners." (Mark 2,17.)

Among them he met with the readiest response. They shall precede the religious-by-profession into the kingdom of God. (Matt. 21,31.) Throughout the Gospel picture we see Jesus as the congenial guest who is at home in the company of all classes of his contemporaries. He condescends to none; he defers to none. When he crosses with the regular requirements of religious respectability, he seems unconscious of it until the guardians of convention call his attention to the irregularity of his conduct and associations. The whole of Jesus' known life is an unspoiled expression of his religious experience.

Jesus sets the child mind as the indispensable foundation for the erection of a solid religious structure in our human life, and he is here true to the very best of humanity's religious genius. Piety in its highest and most convincing forms always rests upon this solid substratum. This fundamental demand strikes upon the modern ear like a strange, unintelligible sound. The modern mind feels that the harmony of its life is disturbed by the introduction of a thing so elemental, and the spirit of this demand seems to bring a harsh, unbearable clash to the modern mood and temper. But the modern mind must possess the principal marks of the child if it is to become religious in the sense of Jesus. And the very practical question arises: Can the modern mind gear itself into this fundamental position of Jesus? The modern mind is convinced of its maturity; it is clearly conscious of having outgrown the naive, the childish and the primitive. Can it become as a little child in its attitude and feel that to it belongs the kingdom of heaven?

There are elements in the modern make-up that seem opposed to this requirement of Jesus. The modern mind prides itself on its knowledge, very justly in the fact that it has cleared up much of the mystery that confused and awed primitive man and that still arouses the wonder of the child. Modern man knows more about the world in which he lives, he feels more at home in it than did primitive man. Many of nature's forces which primitive man feared and fled modern man has mastered and drafted into his service. This tends to rob the modern mind of its native and natural simplicity in the whole of its approach to life. A justified sense of pride in attainment and accomplishment exposes the modern mind to the danger of losing its sense of wonder. The whole of our experience seems to conspire to take this from us. With all of our insight into the laws and operations of the universe and our own earth we may never become insensible to the fundamental mystery of our existence without a hopeless impoverishment of our experience. The laws which we discover are not of our making; the mighty forces which we command do not originate with us. Primitive and modern man alike stand in the presence of the wonder-world. Man sleeps and rises night and day, but the earth bringeth forth fruit of itself; man knoweth not how. In our better moments we are sensible to the fundamental mystery of our existence, but according to Jesus this consciousness of living in the presence of the wonder-world must be the constant content of our experience. Slowly we are realizing that learning is not dangerous to elemental religion, that after all the real wonder-world is at the end rather than ahead of the learning process. The child is sensible to the wonder-world that baffles his understanding, but when we meet the most critical scientific spirit in its finest form we find that it is supersensible to this wonder-world. With all of his in-

vasions into the unknown modern man will always find
something beyond that arouses his awe and wonder, that
calls forth the reaction of deep reverence, and he will
never press his path beyond the presence of the Divine.
In elemental experience he will feel himself one with the
Psalmist, in whose piety Jesus himself grew up:

"What is man, that thou art mindful of him? and
the son of man, that thou visitest him?
"For thou hast made him but little lower than God,
and crownest him with glory and honor."   (8,4-5.)

Our modern life is infinitely complex, almost hopelessly
complicated. The very flood of things overwhelms us.
A baffling maze of materials presents itself to us for apprehension and assimilation. The very eventfulness of
our existence is distracting. It becomes increasingly difficult to make an assessment of our experience and
to single out the essential and fundamental. The very
pressure of life from without robs the modern mind of
the native right to retreat and retirement. Reflection
concerning the fundamental aims and ends of life is
sporadic; we practise it only as time permits. We are
very rapidly losing the fertile faculty of imagination that
sees in life more than appears on the surface. Our
world is becoming less and less suggestive as we become
less and less suggestible. The pressure of the practical
makes us the creatures of regularity and routine. Life
is plain and prosaic, and for many of us moderns it settles
down to a dull, drab, dreary existence even when we are
surrounded by comparative physical comfort. Men and
things become monotonous to us. There is little in them
or in us to stimulate meditation concerning the Divine.

232 THE RELIGION OF JESUS

And the reflections of Jesus on all the elements of human
experience, according to which life is plain at no point
and which learns daily lessons of the Divine, strike us as
a beautiful pastoral idyl, quite possible in the sunny hills
and plains of Galilee but out of all harmony with the din
and discords of our modern industrial world. The modern mind at this point surrenders its hold on Jesus and
leaves him to join that small circle of humanity's idealists
and dreamers to which it feels that he belongs.

In the modern mind there is only a limited sense of dependence. Our command over the physical and natural
world generates a sense of self-sufficiency. Our evident
attainments and accomplishments encourage us to rely
on our own resources. What have we not done on our
own account? What is there left undone that we do not
expect to do in the not-too-distant future? We feel that
we are dependent upon the material and social order, but
we are confident that our own modern methods will result
in satisfactory distribution and adequate adjustment.
Our sense of dependence seldom reaches beyond the world
of appearances. We feel little or no need of more-than-
human supplementation. Seldom do we take refuge and
resort in the religious approach to the problem of living
human life individually and collectively. We feel that
the necessary illumination is only a question of time and
that the requisite strength is only a matter of more mature
growth and development. We are willing to undertake
life on the basis of our own resources. This is commendable enough except for the fact that behind this
willingness there is no commanding religious conviction
concerning the ultimate dependence of the human on the
Divine.

The modern mind is not characterized by unreserved

trust and confidence in its approach to life. It is ultra-sensitive to the hard and harsh facts of existence. It feels that it is caught in a desperate struggle for survival. A withered flower in the field, a fallen sparrow, do not suggest the provisions of Providence, but both appear as victims of a natural order that seems indifferent toward the fate of its offspring. Only the more favorable facts, in our better moments, suggest that after all the world is friendly toward us and perhaps has our ultimate good at heart. But our general mood is skeptical rather than confident and trustful. We feel that the universe is hostile rather than helpful. In our modern maturity we find it difficult to retain any appreciable measure of the child's instinctive faith in the essential goodness of things. The flow of our feeble faith is checked by the first jam of contrary facts. It is not strong enough to sweep its own course clean and find its way to its ultimate outlet. Momentary disturbances and discouragements strike us as permanent and necessary. They cause us to acquiesce rather than augment our aggressiveness. The fact that the sun shines on the evil and the good alike, that the rain falls on both the just and the unjust, hinders rather than helps our faith. We seek a fitness that will enable us to survive rather than a faith that will cope successfully with all the emergencies of our existence.

Modern men may be said to possess a sense of security in their relation to the physical side of their existence. With a commendable courage they are willing to take the physical risks involved in the living of life. But when it comes to the psychic and social side of existence modern men are not so secure. With all their mastery of the physical universe they have not yet mastered themselves. Modern men have yet to learn the secret of living together. Every ramification of our contemporary social order is invaded by a feeling of insecurity. Men do not trust the best in themselves, still less do they trust to the presence and appearance of the best in others. We hesitate to live and act at the impulse of our finer instincts. We suppress our nobler sentiments for fear that they may be rendered ridiculous. We have not yet learned that their full release is the only hope for a sense of social security. History should teach us that humanity has made its greatest steps forward, that it has always experienced an elevation and enrichment of life when men have dared venture upon life, trusting to the best in themselves and in others, acting upon their best instincts and impulses. This submerged fear inhibits the free flow of social and individual life. We shall never experience a sense of security, we shall never feel that we are really out of harm's way, until we learn to trust the human constitution at its best. We are the doomed victims of social despondency and despair until we learn the lesson of Jesus: That men are of more value than many sparrows, not one of which falleth without the knowledge of the Father.

The modern mind has not been able to retain a wholesome and sunny optimism. The sense of social insecurity has robbed us of it. The outlook for the future is that of great advance on the material and scientific side. But the modern mind is moody, at times almost morbid. Our spirit is caustic and sour, sometimes even callous and stale. The spiritual outlook is not bright because men in their many conflicting interests do not seem to understand each other. Our modern attempts at mutual understanding are pitiable. They hardly touch the surface of our social problems. Conferences result in compromises and concessions, but they end with the parties as far apart as ever in feeling and faith. Over the countenance of our modern civilization there comes now and then a touch of color that suggests the warmth of good will, but usually it turns out to be only the flush of the fever that is at work within us. Over our lips pass repeated expressions of confidence when all the while we are skeptical at heart. The prospect of the future is not sufficiently commanding to carry us through a painful present. We are guided by the considerations of caution, by the policies of prudence, rather than by the fundamental ends of human life. We have openly rejected the opulent optimism of Jesus according to which the future is good because it is God's. When Jesus says, "Why are ye fearful?" his words come down to us like a distant echo which we feel was not meant for our ears. We live in the world of fact and seldom rise to the higher realm of faith. Practical realism rather than religion is the source of our life-outlook. It is for this reason that our optimism, so sporadic in its appearance, is short-sighted and equally short-lived. It is not something with which we can confront the whole of life and bid defiance to all the conflicting elements of our experience. And it is for this reason, in turn, that modern man shows himself bankrupt of resources in coping with the great crises when they arise.

To accuse the modern mind of pretense in the hypocritical sense would be unfair, but we do succeed in deluding ourselves about ourselves. We are not frankly and fully what we think and feel. There are too many restraints of every kind. A great part of our thinking, feeling and faith comes to us by social inheritance and imitation. We hesitate to cross with established usage even when our best impulses are at work, even at stake.

We lead a restrained existence. We are held in by custom and convention, by what is expected of us, by considerations of propriety, culture and civilization. The modern social order and system is not hospitable to individual and group innovations; it is not friendly toward the introduction of those personal factors which might disturb and eventually improve it.

Much of our modern religion is self-delusion. The modern mind would resent a charge of irreligiousness, but much of our religiousness is only imaginary. Like certain psychopaths who suffer from imaginary health, we suffer from imaginary religion. The religion of the modern mind has not kept pace with our modern intellectual development. In form and content the modern notion of religion is often crude; often it hardly transcends *taboo*. So far as we are religious, we are overly self-conscious about it; we are constantly on our guard. Our religiousness often amounts to little more than a psychological complex. If it is touched upon in the way of criticism, even with the hope of improvement, we have a terrific discharge of zeal for the faith, a veritable deluge of religious prejudice. Seldom in our corporate life do we completely forget ourselves at the impulse of true religion; seldom are we so engrossed in doing the work of the world religiously that we forget ourselves and later wake up to the fact that we have been religious. And yet this is the very pulse of genuine human piety, the seat of its life. A social order in which men are not permitted to forget themselves may not be called religious in the sense of Jesus. Self-consciousness is fatal to all genuine piety. The forgetting of self, even the utter abandonment of self, is absolutely necessary to all religious experience, individual or group, that is to attain any degree of purity and power.

Such are the elemental foundation stones of religious experience: a native and natural simplicity that discovers the wonder in the world, an intense sensitivity and susceptibility to all that experience offers for apprehension and assimilation, a clear sense of dependence upon the Divine, an unreserved trust and confidence, a sense of absolute security, a wholesome optimism, a lack of pretense and self-consciousness. Whether the modern mind with its peculiar make-up and mood is disposed to accept or to reject this fundamental position concerning the relation of the child mind to real religiousness is a matter of no great importance as far as the truth of Jesus' position is concerned. It is not just the peculiar personal position of Jesus. The student of the history and psychology of religion knows as a matter of hard historical fact that this elemental approach and attitude toward the whole of life, which Jesus chose to illustrate in the child, is the one indispensable condition for the appearance of genuine religious experience. Religious biography teaches us that the more elemental the religious experience, the greater is its purity and power. However, the attitude of the modern mind toward this position is of greatest practical importance. If the modern mind chooses to reject a thing so elemental, it can not be religious in the sense of Jesus. And the psychology of religion will add that it can not otherwise be religious at all.[1]

---

[1] This demand of Jesus—*The Child Mind* presenting *Religion as Elemental Experience*—has its natural companion—*The Religious Reference* presenting *Religion as Social Experience*. This social demand of Jesus is reserved for special study. Cf. p. xi.

WESTERN CHRISTIANITY—THEORETICAL AND ACTUAL

Religion as Commanding Experience

Of recent years, particularly since the Western World has demonstrated that it is capable of sinning on such a tremendous scale, our Western Christianity has come in for a volume of criticism at the hands of the East, especially at the hand of Indians, for its deliberate departures from Jesus. The Indian mind with its rich religious genius has pointed out in no uncertain terms the great disparity between Western profession and Western practise. The Indian has gone even further. He sets our Western Christianity at a deep depreciation and at the same time feels a growing and gripping appreciation of Jesus that amounts often to a devoted discipleship.[2] The Indian mind is accomplishing "a dissociation of Jesus from the West." The Indian "is making a remarkable discovery, namely, that Christianity and Jesus are not the same—that they may have Jesus without the system that has been built up around him in the West . . . Christ without Western civilization."[3] From the Jewish angle, Rabbi Klausner, of Jerusalem, writes: "Christianity has stood for what is highest ethically and ideally, while the political and social life has remained at the other extreme of barbarity and paganism. . . . This can never be the case . . . where nation and belief are in-

---

[2] I have in mind particularly the criticisms of Gandhi and Sadhu Sundar Singh. An excellent book on this reaction of the Indian mind is that of E. Stanley Jones, *The Christ of the Indian Road. See also* the article by Professor Woodburne, "The Indian Appreciation of Jesus," *Journal of Religion*, VII (January, 1927).

[3] From, *The Christ of the Indian Road*, pp. 12f., 57. Copyrighted 1925, by E. Stanley Jones. Reprinted by permission of The Abingdon Press.

separable."[4]   And in our better moments, we of the West know that these observations from the East are words of wisdom. We of the West must confess that we have never pressed close to the heart of all that Jesus represents and can accomplish for our human life.

If we are conscientious and courageous enough to turn to an analysis of our Western Christianity and the various elements of its religious experience, we shall find that it has regressed into a religion of respectability. We are Christian by convention and confession, but we are not Christian either in character or in conduct, that is, if we understand Christianity as a reproduction of the personal piety of Jesus. In a sense, Christianity has been too successful in the West, for it has become the common convention of Western peoples to profess it. It is a tragic case of what were originally commanding elements of experience being forced into the theoretical background and left there entirely apart from the arena of actual life. This is always the danger that threatens a religion that in its essential substance represents a high order of values. The best that it offers is crystallized into convention and confession, and it ceases to create character and to control conduct. When a religion degenerates into a convention, it is dangerously near corruption; at least, it is rendered incompetent for the meeting of the vital problems of human life. The Western World is officially Christian, but in our character and conduct we cater to considerations of respectability rather than respond to the fresh and strong impulses inherent in our faith. Our Western Christianity is too comfortable in its religious conventions, too complacent in its religious confessions. The vigorous and vital elements of a relig-

---

[4] *Jesus of Nazareth*, by J. Klausner, p. 393. Courtesy of The Macmillan Company.

ious faith that is actually the commanding factor in the whole of an experience have gone out of it. Our religion takes on the form of theological theories rather than of a whole life-experience with a theocentric control. We are exceedingly zealous in keeping our Christianity theoretically pure, but in actual life our faith is powerless.

Our religious customs and conventions, creeds and confessions, have developed into a highly complicated and elaborate system, but religious experience wherever it is deeply serious is usually extremely simple. It furnishes a single center about which the rest of experience finds its natural but subordinate place. Our Western Christianity is not sufficiently simple to be deeply serious. We have forgotten, if we ever knew, that the pure and powerful religious spirit finds convention and confession poor conductors for the life-forces that it feels. The great prophets have always been men of simple spirit; their very simplicity has contributed to their greatness. They have always been the foes of conventional religion whether in the form of cult and ceremony or of creed and confession. All without exception have been sinners against religious conventions, not the least of whom was Jesus who went straight across some of the most sacred traditions of his people in response to the experience of God that commanded him. And Jesus demands of his disciples a courage that will break with any or all convention, no matter how firmly established or how long revered—a thing that our Western Christianity seems to fear most. Never was a more terrible indictment against a religion of respectability uttered than fell like a sharp shaft from the lips of Jesus,

"Verily I say unto you, that the publicans and the

harlots go into the kingdom of God before you."
(Matt 21,31b.)

The social successes of Christianity in the West, if we
may speak of such, have been sporadic and detached.
Now and again, a group will declare itself publicly for
the *Golden Rule* and actually conduct itself accordingly
in the settlement of any frictions. But the major phases
of our group life in the West have never been religious in
the sense and spirit of Jesus. From the standpoint of
its application to the great human problems of living together, the religion of Jesus is like certain rivers of his
own East that rise fresh and pure in the mountains, flow
with a rapid torrent down to the upper plains, rendering
fertile the neighboring districts, only when they reach
the dead level of the desert to seep out of sight in the
hot sands without ever reaching the great bodies where
the bulk of the world's life goes on. The Western World
has never even approached the higher ranges of religious
experience on the level of which, according to Jesus, the
whole of human life is to move. The social aspects of our
Western Christianity confine themselves to sentimentali-
ties. It has never gone further socially than a religion
of humanitarianism. When we do seek to find social
salvation we seldom get further than programs and propaganda, conferences and committees, surveys and statistics, methods and merely mechanical means. A social
salvation in the sense of creating group character and of
controlling group conduct Western Christianity has yet
to offer and to accomplish.

Our Western Christianity presents not more than a
pale semblance of all that Jesus represents in the way of
religion. In our Western experience of religion there is

little outside of the theoretical background that suggests the commanding elements of Jesus' personal religious experience. The distinctive things that made him as a religious personality have become for us mere matters of tradition. The Western Christian conscience has allowed itself to be persuaded of the impracticability and impossibility of Jesus' great goal for human life, and in this very retreat Western Christianity has surrendered what he held fast even at the price of life itself. The modern Christian attitude toward the distinctive elements of Jesus' faith may be characterized as Professor Hocking characterizes the popular attitude toward an "ideal": "Something which everybody is expected to honor and nobody is expected to attain."[5]

The religious positions of Jesus often conflict with our prejudices—religious, social, personal, intellectual—and the usual Christian attitude is: So much the worse for the positions of Jesus. This affront is not thought or uttered, but our actions disclose our attitude. This ignoring of Jesus' demands is due to the fact that we do not possess a religious experience that corresponds to his. What for him was actually commanding has become for us purely theoretical. We accept Jesus in theory, but we reject him in practise. Where he refused to concede we are content to compromise. We lack the courage necessary to conquest, the confidence necessary to conquer. We follow him afar off. We Westerners are denominational by conviction, Christian by confession, disciples of Jesus by convenience. At the hands of the Western World the person of Jesus has suffered that paradoxical fate of being deified and denied at the same time.

---

[5]*Human Nature and its Remaking,* p. ix.

The Western Christian experience of God is impoverished. The experience of God as high and holy lies in the remote background. It is not a commanding conviction that stands out clearly in the forefront of all that we seek to be and to do. Our modern reverence is theoretical rather than actual, impersonal rather than personal. The will-to-worship seems to have departed from us. Worship recalls men to the fundamental meanings of their existence and forces them in turn to face the tasks of life in the light of these meanings. Reverence for God, reverence for man as His creature, reverence for the whole of life as His gift, we do not seem to feel except in our better moments or at times of our more favorable experiences. Religious reverence does not stand out as a commanding attitude of the Western Christian mind, for we do not seem to approach the whole of our life as a sacred obligation of man to his Maker. In the major phases of our Western life we do not seem to think, to feel, to act or to live as in the presence always of a high and holy God.

There is no element in its religious thought that Western Christianity clings to more tenaciously than to the Fatherhood of God, which it ascribes, with all reverence, to Jesus as his great contribution. But this too has retreated into the background of our Western religious life. Jesus' experience of God as living and loving Father we affirm and accept but it is not a commanding conviction that we share. We seem unable to build it into our social structure as the basis of all human intercourse. The modern social order puts its own value on man, estimates his worth, but not from the religious point of view of Jesus according to which all men are His children. We judge men in the light of their backwardness or progress in culture, on the basis of their abilities and attainments, not in the light of their native attitudes and aspirations as potential sons of the Divine whether they are conscious of such or not. We judge men on the grounds of race, color and economic condition. We seem to have lost Jesus' scale of human values according to which even the least of humankind possesses infinite worth. Jesus' scale of human values is completely shattered by our modern social, racial, political and class strifes and hatreds.

The infinite worth of man Jesus set at the very foundation of all social structure, and this religious approach permits no social distinctions and discriminations. Jesus was never self-conscious in his contacts with any class of his contemporaries. He is with all and for all alike: rich and poor, scribe and Pharisee, lawyer and rabbi, publican and sinner, distressed and outcast, neglected and needy. Paul was never truer to the religious experience of his Master than when he wrote,

"There can be neither Jew nor Greek, there can be neither bond nor free, there can be no male and female; for ye are all one *man* in Christ Jesus." (Gal. 3,28.)

It was Jesus' experience of God as Father out of which the *Golden Rule* came,

"All things therefore whatsoever ye would that men should do unto you even so do ye also unto them." (Matt. 7,12.)

In this single sentence Jesus has set a social task that will tax the Christian world to the limit. It is the only solid

principle that will hold human contacts within bounds
and keep them wholesome.   But it is more than a moral
check, more than an ethical purgative.   It is the experience
of God as Father in action, aggressive because it feels
the initiative and impulse to good upon and within itself.
With this word Jesus breaks down the last restraint in
the way of the social will to goodness.   But it is only
another of those words of his that we admire and advocate but do not actually adopt.   As a principle of group
conduct it is already one of the hoary treasures in the
Christian scale of theoretical values, as promptly praised
as it is poorly practised.   Our enthusiasm for it exhausts
itself in praising the positive form given it by Jesus over
against the negative forms in other religions.   As an
ethical enterprise the *Golden Rule* has never appealed to
us.

Jesus' words on service and sacrifice as the only adequate spirit for the living of life have found great souls
who have been his true followers.   But our Christian
West lives its life with these maxims consigned to the
theoretical background.   In the major aspects of our
Western life a sense of mastery dominates over all sense
of ministry.   But in the religious experience of Jesus the
minister is the master (Mark 10,43-44),

"Whosoever would become great among you, shall
be your minister; and whosoever would be first among
you, shall be servant of all."

It was a commanding conviction that brought Jesus, not
to be ministered unto, but to minister.   (Mark 10,45a.)
But this word strikes us as another of those puzzling paradoxes that were intended to please rather than to be

practised. However, for Jesus, service and sacrifice are more than mere slogans and catch-words, pious preachments and lofty ideals; they are to be actual, unremittingly basal practises in our human life whether on a minor or on a major scale. The cross can never be removed from religious experience for it is an integral element in human life. The Christian world has yet to learn that the cross is more than a theological theory, a soteriological scheme, a salutary symbol. It has yet to learn that service and sacrifice are the only principles and practises that will enable men to live together on a religious basis commensurate with the pure spirit of Jesus.

The religious mind feels the need of divine forgiveness. For his shortcomings, failures and sins man feels that he can not make adequate atonement with his Maker. As a principle of personal piety, then, the forgiveness of sins springs from a sense of sheer desperation on the part of the religious consciousness. God *must* forgive, otherwise man is hopelessly lost. The forgiveness of sins was one of the pivotal points in Jesus' message of God as living and loving Father. In a parable like that of the prodigal son we see that he lays this divine disposition and this human quest at the very heart of man's relation to his Maker. Jesus himself assured penitent humans of the divine forgiveness. It is a cardinal petition in the great prayer which he gave his disciples. (Matt. 6,9-13.) The forgiveness of sins as the divine disposition toward men Western Christianity has preserved from Jesus. The Christian of the West has always felt that God not only must but does forgive, and this confidence has found expression in our Christian creeds.

But in the religious experience of Jesus the forgiveness of sins is something more than just the basis of the human hope for mercy from the Divine. It is more than a principle of personal piety; it is a social practise. And he even went so far as to base the divine forgiveness upon the human disposition to forgive:

"And forgive us our debts, as we also have forgiven our debtors. . . . For if ye forgive men their trespasses, your heavenly Father will also forgive you. But if ye forgive not men their trespasses, neither will your heavenly Father forgive your trespasses." (Matt. 6,12 14-15.)

Thus Jesus lays the forgiveness of sins as a foundation stone in the social order. But forgiveness as a principle and practise of social conduct in human relationships has followed the path of other commanding elements in the religious experience of Jesus: It has its honored place in the gallery of theoretical Christian values. As a principle and practise of men living together as groups it has never been able to command our Western conduct. We seem never to have thought of carrying it over into the major phases of our complex civilization and culture. The West, Christian by confession, is commanded by the disposition to retaliate, to recompense in kind, to require reparations, and to mete out revenge rather than to forgive the sins of brothers and enemies.

At this point our Western Christian conscience has become corrupt, for we have surrendered a principle and practise of Jesus. We admire its sublime idealism and implications, but we are convinced of its impracticability, even of its impossibility for us. In reality, it is one of the greatest of Jesus' contributions to the universal human problem of living together. We possess sufficient religious intelligence to know that forgiveness as a social practise is not a weakness but requires a superb moral strength. We hesitate, however, to trust the forgiven. But according to Jesus, forgiveness human and divine does not cancel responsibility for rigid moral character and conduct. Forgiveness in the religious life of Jesus was a moral force, an ethical power, for the reconstruction of life even from the most shattered materials. This applies to the forgiver as well as to the forgiven. It means a restoration of social faith and feeling in harmony with the spirit of forgiveness. In his demand for forgiveness as a social principle and practise we see how hard and heavy are the demands which Jesus places upon his followers and what a wide gap yawns between his religious experience and ours.

At the very heart of Jesus' feeling and faith we found the kingdom of God, but this great object of his personal religious aspiration does not survive in our Western Christianity save as a pious phrase or in the diluted form of the church as the kingdom. What it meant for Jesus and what he meant by it, it no longer means for us. It strikes our Western Christian conscience as too Utopian. For Jesus, however, it was not just an alluring adventure but the goal of all human life that wills to make itself worthy. It too has found its way into the theoretical background of our Western Christian thought. It is one of those many impersonal beliefs that we hold, but as a conviction that would alter our social character and conduct it is lost to us. Slowly but surely, Western Christianity has relinquished its hold upon history. We lack the stamina of soul, the constitutional courage necessary for an organized human life on the scale and in the spirit of the kingdom of God. A Christianity that does not take seriously the faith, hope and expectation of a higher and better order of life for all men everywhere does not merit the name it bears.

The pride of the West has been its culture and civilization, and Christianity has come in for its share of credit in this production. The West is quite satisfied with its Christianity, but there are elements in the religious outlook of Jesus that it fears because they seem opposed to cultural progress. But there is nothing in the religion of Jesus that conflicts essentially with true culture and civilization. The best forces for such progress come from Jesus himself. But certain elements in our modern life can not hope to escape his sharpest criticism and condemnation. He gives us no philosophy of civilization, but he does give us a religion for the living of life. Culture and civilization must have religious goals and ends. Progress must mean purification and perfection of human life as well as increase of knowledge and means of material existence. Renaissance must mean more than intellectual illumination; it must have its religious significance, resulting in a recovery of man's moral sense and a regeneration of his ethical power. Religion is always conditioned by the state of culture and civilization in which it appears, but in its best form it must be the commanding element that gives a culture and civilization its distinctive character.

The kingdom of God in the experience of Jesus means all that is highest and best for humankind; thus it carries with it its own cultural implications. The work of the world lies at the very heart of his religious faith and is its immediate task. Religion in the experience of Jesus does not withdraw its best from the world, but the human problem of living together is the very field in which religion is to make its greatest contribution. And it requires no great power of insight to discover any disharmony between our social situations and the religious ideals and demands of Jesus. Christianity has been a very powerful force for culture in the West, but it has not yet pressed its way into the controlling centers of the Western group mind. Organized Christianity has been on the throne in the West but it has misunderstood its task as temporal power. It has as yet never been able to sink the best of its genius into the national and economic mind of the West and produce peoples that are Christian in their national and economic life. Jesus, like Isaiah before him, would look upon political prudence and intrigue, upon economic exploitation in the East or West, not only as a breach of faith with man but as a break of faith in God.

The greatest weakness of our Western World is the complete lack, in the major phases of its life, of any clear consciousness of call and commission higher than the demands of culture and civilization. We seem to have lost all sense for the more ideal things of religion, according to which whole peoples seek to know and to perform the divine will in every phase of their life. Individuals and groups, peoples and states, cultures and civilizations, must possess a consciousness of high call and holy commission to a complete cooperation with the Divine. Our modern social problem in the West is really religious rather than economic, political and so forth. For us, it is not a question of what religion, but the question of building the best of our religion into the very nerve and fiber of our Western life. Apart from the highest religious aims and aspirations there is no hope of a secure social structure. We have yet to learn that a sense of responsibility to men must grow out of a sense of responsibility to God. Our social successes in the future will depend upon our ability to make this religious reference and to apply it to every aspect of our group life.

The Christian West possesses only a fractional faith. It touches portions of our life, but it is not strong enough to command the whole. Our Western faith is trivial rather than triumphant; it will not meet the pressures of our Western life. It fails to function in time of crisis, nor will it bear up under the strain of routine. Our Christian West lives along its make-shift existence, trusting in practically everything except the truths that Jesus lived by. Jesus committed himself to a very different order of values from that to which we trust our fates and fortunes. We trust to power, prestige and profit, the very things which he declared, and which history has showed to be, perishable and perilous. We have not yet learned what religious faith is, and yet Jesus declared it to be the greatest power accessible to human experience. Faith is more than something that we hold; it lays hold on us. It is not just something that we entertain; it is something that enlists us wholly in its service. It is in the power of a religious faith to make and remake men, individually and collectively, that the grounds of its validity must be sought. If Christianity is to assert itself socially in the West, it must mean the redemption, recovery and restoration of our group life. In the words of Jesus we are a "faithless generation." We suffer from a shortage of spiritual life in our group issues. In our pride of physical strength we are struck suddenly sick at heart, and in time of crisis show ourselves utterly bankrupt of religious resources.

The pressure which Jesus puts upon his followers is

tremendous. To live the whole of our life with the religious reference seems a task far beyond our poor powers, yet it stands as his unremitting requirement. His social message is not an elaborate discourse that digresses into all the channels through which our group life flows. His answer to the social question is simply the religious reference for the whole of human life. The religious interest must command us completely; there is no other secure and safe approach to our social frictions and strifes. A civilization and culture like ours that does not set the best of its religious values at the very center of its hope for the future, be it immediate or remote, that does not feel them as the commanding elements in its group experience, and that does not sense the tremendous moral pressure which these religious values bring to bear upon group character and conduct in the present, can not be regarded as belonging in any real sense to the discipleship of Jesus. Western Christendom has yet to learn the elementary things of its professed religion.

Conventional and confessional Christianity in the West has failed as a social religion because it has been little more than a religion of convention and confession. Christianity in the West must come to a new and fresh understanding of itself and its task. In its fear for its preserved purity it has lost its power. We very devoutly worship Jesus, yet we are not disposed to work with him. We deify him rather than commit ourselves to his discipleship. The religion of the future in the West will not be a new religion, but a new and fresh devotion. It must be the religion of Jesus, and the essence of a religion that names itself after him must be devoted, undivided discipleship. Any deviation from this clear construction is a departure from the plainest and most staggering of all Jesus' demands, "Follow me."

DISCIPLESHIP

Religion as Participative Experience

The Christian religion from the very outset has been Christocentric; all of its thought, feeling and faith has focused upon the person of Jesus as the one great center of loyalty. The conception of Jesus' person has been the touchstone of orthodoxy and has formulated the articles of the Christian creeds. Any doubt carries with it the brand of heretic and unbeliever. Historical Christianity has always been sure as to who Jesus was and has made corresponding demands upon its adherents. Thus historical Christianity has demanded first of all the sharing of *a faith about Jesus* rather than a sharing of *Jesus' own personal faith.*

The student of the life of Jesus is keenly conscious of the fact that there is a very definite disparity between the demands of historical Christianity and the demands which the historical Jesus made upon his own personal followers. This disparity is not to be stated in any abstract theological phraseology but in the simple language of the psychology of religious experience. It is the disparity that exists between religious object and religious subject, between the object believed in and the believer, the extreme opposites in religious experience. For historical Christianity, Jesus has always been a religious object, even in the absolute sense, but for the historical student, Jesus of Nazareth was a religious subject on the basis of the best New Testament sources.

In the first three Gospels Jesus never presents himself as a religious object. He speaks and acts with authority; he issues his commands and makes his demands upon his followers; he calls and rejects, but all that he says and does and is, is always at the high call and holy commission of Another. Rather than being a religious object, the Jesus of the first three Gospels has his religious objects to which he devotes himself with the whole of his exclusively religious consciousness. Rather than setting his own person as an object of belief, Jesus himself is the great believer. There is just one great religious object in his experience, God the Father whose kingdom will come. He never ascribes to himself divine prerogatives. His cures are not his own; it is by the Spirit of God that he casts out demons and heals the afflicted. (Matt. 12, 28.) The kingdom which he announces is not his own; it is God's, and will come when God wills. In every aspect of his personality and work Jesus remains rigidly religious. Not once does his thought of and for himself transcend the limitations of the pure religious consciousness. Even when his thought rises to the exalted heights of the Messianic dignity, he remains religious: He is or is to be the Messiah according as the Divine wills.

There is one aspect of Jesus' work which some scholars of strong theological disposition regard as a clear instance of his transcending the limitations of the human consciousness: His assurance of forgiveness to penitent persons. It is true that Jesus announced the divine forgiveness of sins. It was a fundamental theme in his thought of God and he did not hesitate to assure it to particular persons such as the paralytic (Mark 2,1-12) and the penitent woman in the house of Simon (Luke 7,36-50). However, Jesus is not himself forgiving sins in the sense that God alone can forgive. In a contention on this very theme such as we have in Mark 2,1-12 it is clear that he is not ascribing to himself the divine prerogative. Jesus himself says that his word, "Thy sins are forgiven," is synonymous with, "Arise, and take up thy bed, and walk." And the incident closes with public attention centered upon the cure rather than upon the contention. (Mark 2,12.) The general public present feels that it has witnessed a mighty deed of a prophet of God and there is no hint to the effect that it has to do with a blasphemer. Jesus is never approached by any one with the request for the forgiveness of sins. He does not forgive sin, but assures penitent sinners of the divine forgiveness. It is to God alone that men are to pray for the forgiveness of sins:

"God, be thou merciful to me a sinner" (Luke 18, 13);
"Forgive us our debts" (Matt. 6,12).

In the first three Gospels Jesus never sets himself among the objects which he presents to his disciples and to his contemporaries for religious devotion. He never demands that others believe *in* or *on* him. There is only one passage in the first three Gospels in which he is represented as requiring belief in himself, and this is a very clear Christianization:

"And whosoever shall cause one of these little ones that believe on me to stumble, it were better for him if a great millstone were hanged about his neck, and he were cast into the sea."[6]

---

[6]Mark 9,42. In some of the best manuscripts of this Markan passage the phrase *on me* is not found. *See* Matthew's parallel: 18,6.

This passage is an extract from the religious experience of the earliest Christians and is quite foreign to the religious experience of Jesus. It is only in the Fourth Gospel that Jesus is represented as regularly requiring belief in himself.[7] In the first three Gospels there is not a genuine passage in which he demands faith in himself in the sense that he demands faith in God. He cured only in the presence of a warm personal confidence in his ability to help and to heal, but never once does he set himself as an object of religious devotion. The whole theme of his message from beginning to end is,

"Have faith in God." (Mark 11,22.)

The strict Jewish monotheism that was nerve and fiber of Jesus' experience of God would make it impossible for him to set himself as a religious object. Apart from this monotheistic background that is always clear and distinct in the Gospel picture, there is not a single element in his own personal experience of religion that would suggest an exaltation of his own person for religious devotion. As Professor Wernle writes: "Of no man did Jesus require a belief in his own Messianic dignity as a condition for entrance into the kingdom of God, to say nothing of his having thought that belief in his Messiahship could in any way be a substitute for faith in God and love of men."[8]

In all the debates that historical Christianity has waged on the humanity of Jesus the heart of the issue has been neglected. The principal question is not whether Jesus' words and attitudes at any particular points transcend

---

[7]Cf. John 6,35; 7,38; 11,25-26; 12,44 46; 14,12.
[8]*Jesus*, p. 192*f*.

the limitations of human consciousness. The human consciousness is of such varied forms and manifold content that it becomes a purely relative term dependent upon the stage of its development. In form, the human consciousness may be high or low; in content, it may be rich or deeply impoverished. At the beginning of chapter three, we sought to show that Jesus was conscious of genuine human limitations—limitations of knowledge, power and personal worth which appear in the religious consciousness in its highest forms and in its richest content. The principal question on the humanity of Jesus is better framed: Does he at any point in word, deed or attitude transcend the limitations of the genuinely religious consciousness? And on the basis of the first three Gospels themselves the historical student must answer in the negative.

Not for a moment does Jesus cease to be really religious, and from the historical and psychological point of view, it is impossible that he presented himself as a religious object. All the way through our study down to this point we have seen that he is a religious subject, consciously an experient of religion. He is a man of religious faith; he believes in God and His kingdom, which faith calls forth all the corresponding emotions. His self-consciousness is exclusively religious, in attitude, aspiration and expression. For Jesus to have presented himself as a religious object, when in reality he was a religious subject, would involve a contradiction of the religious consciousness that is impossible on a basis of psychic health. The idea that he presented himself as an object of religious devotion is a psychological impossibility.

Historical Christianity has held both to the deity and

to the humanity of Jesus, a paradox that is possible in religious faith but quite out of the question as historical and psychological fact. The church has been able to maintain this paradox because it ascribed to Jesus a theoretical rather than an actual humanity. But when we come to confront the first three Gospels and their picture with the question: Religious object or religious subject? then there is but one answer from the historical point of view. The man who prayed to God as Jesus prayed can never have regarded himself or have presented himself as a religious object. As Professor Mundle writes: "If we turn our attention to the question as to how the Christ, with whom faith has to do, and the Jesus of history, the object of historical research, are related to each other, we shall have to say that the historical Jesus was never an object of religious faith and by his very nature could not be."[9]

Many protests have been made against the distinction between the Jesus of history and the Christ of faith, but it is more certain to-day than ever before that the two belong to very different realms of experience and that they may not be identified in the historical sense. The Jesus of history was a religious subject; the Christ of faith has never been other than a religious object. The one is a fact of our human history; the other is the creation of an enthusiastic faith. The personal religious experience of Jesus is different both in form and content from the religious experience of the first Christians. In form, the religious experience of Jesus is *theocentric*: All that he thought and felt and believed in the way of religion centered upon God and His kingdom. In content, his relig-

---

[9]"Der Christus des Glaubens und der historische Jesus," *Zeitschrift fuer Theologie und Kirche* (1921), p. 212.

ious experience includes just a single object of worship, the high and holy God of Israel who is also living and loving Father. In form, the religious experience of the earliest Christians was *Christocentric*: The whole of their hope of salvation was connected solely with the person and work of Jesus. In content, their religious experience permitted the appearance of a second religious object; along with God the heavenly Christ takes his place as an object of devotion on a plane with God Himself. This is especially clear in the vision of Stephen,

> "Behold, I see the heavens opened, and the Son of man standing on the right hand of God." (Acts 7,56.)

In such a religious experience a human historical figure has become completely deified.

As one moves from the simpler experience of Jesus to the more involved experience of the earliest Christians there is evident a great development, even more, a total transformation. In the experience of the earliest Christians Jesus became something wholly other and different than he was for himself in his own personal experience. In the religious experience of Jesus we find only the Father-God, but in the early Christian community the Son takes his place alongside the Father as equally worthy of religious devotion and worship.

Upon the historical appearance of Jesus Christian thought has erected a whole scheme of salvation. His human life was only an incarnation, an episode in finite existence, merely a single scene in the great divine drama that moved toward the redemption of men. About his person great systems of thought have formed, all shadowy tributes to his religious greatness. With none of these theories does the historical student have any quarrel. They are, for the most part, genuine reactions of genuine religious faith to all that it has been able to find in him. The most orthodox person can not find greater religious significance in Jesus than the historical student finds. No Christian of history accepts the religious significance of Jesus with readier heart than the modern historical disciple, and he feels that he is nearer Jesus and what he meant that his followers should be than any generation of Christians since his death. But the historical student will not locate this religious significance in the weird web of theology that has obscured the real Jesus from our sight. He will find that he can state his experience of Jesus in much simpler language than has been able to satisfy Christian thought in the past. He feels that the church has never esteemed its Lord too highly, but he does feel that the church has made of Jesus something that he never was as a matter of historical fact and that in the process the church has turned a deaf ear to his call to discipleship. The historical student feels that the religion of Jesus requires more than the adoration of his person. He feels that for the church Jesus has become a highly idealized and theoretical figure and that his greatest contribution to mankind, his religious experience, has been almost wholly ignored and neglected.

For Jesus, as for us, religion was not a divine scheme but a human problem, a problem which he faced and sought to solve for himself in the light of all that he could learn to know of God and with the full earnestness of his soul. He never sets his own person at the center of a system of salvation. He speaks out of the highest personal and prophetic conviction:

"Verily I say unto you, This generation shall not pass away, until all these things be accomplished. Heaven and earth shall pass away: but my words shall not pass away." (Mark 13,30-31.)

But he never attaches the religious hopes of mankind exclusively to his own person. He never set himself as the sole mediator between God and man as Christianity of the absolute type has done. In his presentation of the religious relationship of man to his Maker there was no mediator, for there was no need of such. In the experience of Jesus the way between God and man is cleared. In a parable like that of the prodigal son (Luke 15,11-32) we see how simply he conceived of man's relation to his Maker—the repentance and return of wayward children to a loving and forgiving Father.

The cross of Jesus has almost broken down under the weight of the theories of atonement that have been heaped upon it. But Jesus himself attached no expiatory or propitiatory significance to his death; he fitted it into no scheme of salvation. The cross was his own personal religious problem which he solved in the light of the divine will for himself. God in his experience needed no objective atonement: He seeks only a simple and whole-hearted obedience. In his thought the religious redemption of men is exceedingly simple. It is a direct drive to the heart of the loving Father who forgives because He loves.

The Christological speculations that have dominated Christian thought and Christianity's understanding of itself and its task have no counterpart in the thought of Jesus—the relation of Son to Father, of Father to Son, of the two natures, the unity of the trinity, and the trinity of the unity. There is nothing theological or theoretical in his thought of himself. His relation to the Father is simply and plainly religious, the difficult matter of learning and performing the divine will. The church has never permitted any skepticism on this point of Jesus' identity. But on this point of such dogmatic certainty in Christian experience Jesus himself was silent. From Jesus himself in the first three Gospels we have not a single unequivocal statement; and what and how he esteemed himself remains hidden for ever in the inner recesses of his own soul. But it is certain that his thought was never egocentric, that he never conceived of a religion that hinged wholly and solely upon theoretical conceptions of his person, their acceptance or rejection.

The fact that Jesus has so little to say of himself constitutes one of the most hopeless problems in the history of the life-of-Jesus research. His own person he neglects to discuss; never once in his public message does it come to the forefront, where it has always been in Christian thought and faith. It is with the kingdom of God that he connects the religious hopes of the future. He is not consumed with the thought of himself but with the great cause of God which he champions even to the cross. His own person he relegates to that dim background where it never comes to light except as it can serve and sacrifice for God's kingdom. His own personal fates and fortunes never once alter the essential content of his message; from first to last, the kingdom is everything. It has claimed him for its very own to do as it wills. By it he is carried far out beyond any thought of himself. He sets no Christological confessions as necessary conditions for participation in the kingdom. He even warns his

disciples against a too exclusive attachment to his person
as a dangerous self-delusion:

"Not every one that saith unto me, Lord, Lord,
shall enter into the kingdom of heaven; but he that
doeth the will of my Father who is in heaven. Many
will say to me in that day, Lord, Lord, did we not
prophesy by thy name, and by thy name cast out
demons, and by thy name do many mighty works?
And then will I profess unto them, I never knew you:
depart from me, ye that work iniquity."   (Matt. 7,21-
23.)

And a modern Christianity that interprets its experience
and its task solely in the light of orthodox conceptions
and confessions concerning Jesus' person is treading upon
treacherous ground.

When Jesus comes to speak of those things which
matter most in the sight of God, he always speaks in
terms of the divine will, never in terms of the acceptance
or rejection of his person. Entrance into the kingdom
he makes absolutely dependent upon the performance of
the divine will which he presents in the simple but difficult terms of rigid ethical character and moral conduct.
The great question which historical Christianity has set
before the world is: What think ye of the Christ? But
the questions which arise out of the religious message
and experience of Jesus are of quite a different order.
What think you of God and His kingdom? Is God your
Father? Are you His children? Do you perform the
Father's will? Such questions can not be answered in
abstract theological terms, for they are the pressing
problems of a practical and living piety with which Jesus

confronts his followers. Each must answer them for himself. Organized Christianity can not answer them for him nor keep him from answering them for himself. The follower of Jesus can not answer them in the terms of doctrine and dogma, creed and confession, officialism and orthodoxy; all such is too impersonal.

Jesus did not demand that his followers believe *in* or *on* him, but that they believe *with* him. To be sure, the command, "Believe with me," is not to be found in his words. Nevertheless, it is the undertone and import of everything that he has to say, whether in public or in private. The great prophet of religion has but one thing in mind in delivering his great message: That his hearers may share the faith that possesses him. Sharing belongs to the very genius of religious faith. Religion is not so much a process of teaching and learning; it is rather a process of communication and impartation. It is less the mastery of a subject-matter, more the sharing of a spirit. The whole inclination and disposition of Jesus was to share what he himself had sensed, sought and secured as permanent religious values. He sought to share his faith in God as living and loving Father, his faith in His kingdom, in short, the whole of his experience of God and His meaning in human life and history.

The religious faith of Jesus does not come down to us in the impersonal terms of doctrine and dogma, creed and confession. It comes to us in the intensely personal terms of fears and hopes, apprehensions and aspirations, fundamental life-convictions and certainties, utter consecrations and commitments of self. Too often historical Christianity has sought to indoctrinate and dominate rather than to impart and communicate. In this conception of itself and its task historical Christianity has

made a wide departure from the religion and spirit of
Jesus, who had no such impersonal methods and programs.   He trusted himself and his cause to deeper
forces—to the ignition of interests, the firing of faith,
the contagion of convictions which result in corresponding character and conduct.   Such are the sources and
sorts of spiritual stimulus to which he committed himself
entirely.

Jesus not only challenged his followers to believe *what*
he believed but to believe *as* he believed.   They must
share the manner as well as the matter of his faith.   The
religious faith of Jesus is a personal passion that consumes him entirely.   However, it is not a source of nar-
rowness and dogmatism.   He formulates no statements
for repetition but he demands a consecration, a launching
of the whole life in the implications of a deep experience
of God that sets all else at stake.   Religious faith in his
experience is something that calls and claims, something
to which men commit themselves, which commands them
and in the service of which they are ready to consume
themselves.   In this respect Jesus' religious demands are
wholly unconventional, but they are absolutely uncompromising.   He demands that faith possess a fervor that
is sufficiently strong to make it commanding.   Faith must
be with feeling, only thus can it come into its own as a
source of enthusiasm and energy that men actually live
by.   In the religious experience of Jesus faith becomes a
life-enterprise, and he demands that it be just such for
his followers.

Such are the religious demands of the historical Jesus.
But, as Albert Schweitzer says, modern Christianity fears
the *all-too-historical* Jesus for he registers a condemna-

tion unpleasant to the comfortable modern view which Christianity entertains of itself and its task in the world. Historical study makes Jesus too enthusiastic and entirely too confident for modern Christianity to feel at ease and still profess discipleship. It reminds modern Christianity of its losses and relapses from *the religion of Jesus*. It is much more comfortable to confess *a religion about Jesus* than it is to strive to live *the religion of Jesus* after him. The *Apostles' Creed* is easily repeated, but to believe *what* Jesus believed and to believe *as* he believed is a very different matter. To believe that God is a living and loving Father, that all men are His children, that God has a kingdom, that it can and will come, and that soon, and to devote the whole of human life, personal and social, to preparation for its coming to the extent of exhausting life itself in the kingdom's service, is a difficult religious task. But just such is *the religious experience of Jesus,* and over against its richness and reality our modern Christian experience appears as woefully impoverished and unreal. The things that were commanding for him are not commanding for us as he meant that they should be. To seek to share an appreciable measure of the religious experience of Jesus is the great task of his followers.

There is just one great demand of Jesus: "Follow me." It is the only command he ever gave a disciple. This simple command springs from a depth of religious conviction and certainty that is amazing. Such could be born only of a tremendous confidence in his experience of God as valid and wholly true. Such a command can come only from a religious personality that is entirely sure of itself. The very ease with which this simple command is comprehended is deceptive. It is at once clear

even to the plainest intelligence, but it lays the heaviest
of demands upon the moral will of the individual and the
group. In such a simple statement Jesus loads human
loyalty to the limit. The simple way of Jesus is not
smooth; it is straight and narrow; few are they that find
it and still fewer they that enter in thereat. (Matt. 7,14;
Luke 13, 24.) The yoke which Jesus places upon his disciples is not easy; his burden is not light. It is easy
enough to dogmatize about the morals, ethics and religious teachings of Jesus, as has become our Christian habit.
It is easy because all generalizations are easy. Generalizations involve capacity for conception of ideals, even
conviction concerning their truth. But to try to live the
religion of Jesus after him, to clothe it with our contemporary human flesh is a very different and difficult matter.
We possess the enthusiasm that will praise but hardly the
energy that will enable us to practise. The task which
Jesus places upon his disciples takes all the exaggeration
and hyperbole out of a passage like Mark 10,25 :

"It is easier for a camel to go through a needle's
eye, than for a rich man to enter into the kingdom
of God."

It is not surprising that his disciples replied,

"Then who can be saved?"   (Mark 10,26.)

Thus Jesus has greatly simplified our understanding
of religion. The religious life is simple and single. It
presents its difficulties, not to the intelligence, but to the
moral will. In his simplification he has rendered religious living infinitely more difficult. Religion must build

itself into the very structure of individual and group life.

Creed and confession will not bring us into the faithful following of Jesus, for it is in the moral field of character and conduct that genuine religious experience seeks and finds its natural expression. If, in our own day, in the midst of conflicts between fundamentalism and modernism, between evolution and anti-evolution, we could learn that first lesson in the following of Jesus and take the first feeble steps in that direction, our religious life would be infinitely enriched and we would experience a fresh burst of religious energy.

Religion is not a matter of views that are piously phrased and that are accepted and entertained unquestioned and unchanged. Genuine religious experience casts no conscious thought in the direction of its departures from the past; it takes no pride in its loyalty to what has been. Wherever vital and genuine, it is simply and wholly itself, equally indifferent toward any newness and oldness that it may represent. It prides itself neither in its orthodoxy nor in its originality because it is never self-conscious enough to turn to such an analysis.

The religious experience of Jesus demands more than recognition, respect and reverence. It is something that by its very nature and genius demands reproduction. And his true follower will be less inclined toward interpretation, more disposed toward imitation. Jesus called men to be his followers; workers with him, not worshipers of him; sharers in a life of service and sacrifice; contagious centers of conviction concerning God and His cause among men, not confessors of creed; sources of spiritual stimulation and inspiration; dispensers of the great good-news, not defenders of doctrine and dogma; agents of a Will that is high and holy, living and loving;

heralds of hope and helpfulness, not hounds of heresy; organs opposing oppression and opening up the clogged sources of optimism, not organs of officialism and orthodoxy; disciples of his in devotion to God and men, not deifiers of his person; champions of the divine cause, not police of the purity of religious opinions.

If we survey carefully the goals and objectives for attainment which Jesus set before his disciples, we find that they are exclusively religious. He throws men into the midst of a theocentric existence: God is to command every center of human activity and interest. It is for God alone that men and their brothers exist. Thus Jesus strips the religious life of all its adornments and accretions. He lays bare the very heart of the whole matter. At the center of life, personal and social, he anchored a commanding experience of God that has its natural issue in corresponding character and conduct. Religious faith he charges with a warmth of feeling that results in the launching of the whole of life in the quest of the divine will.

In Jesus' religious demands we strike upon the prophetic genius for concentration and compactness. Amid a multitudinous variety he singles out the one or two major matters. He accomplishes a radical reduction in religious requirements. His demands are the simplest and plainest, yet the highest and the most difficult of performance. He brought about a radical revaluation of all religious values: The last shall be first, the first last; the least shall be great, the great least.

For Jesus the demands of religion are as various and uncertain as the demands of life itself. The most pressing demands upon one disciple may never even face his nearest neighbor. Each individual and age must meet its own problems in its own way, but always at the dictates of a commanding experience of God. Religious living in our human world can demand the greatest variety of conduct in concrete instances: Now it may be a cup of cold water, again help to a sufferer, still again the forgiving of one's brothers, the overcoming of evil, or the triumph over temptation, whether in individual experience or in the major phases of the world's life as a whole. Reverence toward God and righteousness toward man as the poles of individual and group experience of religion constitute the inexhaustible program of Jesus. This is infinitely removed from immediate realization, but it furnishes us a task both for to-day and for to-morrow.

Jesus calls men to be his coreligionists, to be sharers of his faith, his fellow-crusaders in the quest of God's great kingdom.

CHAPTER V

The Religious Authority of Jesus

Jesus is the most puzzling and paradoxical personality of our human history. Although the peculiar character of his genius made him a son of the East, it is in the West that his person has had its strange fates and fortunes. Jesus has had a double history: on the one hand, the plain prosaic career of the prophet-preacher of Galilee; on the other hand, the triumphant Son of God to whom the Western World has attached its religious hopes. The Jesus of history was a genuine child of the Jewish people with the blood of ancient Syria in his veins, but in the faith of his followers he became Westernized. The Christ of faith, body and soul, is the product of Western piety. Christianity had its birth in the homeland of Jesus, but the very disposition to see in him a religious object is Greek rather than Galilean. The Christ of faith was girded for a career in the world on Greek soil and was clothed in full splendor by the Greek intellect and imagination. Even Paul was more Greek than Jew in his conception of the person of Christ. The history of Christianity is simply the story of the gradual suppression of Galilee by Greece. Galilee has never been much more than the scene of a pleasant pastoral idyl, a sort of soothing prologue that failed to set the theme for the great drama that was enacted in the West.

GALILEE AND GREECE

From one point of view, it seems strange that Jesus should be reckoned among the great. Judged by the

271

outward phases of his life and work, there is nothing specially striking or remarkable in his historical appearance. He lived his life to the early maturity of the East in the little village of Nazareth of Galilee without leaving upon the village folk the impression either of growing wisdom or of promising personal powers. He left private life for engagement in his public work,

> "In the fifteenth year of the reign of Tiberius Cæsar, Pontius Pilate being governor of Judea, and Herod being tetrarch of Galilee, and his brother Philip tetrarch of the region of Iturea and Trachonitis, and Lysanias tetrarch of Abilene, in the highpriesthood of Annas and Caiaphas." (Luke 3,1-2a.)

Such is the most elaborate historical setting which one of the few records that have come down to us gives for his public life and work.

Jesus' public work confined itself to his own native land, a small and remote province of the Roman Empire. He never came into contact with the life of the world at large as did his great protagonist, Paul. He attracted little or no attention in the world of his day and was practically unknown beyond the borders of Galilee prior to the last week of his life. Contemporary Roman and Jewish historians accord him at best not more than sporadic, usually doubtful mentions of his name. What we know of him in the way of literary records was produced and preserved by his followers.

Jesus died a young man, probably not more than thirty years of age. He did not have a long, but an abruptly short career, probably a few months in length. Approximately the last year of his life he spent in public.

Although he confined his work to his own people, he did not win them to his cause and he came to influence but few of his contemporaries. His work in the capital of his nation was brought to a tragic end within the space of a week. He did not die, as other great men have, with his followers numbering thousands, hundreds or even scores. His personally chosen circle of companions fled from the scene of his arrest after one of the trusted twelve had betrayed him into the hands of his enemies. Only a few faithful women from among his following witnessed his death and burial.

Such are the prosaic aspects of Jesus' historical appearance. Yet from another and more familiar point of view, the fates and fortunes of the person of no man are comparable to those of the person of Jesus, nor has the influence of any man on our Western life been so imposing and ineradicable. "Jesus lives in humanity to an extent and in a way never experienced by any other human being."[1] In the history of Christianity, at some time or other, there has not been a major concern of man's life, hardly a minor concern, whether joyous or sorrowful, hopeful or full of fear, that has not been attended by sincere invocations through and to him.[2] Over against the prosaic features of Jesus' historical appearance stands an ancient and triumphant religious faith that attaches itself to him and of which he was at once the object, a faith that, paradoxically enough, produced and preserved this prosaic account in which it felt itself enriched and which in turn it enhanced.

The figure of the Nazarene has always had about it a peculiar and invincible fascination that has increased

---

[1]Loisy, *The Gospel and the Church*, p. 125.
[2]*See* Heiler, *Der Katholizismus*, pp. 161-236.

rather than diminished with the passing of even long periods of time. Through nineteen centuries Jesus has been the source of a strange stimulation for the religious imagination, one of the most potent factors in the life of individuals and institutions. To the ever-growing portrait of Jesus each people that has accepted Christianity has contributed of its native genius. Each has offered tribute of its best talent—art, poetry, music, philosophy, even mythology. About his head each has cast its own glorious halo and crown, the last more splendid than the rest.

The historical expressions of Christian experience are most multiform and of infinite variety. Every principal phenomenon known in the history of religion, primitive or cultured, has appeared in Christian worship. A great, highly-organized and powerful institution claims Jesus for its very own, as its founder and perfecter, and it feels itself commissioned by him as the guardian of his cause and faith. There are signs, symbols, images, formulas, prayers, incantations, liturgies, benedictions, consecrations, celebrations, mysteries, sacraments, sacred rites, rituals, confessions, creeds, high services, holy performances, hymns, rhythmic chants, offerings, contributions, whole calendars of feast and holy days—all in the name, honor and worship of Jesus. All constitute a tremendous tribute to him and originally all were endowed with the most treasured sentiments and emotions of the Christian consciousness. Yet the whole array presents an elaborate system of religious worship, whether Catholic or Protestant, quite far removed from the simple scenes in the Galilean synagogues, quite unlike the prophet of the kingdom of God who preached on the mountain, by the countryside, from fishing boats, in village streets and marketplaces, and who himself sought out the silence and seclusion of the desert solitude to pray to his God. When one reads the simple New Testament story of Jesus and then surveys simply the objective side of Christianity's history and development, the very proportions of the final issue are almost inconceivable. A Galilean witness of Jesus' ministry could not believe his eyes if he were permitted to see.

If we turn to the subjective side of Christianity's history, to the development of its mind and faith, the outcome is even more amazing. "Christianity has had a history as has no other religion."[3] At a surprisingly early date it won its way as the official religion of the Western World. In the course of its triumphant march from East to West it wrought radical changes and made remarkable contributions to the life of whole nations and peoples. But Christianity did not emerge from this process unscathed, and the changes wrought in itself are quite as radical and remarkable as those it was able to effect. In its history, early and late, the Christian faith has gone through various developments, transitions, alterations, eliminations, additions, accretions, outgrowths, aftergrowths and overgrowths which separate and distinguish it very clearly from the simple yet profound faith that possessed the soul of Jesus.

The person of Jesus became the perennial source of speculation wherever Christianity struck permanent root. About his person there evolved great systems of thought, elaborate and intricate structures of belief, theologies and Christologies, schemes of salvation, doctrines and dogmas, creeds and confessions. Faith became fixed and

---

[3]Bousset, *Das Wesen der Religion*, p. 176.

formal; beliefs became impersonal and official, and with officiality of belief came orthodoxy of opinion. The historical Jesus was enveloped in a mystical, mythical and metaphysical atmosphere that hid him from the eyes of even the believing Christian world. Theology and philosophy in Christian garb overgrew and obscured the religion of Jesus, the simple yet strong sources of spiritual life which he knew. There came, what Professor Rufus M. Jones has called, "the profound transformation of Christianity from a way of life to an elaborate system of thought."[4]

By the third century Greece had submerged the homeland, and the religion that named itself after a Galilean and that claimed him for its founder had left of him little more than a highly exalted but lifeless figure. Every historical student of first-century Christianity knows that the Greek mind, when it was turned to Christianity, did not cease to think Greek and that the great body of Christian theology and Christology is the free and spontaneous reaction of the Greek genius to the Christian message, the natural outgrowth of Greek thought turned with fervor to a new object of religious faith. As Christianity came into new intellectual atmospheres it experienced fresh expansions of life; as it struck root in different psychic soils it developed outgrowths that were perfectly natural and that are perfectly intelligible to the historical student. But the development of the faith that attached itself to God's great Galilean went so far that only those who are trained by tradition can recognize the Jesus of history in the Christ of faith.

It is at this point that the unnatural element appears.

---

[4] *The Church's Debt to Heretics*, by R. M. Jones, p. 20. Courtesy of Doubleday, Doran & Co., Inc.

Christianity's expansions brought shifts in the centers of emphasis; natural outgrowths became unnatural overgrowths; accretions submerged the original acumen; later developments gradually eliminated the primitive intrinsic deposit. And these acquired elements became more impressive for the Christian imagination, official and lay, than the plain prosaic picture presented in the first three Gospels. They gradually usurped the seats of authority in Christian thinking and feeling; they were accepted as the criterions of infallible faith, and unquestioning loyalty was vouchsafed as the guarantee of religious certainty. At not a few points in Christianity's history Jesus has been lost to the church so far as the things that meant most to him were concerned. In the tumult of its theoretical tributes Christianity has often stood in danger of losing Jesus himself. Exalted estimates of his person have obscured the cause to which he felt himself called and to which he committed himself without reserve; controversies over titles befitting his dignity have often grossly contradicted the simple sincerity of his spirit; and both have raised a barrier in the way of the work he sought to accomplish—the kingdom of God among men.

The common idea is that Jesus founded a religion—Christianity. But it is better history to say: *Jesus became a religion.* Christianity from the moment of its birth was *a religion about Jesus* rather than *the religion of Jesus.* The personal piety of Jesus has played practically no rôle, at least no regulative rôle, in the history of official and organized Christianity. For the general thought of the church, his appearance in history has been primarily an act in the great divine drama of salvation. The exalted elevation and enrichment of man's religious experience, the close approach of man to an adequate understanding and knowledge of his Maker, the infinite contribution to our common human problem of religious living, which came in the form of the personal religious experience of Jesus, have never been commanding centers of interest and emphasis. Instead there has always been a subtle swinging away from this best source of spiritual supply. But the history of religion seems to teach that the priest supplants the prophet, that the institution submerges the individual whose genius gave it birth. Such, it seems, is the fate of any social movement that dares gird itself for a career in the world and that commits itself to the great currents of culture and civilization. There is always, it seems, a slow seeping away of the original sources of strength, a subtle stagnation of spirit, a growing weariness and a gradual weakening of the will to work its original and genial way, a shift in the centers of interest and emphasis in the face of new conditions, concessions and compromises that at the outset would have been unthinkable, changes within, influences from without—all resulting in something quite foreign to the first faith.

Such is the strange and parodoxical picture which the history of Christianity and its faith presents. On the one hand, a plain peasant prophet, a lay preacher of the kingdom of God, a religious subject in possession of the richest and most resourceful religious experience of which we have any knowledge. On the other hand, the Risen Lord, the Christ, the Son, very God, the center of a religious faith, the object of religious reverence. The cardinal claims of the Christian faith are something quite different from anything we hear from Jesus himself. As a matter of the best attested historical fact, Jesus kept his own person so completely in the background that we are not in a position to say exactly what and how he esteemed himself, except as the called and commissioned prophet of the kingdom of God. But as a matter of historical fact also, the person of Jesus occupies, as it has from the very first, the whole foreground of Christian thought. All else sinks into the hardly visible background, including some of the things for which he staked his all.

An infinite number of attempts have been made to reconcile the old alternative set by Strauss in 1835: *the Jesus of history or the Christ of faith*. Theological prejudice has reconciled it because it has never perceived it. Vital religious faith has felt it, yet as is faith's peculiar privilege it has seemed to prosper in its presence. That vital religion can thrive in the midst of the most perplexing paradoxes between faith and fact is clear in the religious experience of Jesus himself. But when it comes to the matter of historical fact, to the question of sources and standards of authority in the Christian faith, the old alternative of Strauss is as live as ever after more than ninety years. It is clearer and more certain than ever because we now know more about Jesus and the beginnings of the early Christian faith that attached itself to him. In such a recent and important work as Professor Otto's *Das Heilige* the old issue is restated: "Is Christianity in general and in the strict sense the religion of Jesus?"[5] In the *Zeitschrift fuer Theologie und Kirche* we find an elaborate article on "The Christ of Faith and the Historical Jesus," by Professor Mundle, who frames the issue more incisively than ever.[6]

The issue will not down for it is too deeply imbedded in the New Testament itself. Over against the religious

---

[5] P. 212. *See* pp. 197-204 on *Christentum und Jesustum*.
[6] Hefte 3 und 4 (Neue Folge, 1921), pp. 192-212, 247-273.

experience of Jesus there is something quantitatively great, something qualitatively new in the religious experience of the first Christians. In the New Testament itself it is quite clear that Jesus was something more and different in early Christian experience, something infinitely more and different, than he professed to be for his contemporaries in general, for his intimate companions in particular, indeed, something infinitely more and different than the content of his own self-consciousness exhibits so far as this is accessible to us. In his own experience he was a religious subject, but in the experience of the earliest Christians he was always a religious object. As such he gave to the Christian faith its distinctive character and content.

Jesus did not have followers as have other great men of history, even founders of religions, who came to influence subsequent generations. Other great men have had followers who took up their work where they were forced to leave it off. They have carried it on, seeking to be true to their master's spirit and to accomplish what he had seen by faith. The followers of other great men have championed their master's cause, preached and propagated his message, taught and expounded the things that he thought and taught. The followers of Jesus did none of these things. They did not take up his work where he was forced to leave it off. They did not propagate his distinctive message. The New Testament itself is not made up of injunctions of Jesus but of faith's fervent interpretations of his person. Outside of the first three Gospels there are not in the New Testament more than a dozen sentences from his religious message. The first Christians preached Jesus himself. Jesus had his own message, the kingdom of God, and the early Christians had their own distinctive message, Jesus himself, to whom they attached the whole body of their religious hopes.

Between the religious experience of Jesus and that of the first Christians there is a complete shift in the centers of interest and emphasis. What Jesus guarded as a sacred secret within the inner recesses of his own consciousness, the first Christians announced to the world as the sole hope of religious salvation. How it was that this shift from religious subject to religious object, from the Jesus of history to the Christ of faith, came about we are not in a position to explain, but it stands as a clear fact in the testimony of the New Testament itself. It goes back to the first faint dawning of the Christian consciousness and it had its birth in the Easter experiences of the original witnesses. Jesus as religious object was inherent in the resurrection faith of the first witnesses. Thus, the most radical change came at the very outset.

Theologies and Christologies required time for formation and formulation, but faith in Jesus as religious object was the work of a moment. It transpired with a flash because it was the one ignition point in the experience of those who claimed that Jesus was alive and that they had seen him. Long before the Gospels were written the Christian faith had received its distinctive features which later were to mark it as a new religion. The belief in Jesus' Messiahship, his divine dignity, and his present exaltation and glorification, was a fixed element that reached back beyond Paul to the resurrection faith of the first witnesses. Paul did not create the Christian faith in Jesus as a religious object. He speaks of himself as the last of the Easter experients. (I Cor. 15,8.) Paul

282   THE RELIGION OF JESUS

was simply the sharer of a faith that was older than his own Christian experience.

In the history of Christianity, from the first Easter morning down to the present, we see the Christ of faith gradually suppressing the Jesus of history, the supernatural and superhistorical object of the Christian faith slowly but surely submerging the human historical subject of the richest religious experience of which we know. This process was only natural, for it was the involuntary outgrowth of the experiences of the first disciples at the center of whose lives stood the firm conviction that Jesus was not dead but lived and that they had seen him. This process of obscuration is at work in the New Testament itself and there it has already accomplished this great shift from religious subject to religious object.[7]

THE RELIGIOUS EXPERIENCE OF JESUS AND THEOLOGY

In the past Jesus has been approached almost exclusively from the theological point of view. Each word of his, each incident in his life, has been fitted into the great systems of Christian thought. Until the last century the Christian interest in what Jesus said and did confined itself to a quest for confirmation of theological theories in his words and deeds. This theological approach reaches back to the New Testament itself and it has invaded even the thought of Jesus. An excellent example of this is found in Mark 10,45:

"For the Son of man also came not to be ministered

---

[7]*The Religious Experience of Jesus in the New Testament* is reserved for special study. Cf. p. xi.

unto, but to minister, and to give his life a ransom for many."[8]

In the first part of this passage we have a genuine word of Jesus, the very essence of whose mission was not to be ministered unto, but to minister. However, the closing clause is a Christian conviction cast about the death of Jesus. That it is of Christian origin is clear from the fact that it looks back on his life as closed; it surveys and appraises his work as a whole. It presents a Christian interpretation rather than a personal conviction of Jesus, who did not regard his death as a part of a great divine drama. His fate was his own personal problem, a pressing perplexity of his own religious loyalty, which he solved in the light of the divine will for himself. Mark 10,45 must be read in the light of Jesus' Gethsemane prayer in which he casts no reflection concerning the significance of his suffering and death for later believers.

Christian theology has seemed to aim at system rather than at a sharing of Jesus' religious experience. At times it has been so systematic that little indeed of his own originality has been left. Traditional theology has never had the right disposition toward Jesus, and no matter how refined and how carefully stated, its formulations will never be able to do him justice, for theology is always more interested in itself than it is in Jesus. Theologians have never seemed to want to be near Jesus as he actually was, to be in his company and to enjoy his companionship. They have exalted him to a towering throne. Between him and us yawns that impassible gulf that separates dignified deity from humble humanity. The historical stu-

---

[8]Luke's parallel passage (22,25-27) does not contain the closing *ransom* clause.

dent who repeats the official creed, as he naturally does because he feels that he senses and shares the religious convictions out of which it came, can not escape the feeling that theology has missed the cardinal centers of Jesus' own religious experience, that it has neglected the religious Jesus almost entirely or has so covered him with theological tributes that he is no longer one of us. This theological Jesus was not the man of Galilee; in fact, the Jesus of theology never existed and by his very nature could not exist, for he is too far removed from a serious sharing of historical and human conditions. The Jesus of Matthew and Mark and Luke is a wholly different figure. He is real in the strict sense. He appears as a man among men. His closest friends are human persons of surprising simplicity, yet he is one of them. They thrill at his touch, grow in the presence of his gracious goodness, learn from his lips the ways of God, and respond to the imposing power of his personality. Theological pride can take no pleasure in such a prosaic picture.

The historical Jesus was most untheological. There is nothing intricate or involved in his religious thinking. In the first three Gospels we have no record of Jesus' delivering a doctrinal discourse or of his discussing some technical theological theme.[9] Without exception, he preached the personal and practical phases of piety—religion as it relates itself organically to the creation of character and the control of conduct. We never find him in a technical theological controversy so characteristic of the religious leaders of his day and people.[10] In his con-

---

[9]These doctrinal discourses appear only in the Fourth Gospel, an excellent example of which is found in 6,52-58.

[10]The one exception is Mark 12,35-37, and this is so exceptional that a number of scholars are skeptical concerning its genuineness.

flicts with the religious authorities he contends for the *elemental* over against the *elaborate* in religion.

With his contemporaries Jesus does not seem to have left the impression of formal learning. Nevertheless, he spoke "with authority," as one who speaks out of great conviction and deep inner certainty. Thus he found his way to the hearts of his hearers as a display of learning would never have been able to do. Jesus had no systematic theology. His only theology was *theologia experimentalis*. Jesus stands as the disappointment and dismay of all those who seek careful formulation and system in religious thinking. Theology is not religion. If it were, we to-day would have little to hope for in turning to him. Jesus gives no theological instruction, rather he imparts religious inspiration. He thought and spoke too much to the point, too little at length, to frame his faith in a formal structure. Nowhere do we see him searching for terms that draw the usual careful distinctions in the treatment of theological themes. His utterances strike at the very heart of religious problems, yet they have all the natural variety that belongs to a vital and vigorous faith. His longest addresses in the first three Gospels are brief enough, and they show no interest in either a full or a formal treatment of a theme.

Jesus never makes even an approach to anything like a formal and full statement of his faith. The *Lord's Prayer* is the nearest approach to such. Here within compact compass we have the great religious beliefs of Jesus, not doctrines and dogmas but vital religious faith. As we saw, it is the finest fruition of his prayer-experience. Now we may say that it is the finest and fullest fruition of the whole of his religious experience, of all that he found God to be and to mean for our humankind. It is his greatest

and most significant utterance. It is the richest single
deposit of his faith, and into it the whole of his religious
life is emptied. In view of its remarkable freedom from
those side-issues that so readily distract and distort the
religious outlook, in view of its brevity and comprehen-
siveness, we might speak of it as the creed of Jesus. It
is his creed in the sense that it presents what he regarded
as of most matter before God. But it is not a creed in
the sense that would make it a formal statement of the
substance of his religious faith. It should be the great
creed of Christianity, and if the authority of Jesus were
actual rather than theoretical with us, it would be our
one great confession of faith. Of the *Lord's Prayer*,
Professor Wernle writes: "A more simple, a more confident prayer certainly has never been uttered. . . . It is
the greatest and grandest confession of all Christian
churches, the only thing that can not separate and that can
bind together, the only thing that confronts us with the
one great issue upon which all else depends."[11]

A thorough reading of the first three Gospels will
teach us emphatically enough that Jesus was not a theologian and that from him we may expect no formal theology. As Professor Weinel writes: "Jesus had no
theology; he was an unschooled man of action."[12] In his
experience of religion he was closer to life than formal
theology can ever hope to be. He was the bitter oppo-
nent of a piety that based itself on learning rather than
on living. It was in a religion of traditionalism that he
saw the greatest danger to the divine cause. He speaks
of the theologians of his day as blind leaders of the blind;
both shall fall into the ditch. He was unremitting in

[11]*Jesus*, p. 94.
[12]*Biblische Theologie des Neuen Testaments*, p. 2.

his arraignment of those for whom conceptions about religion had obscured and submerged religion itself. It was not in the religious constitution of Jesus to accept or to advocate a divinely-revealed, a God-given dogma or fixed objective standard of religious truth. Above all tradition he sets the authority of personal religious experience. He accepted and rejected on the sole basis of tradition's contribution to personal religious loyalty and devotion. The best of the past and the present he confronted with the terrible test of actually stimulating, feeding or giving outlet to the more sacred source-springs that lie within.

Theology, formal and full statements of faith, belong to historical Christianity, but not to its Founder. If Jesus had a theology, if he actually taught it, it failed to register itself as a feature in the picture retained by those who knew him best. The simple and single impression which he seems to have left upon those whose witness is at the base of the first three Gospels is that he was a passionately religious personality. Such theology as appears in his religious thought is simply a dim reflection of the thought-forms in which the religion of Israel, early and late, had found expression. These features are characteristic of Jesus, but they were equally characteristic of his contemporaries. They are not distinctive, and at this point Jesus makes no contribution. But into these familiar thought-forms he poured a solid substance and through them he breathed a new life that was his very own.

Jesus is greater than all the theological systems that have tried to compass him about. He is more than Jewish Messianism, more than the resurrectionism of Paul, more than the Logos of John, more than Greek soteriology, medieval mysticism, the Roman régime, or Protestant piety. All of these are only local interpretations of men and peoples who have been his great and less great disciples. Jesus will bear the weight of all the burdensome theologies that have attached themselves to his person, but his religious significance is in no wise dependent upon any of them. Those who feel that the acceptance of Christianity in its historical forms and statements involves an intellectual sacrifice too great for a religious view of reason, may approach Jesus in complete confidence. Jesus required no intellectual sacrifices. He did not restrict or repress; he released the whole of life. A lamp may not be put under a bushel, but on a stand.

The religious experience of Jesus defies systematization. Religion in his experience is neither a maximum nor a minimum of beliefs. It is rather quantity and quality of life actually lived. To advocate a special theological opinion about Jesus, is to be untrue to all that he represented. He was not the advocate of any opinions about himself. And the religion that names itself after him must be more than definitions and statements about him. Jesus can not be defined by a single doctrine or set of doctrines. No single statement or series of statements will say all that he is for all of his followers. We can not press him into a single phrase, no matter how pithy and pregnant it may be. He can not be cramped within the close confines of any creed—he is too great!

In its traditional emphasis historical Christianity has seemed to forget the original sources of its theology. All of our Christian theology had its origin in vital religious experience. It sprang from a fountain of fervent faith that was in no sense cautious or self-conscious concerning the form in which it expressed itself. Most of our Christian theology comes from Paul, but Paul never thought that he would become Christianity's first great theologian. It never occurred to him that his formulations of his own personal faith would become normative for later Christian thought. His statements of his faith were not framed in a self-conscious way. His only interest was in expressing the controlling elements of his experience of Christ. His doctrines of the cross and resurrection were in no sense formal for himself or for his original readers. They were far removed from theological theories, for both were cardinal centers of his personal Christian experience. Paul felt that he had been crucified with Christ, that he had died with him, and that he had seen the Risen Lord on the Damascus road. Both the cross and the resurrection represented religious realities in his Christian life. They were actual, not theoretical. The theology of Paul is the religion of Paul; it was the organic issue of his faith in Christ. He shows no special interest in the form of his faith, but his faith means everything to him. To separate the theology of Paul from the religion of Paul is to do him injustice, for his theology was part and parcel of his personal piety. Our New Testament theology may sift out Paul's doctrines and end by missing the Apostle entirely.

Theology at its best possesses only a relative value. It is valuable only to the degree in which it is able to communicate to us the original religious convictions out of which it sprang. Much of our traditional theology has lost its original freshness and vitality, for it has become an empty form devoid of the solid substance that once gave it body. The great weakness in the transmission of our theological tradition is that it fails to transmit the rich religious experience in which it had its birth.

Theoretically our theology conserves, but actually it fails to communicate.

The final crucible for all doctrine and dogma is religious experience, the genuineness of the religious experience from which it came, and its ability in turn to reproduce itself in subsequent Christian life. Our theology, inherited from the distant past, is meaningless unless we press behind it to the very pulse of the primitive Christian piety that once throbbed through it. And, in many cases, the recovery and reproduction of the religious experience behind our theology will result in an abandonment of the traditional terminology, because vital religious experience seeks to express itself in its own way, true to itself and its best genius. Faith, not the form, is the living thing. And the task of the Christian to-day, even of the theologian, is not to cling for dear life to an empty shell that is too frail to bear him up but to lay hold of its original faith-content. Actual piety must be the criterion of all theology, for theology is its offspring. In and of itself, theology is barren ground. Individual personal experience is the only fertile soil in which religion can live and thrive and do for human life what it claims. "Experience is the only creative factor in the world's religions."[13]

In the theological emphasis that still prevails in our modern Christianity we need to be reminded that theology is valuable, and can be valuable, only to the extent in which it is the expression of a surging religious life, because of the religious verities and certainties it represents in actual experience. Theologies are worthless unless we enjoy the corresponding experience in which they had their

---

[13]Hauer, *Die Religionen,* I, p. v.

birth. Further, we must remember that it is entirely possible to enjoy the original experience and at the same time desert the traditional theological terminology. One of the great tragedies in the history of Christianity has been the insistence on form and the neglect of faith. Theology has often been identified with religion, and this has resulted without exception in an impoverishment of the religious life. The problem of the theologian who has any sense of religious mission is not to create a more friendly atmosphere toward theology on the part of the modern mind that by disposition is unsympathetic or even hostile toward such. His real task is to take theology out of the remote realm of meaningless abstractions, bring it down to the real world of religious experience, and disclose to all the profound spiritual depths from which it sprang, the primitive piety that stands behind and that courses through it.

Whether we like or not, the drift to-day is away from theology and in the direction of a religious experience that is adequate for the living of actual life. The time has for ever passed when enlightened Christianity can make orthodoxy of theological opinion the touchstone of religious loyalty. The modern religious mind has developed a disposition that is wholly indifferent toward the intricacies of theological speculation. The modern follower of Jesus feels that theology is too far removed from the pressing problem of living life religiously. He feels that doctrine and dogma are cold and formal, that the fire of faith is not in them. He feels that the formal statements of faith are retained even though life has departed from them. He feels that the affirmation or denial of most of our theoretical theology is equally unim-

portant. In Jesus, as in most great religious geniuses,
he finds no stimulus to a systematic statement of his faith.
In our Christian theology he finds little that suggests
Jesus himself. All that is left of him in official creeds is
intangible, vague and shadowy.

Theology may have a place in religion, but when it begins to suppress vital religious experience or is offered
as a substitute for such then the really devout person will
revolt in the name of religion itself. Religious faith,
as Professor Herrmann taught his students, is first of all
a living thing.[14] Beliefs may codify themselves into confessions and creeds, but living faith never. There is no
real religious faith apart from a living subject who experiences it as the commanding element of his conscious existence. All the religiously valid theology can be stated in
a single sentence: God is a living, loving Father. All
else is incidental and accessory.

Christianity, if it is to be what Jesus meant that the
religion of his followers should be, must transcend its
theology, dogmatics and traditionalism. They must be
overcome as primitive Christianity overcame its inherited
Judaism and its apocalypticism. Theology can offer us a
theory, but no actual hope of religious salvation in the
light of which we can live and work. Christianity's victories have not been due to its theology except where such
has been the natural and spontaneous expression of a
deep piety. Christianity's genius has carried it along,
the best of which has been its local loyalties to Jesus. To
its sporadic preservations of the spirit of Jesus, Christianity may ascribe its religious but not all of its successes.

The essence of a religion is to be sought, not in its

---

[14]"Der Glaube ist in erster Linie Leben, nicht Lehre."

formal and theoretical expressions, but in the richness of the religious experience of those who are claimed and commanded by it. Creeds and confessions may force the intellect to a rigid behavior in its speculations, but they do not necessarily contribute to the religious living of the believer. A religion is no more, no less, than what it means and accomplishes in the life of the person who confesses and experiences it.

What is religion? Is it a precious heritage from the past that is to be preserved changeless and intact? Or is religion the commanding element in the experience of living men, the greatest of all forces in the molding and moving of human life from one age to another—sometimes in one form, sometimes in another—but always contributing to the excellence of all that men are, that they can and hope to be? In our odd moments we quarrel over doctrine and dogma. Sometimes it becomes our chief Christian occupation. We pride ourselves on our liberalism or on our fundamentalism, when in reality neither offers any religious hope. Thus we push theology in all its forms into the very center of the religious consciousness, and give it a place to which it has no native and natural right. Such is plain disloyalty to Jesus.

Christianity may have its theology, but if it is no more it is certainly not the religion of Jesus. If we conceive of Jesus in only theological and doctrinal terms, we miss the greatest, grandest and best that he has to offer us. We miss his religion; even more serious, we miss Jesus himself. Jesus is the chief heritage of Christianity, and when we come to see something more sacred and secure in the traditions of our faith than we see in Jesus himself we have come to a very dangerous pass. We have fallen into a really deplorable situation when we begin to think more of our theology than we think of our religion, and especially when we recognize the authority of tradition rather than the religious authority of Jesus, whose every word should be our command. We dread doubt on theological questions, but we are all skeptical of Jesus when it comes to the actual practise of his personal piety and the reproduction of his religious experience.

We to-day rely on practically everything except the faith by which Jesus lived and died. Our modern Christian attitude toward Jesus is about as follows: We believe in him, but we do not trust him. We confess his name, but we are not yet willing to commit ourselves loyally to his leadership. We retain the most exalted beliefs *about* Jesus, but we manifest no real confidence in him and his way of life. His own personal piety is not the principle on which we order our existence. We take our theological theories very seriously, but religiously we desert Jesus.

THE RELIGIOUS EXPERIENCE OF JESUS AND ORGANIZED RELIGION

In recent times a great deal of debate has arisen about the question: Who founded Christianity, Jesus or Paul? The answer to this question depends upon one's understanding of Christianity. If by Christianity we mean Jesus' faith in God as Father and in His kingdom and its coming, such as he preached in the Sermon on the Mount and in his parables, then Jesus was the founder of Christianity. But if by Christianity we mean an organized and official religion, a new faith that involved a definite break with the religion of Israel, competing with other religions of the first three centuries for supremacy in the Roman world, then Paul was the founder of Christianity. The founding of Christianity in the historical forms in which it has appeared is the work of Paul and other early Christians as the result of their Easter experiences.

That Paul and the early disciples foresaw the great institution that was to come and that they consciously laid the foundation for it, is, of course, out of question. Paul and the rest were passionate preachers of their great religious convictions and certainties concerning Jesus. They were propagandists of their faith, not plotters of a program that was to reach down through the centuries. In Paul's day there was little or no official organization; the Christian centers which he established were only mission stations, purely democratic communities, one differing quite naturally from the other. But at the heart of the Christian experience of Paul there were elements that demanded a definite break with the Judaistic past, elements that were actually distinctive, and of this break Paul himself was clearly conscious. In fact, Paul stands as the great first-century progressive who shook from the new faith the shackles of Judaism and who launched it in the great currents of the life of the Roman world. In its historical forms as a new faith, as a system of thought, as an organized religion, Christianity bears the marks of Paul rather than those of Jesus.

Jesus appears before us as a man with a profound experience of religion rather than as the founder of a new religion. He manifests neither the elements nor the efforts of the founders of the great world religions. The idea of founding a new religion over against that of his people's past appears as a conception wholly foreign to the mind of Jesus as revealed in the first three Gospels. He never once gives the impression of inaugurating something wholly new. He often appears as a non-conformist in his conduct. He breaks with certain religious conventionalities of his contemporaries; he openly sets his own experience of religion over against particular precepts of his people's past. But he never establishes between himself and the religious past of his people an open breach. Not once does he proffer a substitute for the ancient faith of Israel. He teaches no new and different God, but the God of Abraham and Isaac and Jacob. He is the champion of the faith of Israel's fathers. As we saw in chapter one, Jesus' own personal piety is inextricably rooted in the best of the religion of his people.

Jesus was not conscious of founding a new faith that would later be transplanted from its native to a foreign soil. The one commanding element of his experience was the kingdom of God and its coming. His one great task was to announce it. But even the kingdom he does not present as something new and strange in the religious life of his people. On the contrary, he paints it in Jewish colors. It is true that he preached the kingdom as universally human rather than as a strictly Jewish value. But in this he was in perfect keeping with his great prophetic predecessor, Second Isaiah (40-66), who first gave to the religious mission of Israel a world outlook. For Jesus the kingdom was God's great goal for his own and for all peoples. (Matt. 8,11.) In his faith in the kingdom he was conscious that a greater thing than the temple or Solomon or Jonah was here, but he never presented it as wholly other, as something entirely foreign to Israel's religious experience in the past.

Every student of the life of Jesus knows that the distinctive elements in his experience of religion were super-Jewish and universally human, that his very appearance in Judaism meant the twilight of the old and the dawn of the new for those who followed him. But in the historical form in which it appeared the religious experience of Jesus was Jewish. He was consciously Jewish in his experience of religion, and he remained such to the very end. Paul, however, was consciously Christian in his experience of religion. There was the break with his Jewish past, the annulment of the law, the Risen Lord of the Damascus road—all distinctive elements of his Christian experience. The very form and content of Jesus' religious experience force the historical student to take a Jewish view of him. If one judges the personal religious faith of Jesus and the Christian faith by their sources, objects and issues, he is forced to agree with Wellhausen to the effect that "Jesus was not a Christian, but a Jew."[15]

The traditional Christian idea is that Jesus, during his lifetime, looked forward to and formally founded the church. But when we turn to the Gospel accounts we find that this tradition rests upon an extremely weak literary basis. The church as a word or plan of Jesus is found nowhere in the Gospels of Mark and Luke. The word *church* is found only twice in the Gospels, both times on the lips of Jesus and both in passages peculiar to Matthew. The first passage comes in Matthew 16,17-19 in which Jesus is represented as celebrating Simon's confession of his Messiahship by a festival founding of the church:

"Blessed art thou, Simon Bar-Jonah: for flesh and blood hath not revealed it unto thee, but my Father who is in heaven. And I also say unto thee, that thou

---

[15]*Einleitung in die drei ersten Evangelien*, p. 102.

art Peter, and upon this rock I will build my church; and the gates of Hades shall not prevail against it. I will give unto thee the keys of the kingdom of heaven: and whatsoever thou shalt bind on earth shall be bound in heaven; and whatsoever thou shalt loose on earth shall be loosed in heaven."

This passage is now commonly regarded as ingenuine and as a later Christian addition. It has no parallel in Mark or Luke who report the confession scene otherwise with as much interest and fulness as Matthew. The utterance itself is too officious to come from Jesus. It is impossible in the thought of the historical Jesus, for it contains the later Christian theory of the church. It is impossible as a situation in his life, for it teaches explicitly the primacy of Peter, a doctrine that can not have arisen before the closing decades of the first century. Matthew reports the substance of this passage a second time (18,18) where it is out of all connection with the Apostle Peter.

The second ecclesiastical passage comes in Matthew 18,15-17:

"And if thy brother sin against thee, go, show him his fault between thee and him alone: if he hear thee, thou has gained thy brother. But if he hear *thee* not, take with thee one or two more, that at the mouth of two witnesses or three every word may be established. And if he refuse to hear them, tell it unto the church: and if he refuse to hear the church also, let him be unto thee as the Gentile and the publican."

This passage represents an earlier and less official type of primitive Christianity than the first. The church is still a democratic community. But this passage is plainly an extract from early Christian discipline and does not go back to Jesus. His original word is to be found in Luke 17,3-4:

"Take heed to yourselves: if thy brother sin, rebuke him; and if he repent, forgive him. And if he sin against thee seven times in the day, and seven times turn again to thee saying, I repent; thou shalt forgive him."

The two passages just quoted belong to the history of early Christianity, and both are late contributions of the churchman Matthew.[16] The church as the official organ of his faith and the future form of organization for his following never figured in the religious outlook of the historical Jesus. In fact, the idea of the church contradicts the whole of his religious outlook. Jesus did not look to the future in terms of centuries, but he thought and spoke of it in terms of weeks and months. In the future he saw only the kingdom of God. The man who spoke Matthew 10,23; Mark 9,1; Luke 22,18 can not have looked forward to an organized future for his following. When he sent out the twelve, it was not as pastors but as hasting heralds of the kingdom. He gave them no ecclesiastical or educational program. They are not to halt or greet any man on the way, for there is no time for such. It is only in the Fourth Gospel that Jesus becomes pastoral, planning and providing for

---

[16]For a recent and fine discussion of this question of the relation of the historical Jesus to the church, *see* Heiler, *Der Katholizismus*, chapter I, pp. 18-43.

his orphaned disciples after his death, promising an Advocate that will fill the gap in their lives.

In Jesus we see none of the plans and preparations for the future such as other great religious geniuses have left with their followers. He founded no order as did Buddha, no school as did Plato, no sect as did John the Baptist. Not a single word suggests that he planned an official and organized religion to survive him. He has about him his personally chosen circle of companions, but there is no hint to the effect that he attempted to organize them either for the present or the future. The only suggestion of an organization among the twelve is in the Fourth Gospel where Judas appears as the dishonest treasurer of the group (12,6), whose duty it was to buy provisions or to give to the poor (13,29). But even these details belong to the Fourth Evangelist's policy of blackening the character of Judas.

Throughout his public life Jesus is utterly indifferent toward numbers in his following; he seeks to avoid the great crowds. Such is certainly surprising on the part of any one who is laying plans for the survival of his work and following after his death. Why he chose just twelve personal companions we do not know. On the basis of a word like Matthew 19,28[17] we might think that the number twelve was a matter of Jewish tradition with Jesus. However, he was not the man to include an unworthy disciple or to exclude a worthy disciple for the sake of a sacred number. If the number twelve was a part of any plan that he had in mind, it was shattered by the desertion of Judas.

Within the following of the Baptist there were ele-

---

[17]"Ye also shall sit upon twelve thrones, judging the twelve tribes of Israel." Cf. Luke 22,30.

ments of nascent organization, religious practises which he seems to have given his disciples that held them together as a group and that distinguished them from other religious sects of the day. The one practise which seems to have distinguished them and to have given their master his popular name, the Baptist, was the religious rite of baptism. A second bond that held the followers of the Baptist together was the custom of periodic fasting which they had in common with other Jewish sects and which brought them into conflict with Jesus and his disciples. (Mark 2,18.) A third bond that seems to have come from the Baptist himself was that of prayer. The Baptist seems not only to have taught his disciples prayer as a religious practise, but he seems to have given them a special prayer. (Luke 5,33; 11,1.) A fourth bond of organization came from the Baptist—a common religious confession which he seems to have heard from those who presented themselves to him for baptism. (Matt. 3,6; Mark 1,5.) Of its exact nature we can say little except that it was a confession of sins, but it seems to have been informal rather than formal, a voluntary response to his message of repentance rather than compulsory.

The following of the Baptist disappeared from history; that of Jesus conquered the Roman world. From Acts 18,24-19,7 we might conclude that at least portions, if not all, of the Baptist's following were absorbed in the Christian movement. But it is interesting to note that John the Baptist had a following of sufficiently strong constitution to survive its master's death, to preserve itself independently for considerable time thereafter, and to carry on its own missionary program far from the scene of its master's work.

Among the disciples of Jesus during his lifetime all

such elements of nascent religious organization are missing. The first personal appearance of Jesus in the Gospel
story is at the Jordan where he is baptized by John.
Jesus, as we said, regarded John's baptism as a sacred religious rite and he participated in it actuated by the deepest and most genuine religious motives. Yet he did not
take over from John this religious rite. He and his disciples observed no custom of periodic fasting. Jesus prayed
as none before or after him, and he taught his disciples
extensively on the practise and principles of prayer. But
we never see him observing specially set hours of worship;
he does not withdraw for calendared seasons of prayer.
The praying of Jesus and his group is instinctive rather
than institutional. For his followers he has no formal
creeds or confessions, no articles for the declaration of
faith, no ceremonies or cults. Even on the last night of
his life he is not founding a religious institution to be repeated in his personal memory as the primitive Christian
community at an early date began to construe it. (I Cor.
11,23-25; Luke 22,19-20.) In Matthew 26,26-29 and
Mark 14,22-25 Jesus makes no reference to a repetition
of the occasion in the future, except as he will one day
drink it anew with them in the kingdom of God. The
original incident seems to be that Jesus is celebrating the
Jewish passover with his disciples and that the cup and
bread are simply a final personal pledge of his faith that
the kingdom of God *will* come. (Luke 22,15-18.)

Jesus appears in the New Testament as utterly indifferent toward organization. In fact, he manifests no genius
for effecting it. From the standpoint of organization, no
great religious genius ever left his following so poorly
prepared to meet the future as did Jesus. He seems to
have trusted to purely personal bonds to hold his disciples

to himself, and during his lifetime it was this more intimate type of bond that held his disciples together. This
personal loyalty and attachment did not stand all the
stress and strain of circumstances. The twelve deserted
him at the scene of his arrest; Peter denied him, and
Judas betrayed him into the hands of his enemies. But
after his death it was the conviction that Jesus was alive
again, that they, the Apostles as well as others, had seen
him, that he was with them "even unto the end of the
world," that welded his former companions into a compact company which later resulted in the Christian church.

With his unconventional religious character and conduct it would be difficult to fit Jesus into any ecclesiastical
system. Judging from his attitude toward the official and
organized religion of his day, Jesus would be a poor
churchman. He made no wholesale revolt against the religious institutions of his day and people. The Galilean
synagogues were a frequent scene of his teaching. His
attitude toward the synagogue is an excellent example of
his religious conservatism, but he never connects the synagogue with the religious hope of the future. Jesus was
never more conservative than when he went as a pious
pilgrim to Jerusalem to celebrate the most sacred of
Jewish festivals. But even into the celebration of the
Passover he pours his own personal faith concerning the
coming of the kingdom. Jesus was always giving himself
to the more personal and informal aspects of religion.
The impersonal and formal he neglected. His experience
of religion was purely individual, apparently quite capable
of dispensing with the institutional.

In his message Jesus stripped off all appearances, outer
casings and superficialities. He ignored prominent elements in the conventional foreground, and out of the dim

theoretical background he would bring up some neglected
or conventionalized issue as a commanding element of religious experience. A religion of cult and ceremony he
rejected once for all in true prophetic fashion, and he confronted his contemporaries with obedience to the divine
will as the essence of true piety. He opposed the elaborate in favor of the elemental, the official in favor of the
original. To religious experience he applied no external
tests, but those searching tests of simple and sincere
living.

Jesus bound man's hope of religious salvation to no institution, no matter how sacred or of how long standing.
He left religion where the very structure and substance
of the human constitution demand that it should be left,
an intimate matter between man and his Maker. Religious loyalty he attached to no religious institution, to no
body of beliefs, but to God himself. He did not regard
faith as a deposit from the past that is to be defended
against all comers. He knew of no such impersonal loyalty. In the experience of Jesus faith must function; it
must have its fruitage in character and conduct. He did
not judge religious living as a calculating and balancing
of religious acts, as a sum of good-works that offsets
shortcomings and sins. For Jesus religion in human experience is the fundamental direction and bent of life
intent upon God and His kingdom.

That Jesus surveyed all the coming centuries and foresaw the necessity of an organization and institution such
as the Christian church is nowhere clear in our best
sources. He looked forward to something far less remote, to a permanent society of God and man accomplished by a harmony of the human will with the divine.
"Thy kingdom come!" is the greatest prayer, purpose and

program of the church. The fact that Jesus did not found a religious organization or an official faith should drive the church, which claims him as the center of its life, to the most searching and conscientious introspection. The church must never forget that the religious experience of Jesus is that of the layman and that Jesus singled out the original rather than the official elements of religion. It must keep in mind that in its official form an organized religion may travel far from its original sources of purity and power, that it may even come to the place where its original life-deposit is neglected, forgotten or even supplanted. It should remember that its officialism and orthodoxy are acquired and that they were not a part of the original acumen. Officialism and orthodoxy may never look to Jesus for a spiritual ally. He fixed no forms of faith; he framed no standards by which theoretical opinions are to be measured. He left man in his experience of God as unhampered and free as man is in any field of his experience. He sought to set men spontaneously and seriously in the quest of God, His kingdom and will, and he cast no care in the direction of what or how they should believe in a formal way.

Religion as the human quest of God is not the sole possession of those who are herded and housed in a cliquish conventionality and who pride themselves on preserving the faith iota for iota. In view of the plain New Testament facts themselves the official and the orthodox, those unquestioning savers of what has been, is not now, and never again will be, should be the most modest and humble in the presence of Jesus. They should read again some of his plain paradoxes about the first being last and the last being first, about the greatness of the least and the leastness of the great.

The religious experience of Jesus stands above and beyond all organization and officialism. His spirit can not be confined to such; it breaks all the bands of institutionalism. A subscribing to statement can never be a substitute for a sensing and sharing of this spirit. In our modern church life we are too self-conscious. Not for a moment are we allowed to forget ourselves and our theoretical opinions. We are so sensitive to our differences that we seldom feel the throb of that flow of spiritual life that should make us one. The secret of successful religious living, according to Jesus, is the complete forgetting of self, utter abandonment to the great goals of God for men. What we should seek is not conformity but unity in the midst of greatest natural variety. We must abandon the idea that the church is primarily a conserving agency. Religion, according to Jesus, is a constructive and commanding force in human life and living. As long as the church conceives of its chief task as that of preserving its heritage pure, just so long is it dispensable as an organ in our human society.

The church, if we judge it in the light of what Jesus sought to accomplish, is first of all an agency for the spiritual recovery and restoration of men as individuals and as groups. When the church calms its conscience with the complimentary thought that it is the kingdom of God on earth, it is dangerously near apostasy and betrays the morbidness of its morale. In the light of the New Testament itself it is inconceivable that Jesus could have regarded any organization or institution as the visible kingdom of God. In his faith the kingdom is of and from God; men may meet its conditions, but they do not make it. The church may feel that it is the representative of Jesus on earth, but it should remember that while it possesses this consciousness of high call and holy commission it is not the direct issue and product of his own planning. Rather should it take up Jesus' own work—that of preparing men for the society of God.

The church should always be humble in its claims, proving its worth and the justice of its claims in the terms of a maximum of ministry. If the church could once become true to the best of its genius, it would not be in need of making claims for itself and its right to recognition, for such would be unquestioned. It could become like a great unpretentious personality, the thoroughness of whose consecration, the simplicity of whose spirit, the certainty of whose convictions, would come as a providential blessing to all men who seek for light and strength to live by.

All great religions have had their source in some passionately religious personality. But it seems to be inevitable that a religion which starts with an intense personality, when it begins to win its way with the masses and finds itself thrown into the sweeping currents of the world's life, should develop into an organized movement that has its official institution with corresponding rituals, liturgies, ceremonies, doctrines, dogmas, confessions and creeds. The purer prophetic religion of Israel became encased in the impregnable armor of the priestly cult of Judaism. Christianity chose Jesus rather than his cause. Whether this would have been a personal disappointment to Jesus we shall never know. But the fact remains that the great cause of God, which he served and for which he died, was almost if not wholly neglected by his confessed followers. The fervent faith that possessed the simpler soul of Jesus was soon crystallized into fixed formulas with different sources, objects and issues. How the Christian church, even when fully conscious of all the good that it has done and of all the human help that it has rendered, can continue to read the Gospel story without a pang of conscience, without a sting of regret and remorse, is a modern psychological miracle. It seems that it might be possible for a religion that is represented by an institution to retain at least a fair measure of the warm spirit from which it sprang and to prevent itself from degenerating into a religion of rigid respectability and cold convention. In the midst of all the impediments that the centuries have loaded upon it, it would be a saving song of human hope if the church could retain a full share of inner independence and freedom such as characterized Jesus.

The great danger that threatens the church is not heresy, but apostasy—a virtual denial and desertion of the faith and spirit of Jesus. Diversity of opinion is not half so dangerous as selfishness, staleness and sourness of spirit. A church that is constantly on its guard can never give itself to and for men as Jesus gave himself. Our modern religious work is half make-believe. We go through the motions, and we delude ourselves into thinking that we are religious. We trust to organization as though religion were merely a matter of mechanics. We meet in conventions and conferences, and we go home with some new complex. We appoint committees and sub-committees. We make surveys and compile statistics. We inaugurate programs with pious slogans and catch-words. We do all this with a sense of satisfaction: Surely we have prospered the work of the Lord. We go ahead in our mechanics-madness as though the eternal order itself were composed of an almighty chairman who follows Robert's rules of order, as though the next world were a spacious accounting-house full of adding-machines, card catalogues and filing systems (for we are modern in our conception of the next world!), a great bookkeeping establishment with countless clerks, an immense information bureau with hosts of angelic apprehenders of our human misdemeanors, as though God were One who listened only to the findings of the recording angel and in the light of the conclusions drawn, started a fresh drive of propaganda among the sons of men.

The religious values represented by the church to-day are theoretical rather than actual. It requires personal devotion to impersonal things. It forgets that such is exactly counter to the human constitution. Men feel that they must center their loyalties on things that mean most to them. Only concrete meanings can command human devotions. When the church degenerates into a school of theology, becomes a mere drill master in doctrine and dogma, congratulates itself on its conferences and conventions—then we may say that the deepest things of religion have departed from it. The church may keep its traditional theories on this or that religious theme, but it must not insist that such is the true essence of a religion that names itself after Jesus. The creeds of the church are products of conflict; its doctrines were framed against foes. They are not the natural and spontaneous expression of the Christian faith in its intimate and personal phases.

For many a liberal-minded modern man of strongly religious inclination theology possesses not more than historical interest. Doctrine and dogma are dead driftwood; officialism and orthodoxy are offensive obstacles; creeds and confessions are crumbling crusts. But still the Master of men, who taught more than these things, stands and calls for him, and he in turn, like the four fishermen and the tax-gatherer, is ready to leave all and follow him. Jesus has lost none of his power over humankind, but men must have a chance to see and know him as he was. One of the chief obstacles in the way of a resolute return to Jesus is an organized Christianity that has ceased to interpret itself and its task in the light of loyalty to all that he was and represented in the way of religion. The pulpit is not presenting Jesus as he was, for the pulpiteer knows little about Jesus, the fulness and sufficiency of his experience of God. The chief task of too many ministers to-day seems to be to assure us that we are good and religious, when we in our better moments know that such is not the case.

From Christian circles we often hear the complaint about the lack of real religious interest on the part of the modern man. But the modern man could just as well complain of the lack of an earnest and effective enthusiasm within confessed Christian circles. He finds little to attract him, still less to command him. Seldom does he hear from the church a message, seldom does he witness from it a show of spirit, that might create within him a permanent purpose to become a better man as an individual and as a member of his group.

The church's great task is to follow Jesus, not to recruit followers of itself. Once the church begins to accomplish this task in any appreciable measure it need never again be concerned about its constituency. There will be no clanish church but a great spiritual society following Jesus toward the great goal for which he lived and worked and died—the kingdom of God in which the divine will is as seriously sought and as perfectly performed on earth as it is in heaven. This may be a radical religious idealism, but it is the clear call of that one great religious figure of history who can command the loyalty and life of modern man, the confident and consecrated figure of the prophet-preacher of Nazareth.

The church may never be able to realize this radical religious ideal set by Jesus. Its success will not be absolute but relative, for the higher the ideal the stronger and more serious are the obstacles of human frailty in the way of its realization. But Jesus was willing to accept followers in spite of all their weaknesses. On the basis of constitutional weakness he excluded none from the quest of the kingdom of God. The church needs to learn to be satisfied with beginnings. Jesus seems to have sought not more than a vital start, a single seed with the germ of life in it. The later stages he trusted to the Divine; for growth and harvest he could wait. One of the plainest lessons of Jesus for his followers is working, watching and waiting.

The very distance of the goal set by Jesus is awful, but this does not justify a resistless resignation or retreat. It calls rather for a resolute return of the church to the genius that gave it birth. The Founder of the past may not have foreseen all the facts of the present, but the nature of the problem is unchanged. Progress is a matter of spirit rather than of system. As a system Christianity has been about as successful as it could hope to be, but as a spiritual movement its work is not yet well under way. If it will trust to its original genius, it can work wonders in our human order. The sources of strength are there if we dare trust them in the most serious matter of our human experience.

What after all is a religious society? One that is capable not only of surviving but that is able to cope successfully with all odds? It would be difficult to find a finer example of such a religious society than that which speaks directly to us through the New Testament. The earliest Christian community was little more than a Jewish Christ-cult, a Messianic movement within the confines of Judaism. In the early chapters of Acts the message of the Apostles moves along the line that the little band with its faith is nothing other than true Judaism, the promise to Israel gone into fulfillment. Even Paul in his more Jewish moments, when his disappointed love for his people comes to the surface, shares strongly of this feeling. It was only in the presence of persecution and adversity that the early Christians realized that they represented a new and different religion.

The New Testament comes fresh and strong from the nascent period of Christianity's history. Consequently its literary expressions manifest that natural variety and diversity that belong to the early stages of any movement. Within the New Testament itself Christianity bears a dozen different complexions. A position that one writer sets forth as fundamental and indispensable another writer will neglect entirely. There is no orthodoxy or officialism, only the first faint hints of such appear in the latest and religiously least significant of the New Testament books. It would be difficult to find a more heterodox collection of Christian writings than the New Testament presents. Each of its writers who shows any measure of religious genius expresses his faith in his own free way. They write under no external restraint. There are no fixed formulas to which they must rigidly adhere in giving expression to the personal faith and feeling back of their pens.

Yet straight through the New Testament there runs a

vital bond of unity, and its writers are essentially one in their faith. It is not an orthodoxy of opinion, nor is it a singleness of statement. The New Testament writers are one in their religious experience. With all of their diversity they are united on the religious significance of Jesus. The religious society back of the New Testament is a community of conviction. Its writers are bound together by common longings and fears, persecutions and adversities, expectations and enthusiasms, consolations and confidences, loves and loyalties, convictions and certainties. They are one, not in form, but in fervor and fidelity of faith.

Only such a religious society possesses the power necessary to accomplish its task in the world. The church must learn again from the New Testament. Its vitality and life are quite apart from external matters. It must be a community of conviction. Religion strikes down to the source-springs, and the church must become a spiritual society of those who live by common fears and hopes, common loves and loyalties. The only valid religious faith is that which can still fear, impart courage, realize hope and nourish love and devotion.

Jesus spoke of the religious life in terms of loyalties and devotions. At the center of human devotions, as the pole of human loyalties, he set God and His kingdom. These his followers are to sense, seek, secure and share; by them they are to be claimed and commanded; to them they are to be wholly committed and consecrated. In the religious following of Jesus there is no place for those traditional divisive forces and factors that have shattered the church's unity. Only a resolute recognition of the cardinal centers of the personal faith of Jesus can bring all right-thinking and right-spirited Christian people together. The religious experience of Jesus is essentially unifying.

JESUS—THE AUTHOR AND PERFECTER OF OUR FAITH

Who was Jesus? What is the truth about Jesus Christ? The answers have been legion. Within the New Testament we read that Jesus was the Messiah, the Son of God, the Risen Lord, the Word become flesh, the Lamb of God, and the Savior of the world. And Jesus was all these things for the New Testament Christians. In the history of the church these primitive answers were retained, but they lost their original simplicity and power. They became parts of elaborate systems of thought in which supernaturalism gave its metaphysical replies; orthodoxy had its opinions; theology had its theories, and faith its fixed formulas. During the nineteenth century, the century rich in its lives of Jesus, historical criticism gave its answers: Jesus was a teacher and a healer, a moralist, a mystic, a reformer, a fanatic, a prophet, a preacher, a religious genius. The answers to the question, Who was Jesus? have always been interesting, and so far as they have come from genuine religious experience they have been and still are inspiring.

But the historical student of the life of Jesus to-day has his own answer to this question. His answer does not come in the terms of Christian tradition, nor in the language of abstract speculation, nor in the pious phrases of the past. It is framed in the light of a careful and conscientious study of the New Testament with a view to the truth and the facts. It does not come on the basis of a single passage, but on the basis of all that the best New Testament sources seem to present and portray. His answer comes in the light of literary records, of the conclusions of a conscientious appraisal of these, of historical probability, and most important of all in the light of the psychology of a living personality the whole of whose being was exclusively religious. For the historical student, Jesus was a religious subject, an experient of religion, in possession of the richest religious experience of our human history.

The historical student feels that the traditional thinking of the church has never done Jesus historical and personal justice. He feels that the person of Jesus is not a problem in abstract metaphysics or in speculative theology. For him metaphysics and theology possess no key that would disclose to us the real significance of his appearance in human history. At best they can furnish only semi-mythological and imaginary interpretations. The historical student sees in Jesus a problem in history, for he actually lived in the first century; in humanity, for he was a serious sharer of our human experience; in religion, for he was an exclusively religious personality. It is only as we approach him as a problem in personal piety that we are true to the state and nature of the facts, and that we come near a satisfactory and helpful conclusion. Jesus then becomes "the author and perfecter of our faith." (Heb. 12,2.)

With religious right the Christian consciousness may state, even formulate, its faith in Jesus. But it must be sure that these statements and formulations express his real religious significance, that they demonstrate clearly the actual contribution which he has to make to our human experience. Further, it must avoid that ancient and religiously atrophying error of identifying faith with its formulations.

We may never under any circumstances surrender the person of Jesus. To strip Christianity of the person of Jesus would leave it utterly poverty-stricken and lifeless. It is in Jesus alone as a human, historical and religious figure that Christianity can lay claim to distinction in the field of religion. All of our religious faith must center exclusively upon what he, by being what he was, offers us. But we must remember that Jesus, not later opinions and theories about him, is the one sure and substantial thing that we possess. All else is accessory and incidental, not essential and permanent. To center all emphasis and interest upon theoretical conceptions of his person is to miss entirely his real significance. We must conceive of him in terms of his contribution to our common human problem of living life religiously. Jesus represents fundamental religious values that are absolutely indispensable to humankind if it is to extract anything permanent from its existence. We must, therefore, make a religious appraisal of Jesus. Any interpretation that neglects his religious experience misses the finest and best that he has to offer and to communicate.

Jesus' contribution to the religion of the race is purely personal. To our human history he gives a human life religiously lived, a human experience religiously exalted, enriched and enhanced. He does not stand as an indefinite and intangible ideal, as an absurd abstraction of pious fancy. He stands rather on the solid ground of history, our great human contemporary, a real man who dared live life exclusively in the presence of God and in behalf of men. Many ingenious inquiries have been made that would disclose the secret sources of his life, the pure perfection of his personality, but all have been, doubtless all to come will be, unsatisfactory. We shall never be able to explain Jesus for the simple reason that the ultimate sources of personality are beyond us, still more so in the case of him who stands as the one gigantic figure on our spiritual horizon. But if we seek the chief contributing cause that made him what he was, we shall have to locate it in the purity and perfection of his religious experience which, functioning as the chief factor and force in his life, had as its necessary corollary a corresponding purity of personality.

Religion as a vital power in individual life is beyond our explanation. It is essentially irrational for those who would discover its origin, operation and manifestations in a life that is religiously lived. In the case of Jesus, there is no need of explanation so long as we may enrich the whole of our life and experience from his own.

The life of Jesus, as we have said already, is the richest and most stimulating body of religious subject-matter that we possess. His personal piety, the nature and substance of his religious experience, is the greatest and most convincing thing about him. In the history of humanity's religious experience Jesus stands supreme, superb and sublime. His faith in God and His kingdom with all that it involves is the most significant contribution which he has to make. He is the founder of the only adequate religious faith. In him, human life is exposed to all that is highest and best in the human conception and experience of religion. In Jesus, faith and fact meet, merge and live. In him we see, and he calls on us to share, all that God and religion at their best may and can mean in human life and experience. The faithful follower of Jesus, then, may look to him, as did the writer of Hebrews, as "the author and perfecter of our faith." (12,2.) Here we have a purely religious approach such as the very substance of the first three Gospels forces us to make. For me personally, this crisp and concise confession in Hebrews is the finest of all statements in the history of Christianity concerning who Jesus was and what he is to mean for his followers.

Those who choose to see in Jesus more than the author and perfecter of our faith have a right to do so. Each has a right, according to the measure of his religious life, to enrich his experience from that of Jesus in every way that he can. But Jesus must mean this to every faithful follower, if he is to mean anything at all. The *plus* which Christian piety may add and has added must be more than impersonal and theoretical abstractions; they must represent religious realities that were present in the religious experience of Jesus himself. Any conception of Jesus is worthy of him that comes from the mind and heart of one who is definitely committed to a determined and devoted discipleship. Wherever he stands as the religious center and authority in individual and group life there is no danger of a too low conception of his person. As Jesus once told one of his intolerant disciples (Mark 9,39),

"There is no man who shall do a mighty work in my name, and be able quickly to speak evil of me."

When all the theoretical attempts fail adequately to comprehend Jesus, then the historical student reserves for himself the religious right to form a new resolve and return to the New Testament, there to win, for himself at least, all that Jesus offers of permanent value and worth for human life and living. The historical student who is compelled to take a religious view of Jesus is in no way disloyal to the essential elements of the Christian faith, that is, if we understand Christianity as devoted discipleship such as he demanded of his followers. Jesus stands at the very center of the religious faith of the historical student, not as a religious object, but as a religious subject whose experience of God is sufficiently rich to demand limitless loyalty. In our modern day when we insist that religion must be real, that faith should function, there is not a finer or more resourceful conception of Jesus and the place he should occupy in the Christian faith than that of Hebrews 12,2.

Wherein lies the authority of Jesus? Certainly not in theology, for he did not teach it. Certainly not in doctrine and dogma, for he preached neither. Certainly not in confession and creed, for he never required such. Certainly not in officialism and orthodoxy, for he founded neither. Certainly not in religious convention, for he broke with it. Jesus is an authority in just one field, that of personal religious experience. He stands in history as the supreme authority on the subject of living human life religiously. And it is just at this point that the social significance of Jesus' religious experience appears, for there is no social religion apart from individually religious personalities. At the very center of our human order Jesus sets a plain yet profound piety that is a source of light and strength sufficient for coping with all the major and minor matters of individual and group life—that is, for those who dare to seek to share it. As the perfecter of the purest personal piety the authority of Jesus will remain until another of the sons of men shall choose God so completely.

Jesus, however, is not an authority on the forms of

religious experience. He never lectures his disciples on either its varieties or uniformities. He gave them no set standards and criterions for judging the forms of religious experience. It was not a problem with which he was forced to deal as was Paul in I Corinthians 12-14. Religious certainty and the genuineness of personal religion he did not base upon its psychological forms of expression. He never prescribed types even for those to whom he devoted most care and attention. How and what they should feel he did not say. To all religious experience Jesus applied but one test, that of fruits. In order to be genuine religious experience must express itself in corresponding character and conduct. He laid no emphasis on the form of religious experience, but on its content.

If we approach the personal piety of Jesus from the standpoint of religious profession, we are amazed at its simplicity and modesty. He who possessed the most exalted consciousness of God's high call and holy commission, who was held by an unparalleled confidence and conviction, makes no profuse profession that springs from experiences past or present. Rather he discourages religious profession and presses on with all his soul in the persistent pursuit of the divine will for himself and all who are like-minded. As psychological types we know next to nothing of his religious experiences. If he had such, he never refers to them; still less does he set them as normative for others. Nowhere in the words of Jesus do the stock phrases of religious witness appear.

Interest in and emphasis upon the form rather than the content of religious experience is characteristic of the history of religion among all peoples. The various Christian sects that have appeared and have insisted on special types of religious experience as the sole sources of religious certainty have not been followers of Jesus in this respect. Conformities in religious experience seem to have had their origin in the ecstatic and strongly psychic beginnings of Christianity such as appear in the early chapters of Acts and in I Corinthians 12-14. But Jesus stipulated no set type of religious experience that should become universal among his disciples and as such give the distinctive features to their faith.

Some scholars, notably Albert Schweitzer[18] and Karl Weidel,[19] have undertaken to estimate the contribution and authority of Jesus in terms of moral will directed toward the highest religious values. They speak of him as the man of will (*den Willensmensch*, Weidel), possessing and in turn imparting a strange and stimulating strength of will (Schweitzer).

Such an appraisal of the authority of Jesus has under it two solid foundation stones. In the first place, it is true to the psychology of religious experience. The moral will is the seat of all personal religion that moves on a high plane; it is an integral element in the fabric of personal religious faith. Professor Hocking writes, "A faith without a large ingredient of will, is not faith at all."[20] Professor Coe writes, "The center of gravity in religion is the moral will."[21] In the second place, the estimate of Jesus in terms of the moral will has under it the solid foundation of the Gospel picture. Any one who has observed so much as the character and content of Jesus' choices can not but be astonished at that won-

---

[18] *The Quest of the Historical Jesus*, concluding chapter.
[19] *Jesu Persoenlichkeit. Eine Charakterstudie.*
[20] *The Meaning of God in Human Experience*, p. 150.
[21] *The Psychology of Religion*, p. xiv.

drous wealth of will which he was capable of launching in the quest of the Divine. Jesus faced decisions and he made them in the most resolute manner. His work demanded deepest determination in the face of disappointment, and he was capable of it. His choice of the divine cause required constancy, unfailing confidence, unflinching fidelity. It required a will, a wealth of will, to believe what Jesus believed. The whole of his experience is an unprecedented exhibition of a vast volume of volition in the service of religion. Further, his religious demands upon his followers were direct appeals to the moral will. No religious leader has ever laid such pressing practical demands on the individual and social will as did Jesus. The discipleship of Jesus requires a real will-to-believe.

There is a strangely stimulating strength of will in the mind of Jesus, but to make him an authority in matters of the moral will only is a much too narrow confinement for the power that he possessed. His passionate personality bursts the narrow walls of will. They may define him on the one side, but they can not contain him. Pure will is definite, sharp and exacting. But Jesus possessed an enthusiastic energy. Pure personal piety is will, but it is more, even though will is its most substantial single element. "Not in the cold, deliberate choice of will, but in the passion of soul is to be found that flood of energy which can open to us the sources of power— mastered by such a passion the soul will admit no defeat."[22]

The thing that characterizes Jesus from the volitional point of view is the depth of his personal devotion.

[22] *The Spirit*, by B. H. Streeter, p. 87.   Courtesy of The Macmillan Company.

Devotion is more than decision and determination. Decision may be clear-cut, extremely self-exacting. Determination may be undivided, even desperate. But in devotion there is a warmth, a glow, a burst, a fervor that make self-denying decision and determination possible. Devotion as it appears in the religious experience of Jesus means the enlistment of the whole self—will, emotion, thought, faith—in the service of something beyond and above self. The will is never at its best unless the subject possesses a sense of being claimed and commanded. Mere selection is far removed from service and sacrifice. Choice is only a mechanical mental process when compared with that entire commitment and consecration of which the religious subject is capable. The will may do police duty, but it takes passion to promote. The power that pushes a personality toward its goal demands will, but it demands more. It operates less under the consciousness of *having chosen,* more in the conviction of *having been chosen.* Above selection in the experience of Jesus stand service and sacrifice; above decision and determination, a depth of devotion that demands all; above choice, a consciousness of call and commission, utter commitment and consecration.

With all of his wealth of will, the attitude of Jesus is never that of self-sufficiency. As we saw in chapter three, Jesus on this as on all points remains rigidly religious. He is fully aware of the weakness of the human will. Therefore, he taught the graciousness of God over against the merit of man. And there is no good reason why we should not regard this fundamental religious position as autobiographical, an extract from the depths of his own experience.

In our modern approach to Jesus we must leave him where and how and what he was, as real as he was—human, historical, religious. We must leave him where he found God and God found him, a religious figure of our human history. Above all, we may not separate him from the religious centers of his life without inflicting grave injustice on him and on ourselves. The religious evaluation of Jesus is the only one that will bring us to him and him to us, the only avenue that will communicate what he has to impart. In all of his life and work Jesus placed himself on the side of humanity. Speculation only separates him from us and makes him increasingly unreal.

There are very definite religious dangers in deification—dangers destructive of Christianity and the chief cause of the church itself. Absolute deification withdraws Jesus and his religious experience from the ranks of men who most need religion. As long as he remains with them, one of them, men may feel that he has something to say to them, still more to impart. They may be reasonably assured that what he became they may at least attempt with courage and in some measure attain. The great majority of modern men who feel that religion is practical and who are convinced that religious living is a hard task claiming their all, will never consent to the removal of Jesus from their ranks, for their only hope is the conviction and certainty that he is on their side. We may take Jesus from the ranks of men of true and deep religiousness and ascribe to him all possible predicates, but the sense of being led and the courage to follow has departed from men and leaves religiously stranded those who are most in need of religious leadership and command. *A religion about Jesus* may fit the pious patterns of the past and satisfy the ecclesiastic and doctrinaire of the present, but only *the religion of Jesus* can recommend and prove itself in the life and experience of modern men who find themselves confronted at every turn with grave moral struggles that threaten to destroy them and their kind. We may admire and adore Jesus, deify and worship him, as our inclinations and inspirations prompt us individually, but we must follow him, believe with him, and seek to share his experience if he is to mean most to us religiously.

The disposition to deify Jesus was natural enough for the first Christians. The very nature and substance of their Easter experiences virtually demanded this. But for us to-day such deification will only keep him remote, out of all contact with the problems of our experience. The whole structure of Paul's Christian faith rested upon the validity of his Damascus vision of the Risen Lord (I Cor. 15,14),

"If Christ hath not been raised, then is our preaching vain, and your faith also is vain."

But the resurrection faith will never claim us as it claimed Paul and its original experients. We may entertain it as a common human hope, we may maintain it for Jesus in particular, but theoretical belief in the resurrection will never solve for us the common human problem of living life religiously in the sense of Jesus.

Our loyalty to Jesus is not a matter of theoretical and impersonal belief. It is a matter of trust, of warm personal confidence in his ability to help. We must approach Jesus to-day as he was approached by those of his contemporaries for whom he did most—with the hope of

high helpfulness from him. The leper came to him with
a confidence that almost staggers us (Mark 1,40),

"Lord, if thou wilt, thou canst make me clean."

The centurion met him with a faith that was new in Israel
(Matt. 8,8),

"Only say the word, and my servant shall be healed."

The woman's reflections are a tremendous tribute (Mark
5,28),

"If I touch but his garments, I shall be made whole."

Jesus and his contemporaries were not separated by
theological theories. Their relation to him and his relation to them was purely personal. They knew him as
a real man of their own life and experience, a knowledge
unhampered by traditions. And even to-day we have a
native and natural religious right to approach him as he
was approached by his contemporaries and as he approached them, so far as careful study can clear the way
for us. In our approach to Jesus we have a right to strip
our minds of everything that has intervened since his
death, so far as this is possible.

To base the religious authority of Jesus on the Immaculate Conception, the Virgin Birth, the historicity of the
nature-miracles, or even on the resurrection, is distorted
devotion to primitive Christian values. His religious
significance does not stand or fall with any of these things.
We must determine the authority of Jesus by those elements in his experience that are vital and life-giving,

those elements that are capable of enriching our human experience in such a way that we become capable of coping successfully with all the exigencies of our existence.

The modern question concerning Jesus is not whether we may or may not speak of him in the terms of deity and divinity. The great question is: How valid is Jesus' religious experience? May we trust his experience of God as true? Is his faith real and reliable? May we live in the faith that the world is good because it is God's, that God is a living and loving Father, that all men of all conditions are His children, that He has a kingdom that will come? Is Jesus' personal piety worthy of reproduction? Is his religion something that we may share? Is it something that we may live by? It is at these points that the religious authority of Jesus is at stake, and only seasoned experience in his devoted discipleship can answer these questions. The historical student is ready to answer these questions in the affirmative. He believes that the religious experience of Jesus will stand until all human experience proves itself to be only a delusion.

The question, Who was Jesus? each must answer for himself with the New Testament before him and in the presence of God. Here our learned text-books in systematic theology will not help us. In the nearness of the historical Jesus we feel that we have come into the presence of the Divine, as near as our human constitution will permit. Again—in Jesus, faith and fact meet, and we come at once into the presence of the human and the holy.

Eduard von Hartmann once wrote that Jesus is "a much too narrow foundation for the erection of a religious structure."[23] But Von Hartmann was judging Jesus

---

[23]*Das Christentum des Neuen Testaments*, p. 15.

more in the light of the historical background of the first century than in the light of the nature and substance of his religious experience. This fallacy of mistaking the form of Jesus' faith for its content is not unknown even to-day. In the form of his faith he certainly belongs to the first century where he remains firmly imbedded as a man of history. But the substance of Jesus' faith is superhistorical. It is solid and sound to the core for, to use a principle of Kant, it is capable of universalization. The religious experience of Jesus is not outgrown. It is the most abiding value of our human history, as commanding and adequate to-day as it was in 30 A. D. We have yet fully to comprehend the religious experience of Jesus and all that it involves for our human life. Religion in his experience leaves no phase of human life and living untouched; it strikes down to the very source-springs of our existence and lays hold on the elemental forces of life in a way and to a degree that offers the only hope for man's future on earth as reasonably religious and righteous.

Religion is a serious matter in human life and experience. Its presence or absence makes itself felt, and life is different. Religion of a high order does result in respectability of life, but respectability is not religion. Respectability is not resourceful enough to rely on in time of crisis. When elemental human instincts, impulses and passions are aroused, whether of the individual or of the group, there is need of something that will carry us out beyond ourselves and the opinions of others and furnish us with powers of inhibition, guidance and control. The Western World ascribes to Jesus a theoretical authority, but it does not accord him an actual authority. It rises instantly against those who dare question the authority of Jesus, but it feels no obligation to order its actual existence after his way of life—an attitude of impersonal rather than personal devotion. If we interpret religion and the part it is to play in human life as Jesus seems to have interpreted it, we shall have to say that Christianity, even at its best, has as yet touched not more than the periphery of our existence.

We to-day must reconstruct our religion, not in the light of Paul, or John, or of later accepted and official dicta, but in the light of the religious experience of Jesus himself. Christianity will never be true to its best genius, it will never accomplish its real work in the world until it has the courage to undertake such a reconstruction. The hope of Christianity and its contribution to our human life is not a rigorous restriction of what may or may not be believed *about* Jesus, but in an unreserved release of all our powers to believe *with* him. It is to share his religious experience and faith that Jesus calls us over the tumults of theology, over the confusion of controversy and conflict. And a resolute return to him will require courage to overcome all obstacles, not the least of which will be our own selves and the delusion of our religiousness.

If Jesus is to be taken at all, he is to to be taken seriously. Surely we are not supersensitive souls whose constitution is not sufficiently strong to appropriate and assimilate the solid subject-matter which is offered us in the form of his religious experience. Surely we are capable of facing the facts and fighting our way back to that great contribution which he has to make. If we are going to be religious, let us be really religious in the sense of Jesus.

What is the preacher to preach and, with his preaching, live? What is the layman to live and, by his living, preach? The answer is simple and clear: the religion, the personal piety, of Jesus which he himself sought to share with his followers.

Jesus came to cast fire upon the earth, that mysterious element of his own East, the fire of his faith. (Luke 12, 49.) Into our human history Jesus has hurled a firebrand. Men may relate themselves to it as they will, but it continues to burn, igniting the fires of judgment upon our human delinquency and wickedness, but for those who have the courage to snatch it up, it illuminates the way out. The very fact that Jesus lived—human, historical, religious—for ever forbids that life should go on unchanged, without elevation, enrichment and enhancement, unless we are to be overtaken by that most terrible of human maladies, a creeping paralysis of the religious consciousness.

Who was Jesus? This study has sought to show on the basis of the New Testament, the history and psychology of religion, that Jesus was a religious subject, an experient of religion, the most religious personality, the possessor of the richest and most resourceful religious experience of our human history. The author is not ready to say who Jesus was, all that he was; but he feels that Jesus is religiously sufficient for all our human needs. He feels that we may actually trust Jesus in the most serious matter of our human experience, that of living life religiously. He also feels just as strongly that Jesus is entirely too intense a personality to be cramped within the narrow confines of intellectual concepts. He strikes the whole of our life, not just the thinking process. The Christian task is not to define Jesus, but to demonstrate him to all who know him not.

THE END

BIBLIOGRAPHY

BIBLIOGRAPHY

BOUSSET, W. *Jesus* (3te Auflage, Tuebingen: Mohr, 1907).

Jesu Predigt in ihrem Gegensatz zum Judentum (Goettingen, 1892).

Das Wesen der Religion (4te Auflage, Tuebingen: Mohr, 1920).

BULTMANN, R. *Jesus* (Berlin: Deutsche Bibliothek, 1927).

BUNDY, W. E. *The Psychic Health of Jesus* (New York: Macmillan, 1922).

"The Meaning of Jesus' Baptism," *Journal of Religion* (Chicago: University of Chicago Press), VII, January, 1927.

CASE, S. J. *Jesus: A New Biography* (Chicago: University of Chicago Press, 1927).

COE, G. A. *The Psychology of Religion* (Chicago: University of Chicago Press, 1921).

DEISSMANN, A. *Evangelium und Urchristentum* (Muenchen: Lehmann, 1905).

The Religion of Jesus and the Faith of Paul (New York: Doran, 1923), translation from the German by W. E. Wilson.

"Der Beter Jesus," *Christliche Welt* (XIII, 1899, cols. 701*ff.*).

FEUERBACH, L. *Das Wesen des Christentums* (Leipzig, 1846).

GOLTZ, E. v. d. *Das Gebet in der Aeltesten Christenheit* (Leipzig: Hinrichs, 1901).

335

GREIFF, A. *Das Gebet im Alten Testament* (Muenster i. W.: Aschendorff, 1915).

HARTMANN, E. v. *Das Christentum des Neuen Testaments* (Sasha im Harz: Haacke, 1905).

HAUER, J. W. *Die Religionen: ihr Werden, ihr Sinn, ihre Wahrheit.* Erstes Buch: *Das religioese Erlebnis auf den unteren Stufen* (Stuttgart: Kohlhammer, 1923).

HEILER, F. *Das Gebet. Eine religionsgeschichtliche und religionspsychologische Untersuchung* (4te Auflage, Muenchen: Reinhardt, 1921).

Der Katholizismus. Seine Idee und seine Erscheinung (Muenchen: Reinhardt, 1923).

Die Buddhistische Versenkung (2te Auflage, Muenchen: Reinhardt, 1922).

HOCKING, W. E. *Human Nature and Its Remaking* (New and revised edition, New Haven: Yale University Press, 1923).

The Meaning of God in Human Experience (New Haven: Yale University Press, 1912).

HOELSCHER, G. *Die Profeten. Untersuchungen zur Religionsgeschichte Israels* (Leipzig: Hinrichs, 1914).

JONES, E. S. *The Christ of the Indian Road* (New York: Abingdon Press, 1925).

JONES, R. M. *The Church's Debt to Heretics* (New York: Doran, 1926).

KLAUSNER, J. *Jesus of Nazareth* (New York: Macmillan, 1925), translation from the Hebrew by Herbert Danby.

LEIPOLDT, J. *Das Gotteserlebnis Jesu im Lichte der vergleichenden Religionsgeschichte* (Leipzig: Pfeiffer, 1927).

LOISY, A. *The Gospel and the Church* (New York: Scribners, 1912), translation from the French by Christopher Home.

My Duel with the Vatican (New York: Dutton, 1924), translation from the French by R. W. Boynton.

MUNDLE, W. *Das religioese Leben des Apostels Paulus* (Leipzig: Hinrichs, 1923).

"Der Christus des Glaubens und der historische Jesus," *Zeitschrift fuer Theologie und Kirche,* Hefte 3 und 4. (Neue Folge, 1921.)

OTTO, R. *Das Heilige. Ueber das Irrationale in der Idee des Goettlichen und sein Verhaeltnis zum Rationalen* (9te Auflage, Breslau: Trewendt & Granier, 1922). English translation by John W. Harvey, *The Idea of the Holy. An Inquiry into the Non-rational Factor in the Idea of the Holy* (3d impression, London: Oxford University Press, 1925).

PARKER, Mrs. A. *Sadhu Sundar Singh* (4th edition, New York: Revell, 1923).

PENNEY, N. *The Journal of George Fox* (Tercentenary edition, New York: Dutton, 1924).

PRATT, J. B. *The Religious Consciousness* (New York: Macmillan, 1921).

SCHUERER, E. *Die Geschichte des juedischen Volkes im Zeitalter Jesu Christi* (2te Auflage, Leipzig: Hinrichs, 1886).

SCHWEITZER, A. *Die Geschichte der Leben-Jesu-Forschung* (2te Auflage, Tuebingen: Mohr, 1913). English translation of the first edition, *Von Rei-*

marus zu Wrede (1906), by W. Montgomery, *The Quest of the Historical Jesus* (2d edition, London: A. & C. Black, 1911).

SELBIE, W. B. *The Psychology of Religion* (London: Oxford University Press, 1924).

SINGH, S. *Reality and Religion* (New York: Macmillan, 1924).

Visions of the Spiritual World (New York: Macmillan, 1927).

At the Master's Feet (New York: Revell, 1922), translation from the Urdu by Reverend Arthur and Mrs. Parker.

STAERK, W. *Die Schriften des Alten Testaments* (2te Auflage, Goettingen: Vandenhoeck & Ruprecht, 1920), 3te Abteilung, Band I, *Lyrik und Weisheit.*

STREETER, B. H. *The Message of Sadhu Sundar Singh* (New York: Macmillan, 1922).

Concerning Prayer: Its Nature, Its Difficulties, and its Values (London: Macmillan, 1921).

The Spirit (New York: Macmillan, 1922).

WARSCHAUER, J. *The Historical Life of Christ* (New York: Macmillan, 1927).

WEIDEL, K. *Jesu Persoenlichkeit. Eine Charakterstudie* (2te Auflage, Halle a. d. S.: Marhold, 1913).

WEINEL, H. *Biblische Theologie des Neuen Testaments* (3te Auflage, Tuebingen: Mohr, 1921).

WEISS, J. *Die Schriften des Neuen Testaments* (3te Auflage, Goettingen: Vandenhoeck & Ruprecht, 1917), Band I, *Die drei aelteren Evangelien.*

Das Aelteste Evangelium (Goettingen: Vandenhoeck & Ruprecht, 1903).

WELLHAUSEN, J. *Einleitung in die drei ersten Evangelien* (2te Ausgabe, Berlin: Reimer, 1911).

WERNLE, P. *Jesus* (Tuebingen: Mohr, 1916).

WOODBURNE, A. S. "The Indian Appreciation of Jesus,"
Journal of Religion (Chicago: University of
Chicago Press), VII, January, 1927.

INDEX OF SUBJECTS

INDEX OF SUBJECTS

Abel 14
Abraham 296
Acts 312
  See Index of Scripture Passages
Ahaz, King 100
Amos 32, 39, 42, 43, 87, 107, 134, 164, 177
  See Index of Scripture Passages
Anti-eschatology 122*f.*
Anti-evolution 268
Apocalyptic writings 108
Apocrypha 7*f.*, 106*f.*
  See Index of Scripture Passages
Apostles 303
  See Disciples
  See also Twelve, The
Apostles' Creed 266
At the Master's Feet 203
Augustine 117

Baptism
  Jesus' 45, 166-168, 189, 302
  Jesus and 51, 302
Bertholet, A. 181
Bethlehem 6
Bibliolatry 27
Biblische Theologie des Neuen Testaments 169, 286
Bousset, W.
  Jesus 77, 85
  Jesu Predigt in ihrem Gegensatz zum Judentum 122
  Das Wesen der Religion 275
Buddha 300
Bultmann, Rudolf
  Jesus xii
Bundy, W. E.
  "The Meaning of Jesus' Baptism" 166
  The Psychic Health of Jesus 23, 125, 128, 149, 191

Bunyan 26

Cæsarea Philippi 189, 191
Capernaum 21, 22
Case, S. J.
  Jesus: A New Biography xii
  Christentum und Jesustum 279
Christianity xi, 160, 170, 238-253, 275-276, 291, 299*ff.*, 316, 324
  analysis of in West 239*ff.*
  and the East 238
    Gandhi 238
    Singh, S. 238
      See Singh
  and the Fatherhood of God 243
  and forgiveness 246-248
  and the *Golden Rule* 244-245
  and the kingdom of God 248-249
  and Paul 289
    See Paul
  and social problems 250-251, 252
  as cultural factor 249-250
  Christocentricity of 253
  contrast with religion of Jesus 139-140
  evolution of 276*ff.*
  faith of 251, 319
  founding of 294-295
  historical 253*ff.*, 282*ff.*
  of first century 276
  of to-day 291*ff.*
  social successes of 241
  reverence of 243
  task of 331
  theories of 259-260
Christians 124, 152, 280-281
  faith of 281
  religious experience of 281
  theology of 283*ff.*
  See Christianity

343

Christliche Welt 170
"Christ of Faith and the Historical Jesus, The" 279
Christ of the Indian Road, The 238
Christology 94, 147, 261, 275, 281
Church 297*ff*., 304-305, 306*ff*.
  apostasy of 308*f*.
  in New Testament 311-313
  task of 310
Church's Debt to Heretics, The 276
  The Psychology of Religion 59, 184, 204, 205, 321
Coe, G. A.
Concerning Prayer—Its Nature, Its Difficulties, and Its Values 184
Creed 268, 275, 284, 288, 292, 293
  Apostles' Creed 266
Cross 25, 26, 261
Cures 168, 228, 254, 256
  cleansing the leper 189
  Gerasene demoniac 154
  Jesus' attitude toward 153-155
  Simon's wife's mother 21

Damascus road 289, 297
Daniel 177
  book of 13, 14, 108
  See Index of Scripture Passages
Das Aelteste Evangelium 169
Das Christentum des Neuen Testaments 327
Das Gebet 26, 27, 102, 170, 171, 175, 178, 180, 187, 193, 198, 204
Das Gebet im Alten Testament 170, 180, 181
Das Gebet in der Aeltesten Christenheit 170
Das Gotteserlebnis Jesu 71, 101
Das Heilige 73, 75, 76, 85, 150, 279
Das religioese Leben des Apostels Paulus 197
Das Wesen der Religion 275
Das Wesen des Christentums 170
David 6, 28, 177
Decalogue 213-214

Deissmann, A. 27
  "Der Beter Jesus" 170
  Evangelium und Urchristentum 12, 38, 39, 49, 79, 138, 170, 193
  The Religion of Jesus and the Faith of Paul 49, 118, 170
"Der Beter Jesus" 170
"Der Christus des Glaubens und der historische Jesus" 258, 279
Der Katholizismus 123, 124, 157, 195, 273, 299
Devotion 322-323
Die Buddhistische Versenkung 170, 171, 178, 198
Die Geschichte der Leben-Jesu-Forschung 122
Die Profeten 152, 177
Die Religionen 140, 290
Die Schriften des Alten Testaments 180
Die Schriften des Neuen Testaments 144
Disciples 151, 184, 267
  lack of organization of 302, 320, 322

Easter 281, 282, 295
Ecclesiasticus 15
Eden 14
Egypt 16
Einleitung in die drei ersten Evangelien 297
Elijah 14, 39, 52, 54, 99-100, 194
Eschatology 122-123
  definition of 108
  of Jesus 13*f*., 108*f*., 113, 123-128
Esdras II 15
Esther 177
Evangelium and Urchristentum 12, 38, 39, 49, 79, 138, 170, 193
Evolution 268
Evolution of religious experience 259
Ezekiel 134
  See Index of Scripture Passages

Faith 212, 223, 275, 292, 314*ff*.
  and world of fact 83-84
  characterization of 64-65, 129
  importance of in religious genius
    62
  never a failure 137
  of Jesus chapter II
  See Jesus, faith of
Feeding the five thousand 189
Feuerbach, L.
  Das Wesen des Christentums 170
Fourth Gospel 51, 281, 284, 299,
    300
  See Index of Scripture Passages
Fox, George 194, 199
Fundamentalism 268, 293

Galilee ix, 3, 7, 9, 86, 154, 162,
    190, 195, 232, 271, 272, 274,
    275, 276, 284, 303
  and Greece 271-282
Gandhi 238
Gentiles 187
Gerasene demoniac 154
*Geschichte des juedischen Volkes im
  Zeitalter Jesu Christi* 179
Gethsemane 9, 26, 76, 158, 163,
    190, 194, 196, 199, 201, 204,
    207, 283
God
  and religious genius 67-68
  as Father 146, 147, 205
    historical background of 78-79
    Jesus' attitude toward 79*ff*.
  as Holy 72*ff*., 146, 148, 217
  attributes of
    ascribed by Christian rational-
      ism 91-92
  belief in 67
  Jesus' experience of 68, 71, 146-
    148
    See Jesus, faith of
  Jesus' faith in, 67*ff*., 107, 223-
    224
    See Jesus, faith of
  meaning of 104
Golden Rule 244-245

Goltz, E. v. d.
  *Das Gebet in der Aeltesten
    Christenheit* 170
Gospels, Synoptic 1, 4, 5, 12, 14,
    15, 16, 19, 20, 22, 23, 36, 47,
    49, 50, 53, 63, 70, 76, 123, 132,
    142, 143, 148, 154, 159, 166,
    168, 182, 189, 190, 195, 196,
    204, 209, 218, 228, 255, 256,
    262, 277, 280, 281, 285, 286,
    287, 295, 302, 321
Greece 271*ff*.
Gospel and the Church, The 57,
    136, 138, 273
Greiff, A.
  Das Gebet im Alten Testament
    170, 180, 181

Hannah 177
Hartmann, E. v.
  *Das Christentum des Neuen
    Testaments* 327
Hauer, J. W.
  *Die Religionen: ihr Werden,
    ihr Sinn, ihre Wahrheit* 140,
    290
Heiler, F.
  Das Gebet 26, 27, 102, 170, 171,
    178, 180, 187, 193, 198, 204
  Der Katholizismus 123, 124,
    157, 195, 273, 299
  Die Buddhistische Versenkung
    170, 171, 178, 198
Herod 31, 39, 40
Herrmann, Professor 292
Historical Life of Christ, The 122
Hocking, W. E.
  Human Nature and Its Remaking
    55, 242
  *The Meaning of God in Human
    Experience* 142, 184, 321
Hoelscher, G.
  Die Profeten 152, 177
Hosea 32
  See Index of Scripture Passages
Huggard, W. A. xii
Human Nature and Its Remaking
    55, 242

Immaculate Conception 326
"Indian Appreciation of Jesus, The"
  238
Interimsethik 122
Isaac 296
Isaiah 32, 34, 39, 100
  See Index of Scripture Passages
Israel 9, 32, 33, 54, 68, 73, 84,
  85, 90, 92, 105, 108, 119, 147,
  151, 167, 175, 176, 177, 178,
  179, 180, 181, 259, 294, 296,
  307
  devotional literature of
    See Old Testament
  religion of as background for
    Jesus 60
I-style (*Ichstyl*) of prophets 36

Jacob 176, 296
James (son of Zebedee) 100
Jehovah 194
Jeremiah 32, 34, 39, 134, 158,
  177-178, 182
  See Index of Scripture Passages
Jerusalem 87, 142, 144, 165, 167,
  169, 222, 238, 303
  as Holy City 34, 87
Jesu Persoenlichkeit 321
*Jesu Predigt in ihrem Gegensatz
  zum Judentum* 122
Jesus
  acts of
    baptism 156-168
    cleansing the temple 169
    cures, 21, 168, 228, 254, 256
    feeding the five thousand 168-
      169
    journey to Jerusalem 169
    journey to north 168
    last supper 169
    number of 166
    prayers 169
      See Jesus, prayers of
    sources for 165
  and alms-giving 89
  and the church 297*ff*., 304-305
  and the cross 25, 26, 261
    See Jesus, prayers of

Jesus—*cont*.
  and cult 87, 304
  and fasting 89, 90, 302
  and forgiveness of sins 246-248,
    254-255
  and historical student 288*ff*., 315,
    327
  and Jewish religion 53*ff*.
  and John the Baptist 38-52
  and Nature 81-82
  and the Old Testament 12, 13-
    31, 85
  and organized religion 294-314
  and swearing 222
  and theology 282-294
  as author and perfecter of our
    faith 314-331
  as Messiah 42
  as mediator 94, 261
  as non-conformist 88, 89, 296
  aspirations of 155-163
    discovery of divine will 157-
      163
    performance of divine will
      157-163
  as prophetic personality 31-38,
    136, 216, 227, 269, 274, 304,
    311
  as religious genius 13, 59-61,
    210-211, 292
  attitudes of
    paradoxes of 148
    toward conventions 86*ff*., 165
    toward cures 153-155
    toward God 146-148, 149, 323
    toward himself 143*ff*., 262,
      278-279, 323
    toward the kingdom 150-153
    toward Nature 221*ff*.
    toward the synagogue 86
    toward the temple 34, 87, 165,
      169
  authority of 133, 273-331
    basis of 326
    in personal religious experience
      319
  baptism of 166, 189, 191, **302**
  birth traditions of 6

Jesus—*cont.*
    characteristics of thought of 115-116
    comparison of experience of with the child mind 219-226
    confidence of 223
    contribution to religion 316
    deification of 325
    dependence of 221-222, 149-150
    devotion of 322-323
    emotions of 147*ff.*
    energy of 322
    entrance into public life 132*ff.*
    eschatology of 122-128
    faith of 11, 264-265, 285-286, 328
        achievement in 79-80
        authority for 95
        characteristics of 65-67, 96, 98, 99
        development of 95
        emphasis of 84-85
        gives philosophy of life 83
        in God as Father 78*ff.*
        in God as Holy 72*ff.*
        in kingdom of God 104*ff.*
        lack of philosophical elements in 92, 93*ff.*
        materials on 63
        non-rational elements in 74*f.*, 96
        reflected in attitude 80, 85
        relation to Christian faith 91*ff.*
        results of 82-83
        sharing of 96-97
        sources for 68-70, 134
    first day in public 21
    followers of 280, 300, 302, 322
        See Twelve, The
    Galilean period of 162
    genius of 159-160
    great demand of 266
    humanity of 142*ff.*, 256-257
    humility of 149
    Immaculate Conception of 326
    inexplicableness of 60-61
    in general experience of religion 37-38

Jesus—*cont.*
    Jewishness of 53, 125-126, 297
    lack of organization of 302*f.*
    lack of self-consciousness of 226
    language of 9, 105
    last supper of 169, 190, 302
    limitations in knowledge of 143-144
    limitations in personal worth of 145-146
    limitations in power of 144-145
        See chapter III
    limitations in study of 1-3
    message and presentation of 35-37, 280
    miracles of 326
    moral will of 321*f.*
    mysticism of 101-102, 194
    Narratives of the Nativity of 5, 7
    not a statesman 35
    of history and the Christ of faith 258*ff.*, 271, 276, 279
    optimism of 224-225
    parables of
        See Parables
    paradoxes of
        See Paradox
    personality of 122, 146, 160, 210, 228, 322
    personal power of 129-130
    personal problems of xi, 163
    piety of 29, 30, 31, 53, 54, 55, 57, 58-59, 68, 80, 129, 139, 159, 160, 161, 168, 182-183, 277, 317, 320, 330
    prayer-experience of 183*ff.*
    prayer-heritage of 175-183
    prayers of xii, 195-209
        after first public day 22, 190
        at feeding the five thousand 190
        at feeding the four thousand 190
        at last supper 190
        characteristics of 196-204

Jesus—*cont.*
  prayers of—*cont.*
    for Simon 196, 197
    in Gethsemane 158, 163, 196,
      199, 201, 204, 207
    Lord's Prayer 196
      See Lord's Prayer
    meaning of 191-192
    of praise 196-204
    on cross 19, 25, 196, 197, 207
    results of 207-208
    See list 196
  religious consciousness of 143-209
  religious demands of 210-270
    discipleship 253-270
    the child mind 219-237
    the living of life with re-
      ligious reference 238-253
  religious message of 105-116
  religiousness of 254*ff.*, 287-288,
    323
  religious outlook of 116-128
  religious task of 131-132
  résumé of life and work of 272-
    273
  retreats for prayer xii, 22, 189-
    195
    See list 189
  scale of values of 243-244
  sensitiveness of 221
  Sermon on the Mount 29, 294
  sense of security of 224
  simplicity of 220
  sinlessness of 160
  temptations of 19*ff.*
  transfiguration of 53-54
  virgin birth of 326
  way of 267
Jesus (Bousset) 77, 85
Jesus (Bultmann) xii
Jesus (Wernle) 14, 55, 68, 79,
  81, 149, 161, 207, 256, 286
Jesus—A New Biography xii
Jesus of Nazareth 239
John (gospel) 287, 329
  See Index of Scripture Passages

John (son of Zebedee) 100
John the Baptist 13, 31, 32, 38-52,
  133, 166, 167, 168
  as fore-runner of Jesus 40*ff.*
  as prophet 39-40, 41
  attitude of Jesus toward 47-48
  Christian view-point toward 40*ff.*
  comparison with Jesus 50-52
  followers of 46, 52, 300-301
  historically inseparable from
    Jesus 45
  influence of on Jesus 46*ff.*
  materials on 41*ff.*
  meets with Jesus 45, 46
  practises of 43-44, 101, 300*f.*
Jonah 136, 296
Jones, E. S.
  The Christ of the Indian Road
    238
Jones, R. M.
  The Church's Debt to Heretics
    276
Jordan River 132, 133, 302
Joseph (father of Jesus) 6, 8
Joseph of Arimathea 124
Journal of George Fox, The 195,
  199
Journal of Religion 166, 238
Judaism 13, 40, 41, 64, 88, 106,
  107, 108, 123, 178, 295, 296,
  307, 312
Judas 300, 303
Judith 15, 177

Kant 328
Kingdom of God 219, 221, 229,
  248-249, 257-258, 274, 280, 296,
  306, 310
  as a new world order 113
  as a realm 112
  as religious cause of Jesus 129*ff.*
  as religious message of Jesus
    105-116
  as religious outlook of Jesus
    116-128
    estimate of 121, 131
    eschatology of 122-128
  as a reign 112

Kingdom of God—*cont.*
as a spiritual community 113
as the supreme value 113-114
entrance into 263
eschatological in form of realization 108-109
Jesus' faith in 67
place in thinking of people 106, 107
presentation of 110*ff.*
time of coming 114
Kingdom of heaven 105
Klausner, J.
Jesus of Nazareth 239

Last supper 169, 190, 302
Leipold, J.
Das Gotteserlebnis Jesu im Lichte der vergleichenden Religionsgeschichte 71, 101
Leviticus 29, 87
See Index of Scripture Passages
Liberalism 293
Logos 287
Loisy, A. 108
The Gospel and the Church 57, 136, 138, 273
My Duel with the Vatican 205
Lord's Prayer 77, 83, 110, 121, 122, 150, 189, 196, 198, 203, 217, 285-286
Lot's wife 14, 28
Luke
See Index of Scripture Passages
See also Gospels, Synoptic
Luther 26, 117, 171

Maccabees I 15
Manasses 177
Mark
See Index of Scripture Passages
See also Gospels, Synoptic
Mary (mother of Jesus) 6, 8
Matthew
See Index of Scripture Passages
See also Gospels, Synoptic
Maturity 219

Meaning of God in Human Experience, The 142, 184, 321
"Meaning of Jesus' Baptism, The" 166
Message of Sadhu Sundar Singh, The 171
Messianism 287
Micah 32, 34, 39, 43, 215
See Index of Scripture Passages
Miracles 326
Miserere 181
Modern mind 98, 116
characteristics of 229*ff.*
religion of 236
Modernism 268
Monotheism 68, 256
Moses 14, 28, 177
Mount Horeb 194
Mundle, W.
Das religioese Leben des Apostels Paulus 197.
"Der Christus des Glaubens und der historische Jesus" 258, 279
My Duel with the Vatican 205
Mysterium tremendum 73, 75, 76, 150
Mysticism 287
of Jesus
See Jesus, mysticism of

Narratives of the Nativity 5, 7
Nathan 39
Nazareth 6, 135, 253, 272
New Testament xi, 41, 44, 45, 68, 74, 253, 275, 279, 280, 281, 282, 302, 305, 306, 312-313, 314, 318, 327, 330
See Gospels, Synoptic
See also Index of Scripture Passages
Noah 14, 28

Old Testament 12, 52, 54, 79, 85, 91, 106, 108, 112, 156, 197, 202, 213, 217
Christian use of 17

Old Testament—*cont.*
Jesus and 13-31
prayers of
and prophets 177-178
David's prayer-literature 177
Hannah's prayer 177
in beginning 176
Jacob's wrestling with angel 176
Moses on the mount 177
Solomon's 177
Otto, R.
Das Heilige 60, 73, 74, 75, 76, 85, 150, 279
Our Recovery of Jesus xii

Palestine 9
Parables
for presentation of the kingdom 138
the importunate friend 186
the Pharisee and publican 95, 186*f.*, 227-228
the seed growing secretly 151, 220*f.*
the sower 152
the tares 151
the unjust judge 186
Paradise 25
Paradox
in faith of Jesus 66
in Jesus' conception of the kingdom 115-116, 138
in Jesus' experience of God 71-72, 77-78, 93-94, 97
in personality of Jesus 58
in Jesus' prayer-life 185, 188
in Jesus' prayers on the cross 25-26
of the greatness of the least 245
Parker, Mrs. Arthur
Sadhu Sundar Singh 155, 192
Pascal 26
Passover 87, 169, 303
Paul 124, 244
and Christian faith 281
and Judaism 312
and problems of religious experience 320

Paul—*cont.*
and reading of Old Testament 16
and religion of to-day 329
as founder of Christianity 294-295
conception of Christ 271
exegesis of 15, 16
faith of 98
language of 160
letters of 2-3
pessimism of 83
piety of 3
prayer-experience of 206
protagonist of Jesus 272
religious experience of 297
theology of 94, 117, 289
training of 8

Penn, William 194, 199
Penney, N.
The Journal of George Fox 195, 199
Pentateuch 28
Peter (Apostle) 24, 297, 298, 303
Pharisees 88, 226, 227, 244
Piety 229
in Old Testament 217
See Jesus, piety of
Plato 300
Plotinus 196
Pratt, J. B.
The Religious Consciousness 184
Prayer
and the pious Israelite 181-182
in Old Testament 170, 202
in primitive Christianity 170
Jesus' estimate of 189
Marana tha 124
of Jesus
See Jesus, prayers of
of Paul 206
See Lord's Prayer
Prayer-Act
and cultured man 172-174
and piety 171
and primitive man 172-173
and religion 170
as personal and social value 174-175

Prayer-Act—*cont.*
  content of 171-174
  in Old Testament 175*ff.*
Prophets 13, 31*ff.*, 107, 108, 112,
  116, 130, 156, 164, 166, 176,
  214, 260-261, 264, 278
  and prayer 177-178
  Jesus as one of
    See Jesus, as a prophetic
    personality
  Jesus quotes 33, 34
Providence 149, 173, 223, 233
Psalms 29, 84, 86, 87, 122, 179-
  180, 201
  See Index of Scripture Passages
Pseudepigrapha 106, 108
Psychic Health of Jesus, The 23,
  125, 128, 149, 191
Psychology of Religion, The (Coe)
  59, 184, 204, 206, 321
Psychology of Religion, The (Sel-
  bie) 184

Queen of Sheba 14
Quest of the Historical Jesus, The
  321

Reality and Religion 81, 206
*Religion of Jesus and the Faith of
  Paul, The* 49, 118, 170
Religious Consciousness, The 184
Religious consciousness
  attitudes of 146
  basis of 141
  of Jesus 143-209
  of primitive man 155-156
  tendency of acts of 163-165
Religious genius 210-211
  See Jesus as a religious genius
Religious literature 137
  See Old Testament
Revelation 124, 152
Roman Empire 3, 78, 272

Sadhu Sundar Singh 155, 193
St. Teresa 205

Satan 23, 24, 64, 154
Schuerer, E.
  *Die Geschichte des juedischen
    Volkes im Zeitalter Jesu
    Christi* 179
Schweitzer, A. 108, 123
  *Die Geschichte der Leben-Jesu-
    Forschung* 122, 153, 265, 321
  *Quest of the Historical Jesus,
    The* 321
Selbie, W. B.
  The Psychology of Religion 184
Sermon on the Mount 29, 294
Simon the Pharisee 227
Singh, S. 155, 171, 192, 238
  At the Master's Feet 203
  Reality and Religion 81, 206
  Visions of the Spiritual World
    156
Solomon 14, 177, 296
Soteriology 91, 94, 246, 287
Spirit, The 322
Staerk, W.
  *Die Schriften des Alten Testa-
    ments* 180
Stephen 259
Strauss, D. F. 128, 279
Streeter, B. H.
  *Concerning Prayer: its Nature,
    its Difficulties, and its Values*
    184
  *The Message of Sadhu Sundar
    Singh* 171
  The Spirit 322
Synagogue 86
Syria 271

Taboo 156, 236
Taylor, Jeremy 131
Temple 179
  cleansing of 169
  Jesus' attitude toward 34, 87,
    165, 169
Terstegen 73
Theology 91, 94, 117, 144, 147,
  183, 209, 246, 262, 275, 276,
  281, 288, 309, 314, 315, 319
  Jesus' attitude toward 282-294

Tobit 15, 177
Trinity 261-262
Twelve, The 31, 135, 144, 189, 273

Underhill, Evelyn 195
Utopia 127

Virgin birth 326
Visions of the Spiritual World 156
Warschauer, J.
The Historical Life of Christ 122
Weidel, K.
Jesu Persoenlichkeit 321
Weinel, H.
Biblische Theologie des Neuen Testaments 169, 286

Weiss, J. 108
Die Schriften des Neuen Testaments 144
Das Aelteste Evangelium 169
Wellhausen, J.
Einleitung in die drei ersten Evangelien 297
Wernle, P.
Jesus 14, 55, 68, 79, 81, 149, 160, 207, 256, 286
Western World 271, 328
Wisdom of Solomon 15
Woodburne, A. S.
"The Indian Appreciation of Jesus" 238

Zeitschrift fuer Theologie und Kirche 258, 279

INDEX OF SCRIPTURE PASSAGES

INDEX OF SCRIPTURE PASSAGES

OLD TESTAMENT

Genesis	Page
3	176
32,22-32	176f.

Exodus	
20	213
34,17-26	214

Leviticus	
19,18	29, 217

Deuteronomy	
5	213
6, 4-5	217
13	20, 24
16	20, 23, 30
8, 3	20, 22
9	177

I Samuel	
2, 1-10	177
15,11	177

II Samuel	
12, 1-15	39

I Kings	
3, 6-9	100
18,25-40	177

II Kings	
1, 9-16	100
5,26	37n
19,14	37n

Ezra	
9, 5-15	178n

Nehemiah	
1, 5-11	178n
9, 5ff.	178n

Psalms	
8	81
4-5	231
19, 1-7	81
22, 1	25, 197, 201
28	106
23	18, 175
27,10	79n
29	81
1	79n

Psalms	Page
31, 5	25, 197
34	160
42	87
43	87
51, 9-15	181
57,17	179n
78, 2	16
82, 6	79n
84	86
89,27	79n
90	142
91	18
11-12	30
103	79
104	81
116, 1-2	176
122	86

Isaiah	
1, 2	79n
10-17	36n
6	37n
3	73
9-10	17
7,10f.	100
9, 1-2	16
24,23	106f.
28,16	178n
29,13	33n
30,15	178n
38,10-20	178n
40,26-31	178n
40-66	35, 107, 296
42, 5ff.	178n
45, 6ff.	178n
48,12	178n
52, 7	107
55, 8-9	73
56, 7	34
61, 1-2	17, 33n, 37
63, 6ff.	178n
16-18	79n
64, 7	79n

355

Jeremiah	Page
3,19	79n
6,11	37n
7,11	34
10,23ff.	178n
14, 1ff.	178n
15,11	178n
16	178n
17,18	178n
18,20-23	178n
20, 7	178n
7-9	37n
11-12	178n
23,18	37n

Ezekiel	
1	37n
3,14-15	37n

Daniel	
6,10	179n
7,13-14	109, 125

Hosea	
2, 1	79n
3, 1	79n
6, 1ff.	178n
6	33n
10,12	178n
11, 1	16
14, 1ff.	178n

Amos	
3, 7-8	36n
8	37n, 134
4, 4	164

Amos	Page
5, 2	36n
16-20	36n
7, 2-3	177n
5-6	177n
14	37n
8,11-13	36n

Obadiah	
21	106

Jonah	
2, 2-10	178n

Micah	
1, 6	36n
2, 3	36n
6, 6-8	156, 214ff.
8	34n
7, 6	34n

Nahum	
1,14	36n
3, 5-6	36n

Habakkuk	
1, 2-4	178n
12-17	178n

Zechariah	
1, 7ff.	37n
3, 1ff.	37n
4	43
13, 9	178n
14, 9	107

Malachi	
1, 6	79n
3,17	79n
4, 5-6	39

NEW TESTAMENT

Matthew	Page
1-2	5ff.
2,14-15	16
3, 1-12	42
1-17	38n
4	43
6	301
7	46n
7-10	42
9	46n
10	46n
12	46n

Matthew	Page
3,14-15	45f., 167
4, 1-11	19
2	89n
3-4	21f.
5-7	22f.
6	30
7	30
8-10	23f.
12	38n, 48f.
12-16	16

Matthew	Page
5, 6	121
17	31,53,86
5,21*ff.*	29n
23-24	87, 165*f.*
34-37	76, 222
36	149
45	81, 223
6, 2-4	89
5-6	89, 185
6	193
7	198
7-8	185
8	82, 92, 202
9	77
9-13	196, 217, 246
12	247, 255
14-15	247
16-18	90
24	129
25-34	81
26	81
26-32	223*f.*
27	149, 222
28-30	81
34	225
7,1-2	76
12	244
13-14	112
14	267
16-18	46n
19	46n
21	112
21-23	158, 263
28-29	133
8, 8	326
11	296
11-12	113
12	35
27	228
9,13	33n
14	38n
10,23	109, 114, 120, 135, 151, 299
28	78
29-31	78, 81n, 224
35	34n
11, 2-7	46
2-19	28n, 47

Matthew	Page
11, 7-9	44
11	48
12	48
14	39n
18	43*f.*
18-19	51
21-24	154
25	77
25-26	196
12, 6	56, 87, 119
7	33n
28	114, 154, 254
33	46n
34	46n
38-42	22n
41-42	56, 119
46-50	8n
13,16-17	119
24-30	150
30	46n
35	16
44-46	113*f.*, 121
52	57
14, 1-2	39, 52n
1-12	38n
3-4	39
5	40
19	190n
23	189
15,36	190n
16, 1-4	22n
13-14	52n
14	31, 38n
17-19	297*f.*
22-23	23
17,10-13	39n
13	38n
18, 3	113, 218
6	255n
15-17	298*f.*
18	298
19,13	190
28	35, 112, 300
20, 1-16	112
21,13	87
25-26	38n, 40n
31	229, 240*f.*
32	38n

Matthew	Page
22, 1-14	112
41-46	15
23, 1-39	88
5-7	227
23	34n, 46n
25,31-46	112
26,26	190n
26-29	302
29	135
36-44	189
39-42	196
73	9
27,46	19, 25, 196
28,19	51

Mark	Page
1, 1-11	38n
2-8	41, 132
2-13	132
5	301
6	43
9-11	132, 166
12-13	132
14	38n
14-15	132
15	67, 105, 120, 151
21-28	21
21-34	191
21-38	21*f*, 162
29-31	21
32-34	21
35	193
35-38	21*f*., 24, 189, 191, 207
40	326
44	87
45	190n
2, 1-12	254*f*.
12	228, 255
17	228
18	38n, 44, 52, 301
18-22	89
21-22	56
3,17	100
19-21	8n
31-35	8n
35	158
4,10-12	16*f*.
11	150

Mark	Page
4,26-29	114, 150*f*., 220*f*.
30-32	114
5,28	326
6, 1-6	6
14-16	39, 52n
14-29	38n
15	31
17-18	39
20	40
30-31	190n
31	192
35-44	168
41	190n
46	189
7, 6-7	33
24-30	168
34	190
8, 6	190n
11-12	22*ff*., 100
27-28	52n
28	38n
32-33	23*f*.
9, 1	109, 113n, 120, 135, 151, 299
11-13	39n
23	99,154
39	318
42	255n
10, 2-12	15
13-16	218
17	145
18	145, 167
25	267
26	267
35-41	125
37	144
39-40	145
43-45	245
45	282*f*.
11,12	142
15-17	34
22	256
23	99
30	167
30-32	40n
12,29-30	33
30-31	217

Mark	Page
12,31	33
34	113
35-37	15, 284n
37	133
38-40	227
13	109, 143
1-2	34
4	125
24-27	113n
26-27	109, 122
28-29	137
30	128, 135, 143
30-31	261
31	128, 143
32	115, 143, 152
14,22	190n
22-25	302
32-42	24, 189
33-34	76n
34	207
36	9, 196f.
38	192
62	109, 122
70	9
15,34	9, 19, 24f., 77, 162, 196, 207
16,16	51

Luke	Page
1, 5	39n
5-25	38n
15	44
13-17	39
25	39n
26-56	8
57-80	38n
1-2	5ff.
2,19	8
22-52	8
41-52	7
51	8
3, 1-2	272
1-18	42
1-22	38n
7	46n
7-9	42
8	46n

Luke	Page
3,9	46n
10-14	42f., 50
19-20	39
21	168, 189f.
23	6
4, 1-13	19
2	89n
3-4	21f.
5-8	23f.
9-12	22f.
10-11	30
12	30
13	24
16	86
16-20	14
16-21	17, 37
17-19	33n
42-43	190n
5,16	189
26	228
33	38n, 301
6,12	189f., 193
27-28	30
43-44	46n
7,18-24	46
18-25	38n, 47
24-26	44
28	48
33	43f.
33-34	51
36-50	254
39	227
8,19-21	8n
9, 7-9	38n, 39, 52n
16	190n
18	189f.
18-19	52n
28	193
28-29	189f.
29	38n
37	193
55	100
10,21	196, 207
11, 1	38n, 189, 301
1-4	196
5-8	186

Luke	Page
11,11-13	82
16	22n
29-30	136
29-32	22n
12,49	98, 330
13,24	160, 267
28-29	35
15,11-32	94, 261
16,16	38n, 48
17, 3-4	299
20-21	114
37	125
18, 2-5	186
9-14	95, 186*f.*
10-13	227*f.*
13	255
14	204
19,41	142
20, 4-6	38n, 40n
41-44	15
22,15	88
15-18	169, 302
17	190n
18	109, 120, 299
19-20	190n, 302
25-27	283n
28	24
30	35, 300n
31-32	196*f.*
40-46	189
42	196
43	194
59	9
23,34	25, 30, 196
43	25
46	19, 25, 196*f*, 207
47	228
24,30	190
35	190

John	
3,22-26	51n, 52
4, 2	51n
6-7	142
6,35	256n

John	Page
6,52-58	284n
7,38	256n
53*ff.*	2
11,25-26	256n
12, 6	300
12,44	256n
46	256n
13,29	300
14,12	256n

Acts	
1, 5	38n
7	144
22	38n
2,22	154
3, 1	179n
7,56	259
10,37	38n
11,16	38n
13,24-25	38n
18,24*ff.*	38n, 301
22, 3	8n
26, 5	8n

Romans	
7-8	56
11, 1	8n

I Corinthians	
9, 9-10	15
10, 4	15
11, 6-10	15
23-25	302
12-14	320*f.*
15, 8	281
14	325
16,22	124n

II Corinthians	
11,22	8n
12, 8-9	206

Galatians	
3,16	15
28	244
4,22-31	15

Philippians	
2,12	160
3, 5	8n
12	98

INDEX OF SCRIPTURE PASSAGES 361

I Thessalonians
  4,15-18 ——————————124

Hebrews
  12, 2 ———————315, 317, 319

Revelation
  22,20 ——————————124n

EXTRA-BIBLICAL WRITINGS

Assumption of Moses   Page
  10, 1 ——————————————107

Didache
  10, 6 ————————————124n

III Maccabees
  5, 7 ——————————————79n

Psalms of Solomon
  17, 3 ——————————————107

Sirach
  23,14 ——————————————79n

Sirach   Page
  23,16 ——————————————79n
  3, 8 ——————————————107
  14, 1*ff.* ——————————79n
  18, 5 ——————————————79n
  51,10 ——————————————79n

Wisdom of Solomon
  2,13 ——————————————79n